Foundation Physics

For Class X

Part-1 of 2

NOTION PRESS

NOTION PRESS

India. Singapore. Malaysia.

ISBN xxx-x-xxxxx-xx-x

Dedicated to our Beloved Prime Minister Shree Narendra Modi ji, whose life gives the Inspiration to every Individual

*If a Man **Decides** to achieve something in his life nothing is Impossible*

कर्मण्येवाधिकारस्ते मा फलेषु कदाचन।

मा कर्मफलहेतुर्भूर्मा ते सङ्गोऽस्त्वकर्मणि॥ २-४७

Karmanye vadhikaraste Ma Phaleshu Kadachana,

Ma Karmaphalaheturbhurma Te Sangostvakarmani

You have the right to work only but never to its fruits.

Let not the fruits of action be your motive, nor let your attachment be to inaction.

CONTENT

TOPIC NAME PAGE NO.

1. ELECTRICITY

2. MAGNETIC EFFECTS OF ELECTRIC CURRENT

TOPIC NAME	PAGE NO.

3. SOURCES OF ENERGY

1 ELECTRICITY

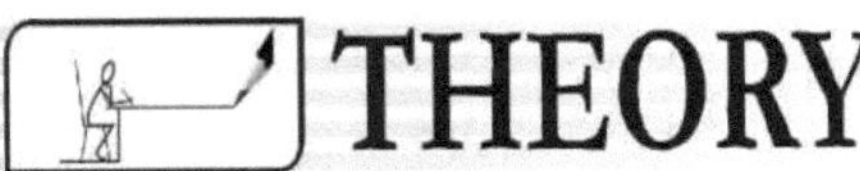

CONCEPT TREE :

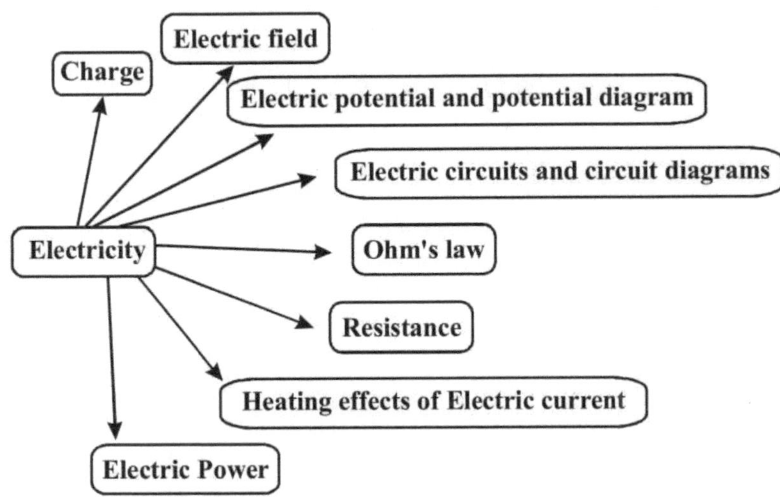

1.1 INTRODUCTION :

Electricity has great importance in the modern society. The modern devices in our day to day life require electricity for their operation. The most clean and convenient form of energy in our day to day life is electricity.

1.2 CHARGE :

Charge is defined as the property of matter. When a charge is at rest, it produces electric field only, but when in motion, it also produces magnetic field. Charge can be positive or negative. The smallest stable possible charge is the charge on an electron.

Properties of Electric Charge :

1. Electric charge is of two types viz., positive and negative charge. Proton is said to be charged positively and electron is said to be charged negatively. The magnitude of elementary positive or negative charge is same and is equal to 1.6×10^{-19} C.
2. Like charges repel and unlike charges attract each other. Thus a proton repels a proton and attracts an electron.
3. The force of attraction or repulsion between two charges is given by Coulomb's law.

4. **Charge is conserved :** Charge can neither be created no be destroyed. The charge from one body can be transferred to another body but the total charge of a system remains constant. This is called the law of conservation of charge.

5. **Charge is quantized :** Protons and electrons are elementary charged particles. Though the charge on them is opposite in nature, the magnitude of charge possessed by them is same i.e., 1.6×10^{-19} C. Charge on a body is always an integral multiple of this value. This is called quantization of charge.

   The charge exists in fixed packets i.e. when a body is charged the charge on it is an integral multiple of the charge on an electron.

   $$\boxed{q = \pm ne}$$

   Reason for quantisation :

   Since, electrons are indivisible, thus, only integral number of electrons can be transferred from one body to another, on rubbing. Hence, the charge bodies will have charges which are integral multiples of the charge on electron.

6. When a body gains electrons, it becomes negatively charged. When it loses electrons it becomes positively charged. The positive charge being bound firmly in the nucleus does not participate in charging.
7. Charge is invariant
8. Charge resides on the outer surface of the conductor. In insulators it remains where it is placed.
9. The electric charge is additive in nature.
10. Charge cannot exist without mass but mass can exist without charge.
11. Charge is scalar quantity and the SI unit of charge is coulomb, denoted by (C).

Note : The smallest possible charge is the charge on a quark i.e. $\frac{2e}{3}$ and $\frac{-e}{3}$, but it is unstable in nature.

Mass of an electron = 9.1×10^{-31} Kg.

A body having a charge of +1C has an electron deficit of 6.25×10^{18} electrons.

The study of electricity is classified into two parts.

1. **Static electricity :** It deals with electric charges at rest and their effects.
2. **Current electricity :** It deals with charges in motion and their effects.

S.No.	Positive Charge	Negative Charge
1.	Glass Rod	Silk
2.	Woolen cloth or fur	Ebonite, Amber, Rubber
3.	Woolen cloth	Plastic
4.	Dry hair	Plastic Comb

This chapter deals with charges in motion i.e., current electricity.

1.3 ELECTRIC FIELD

The region of influence around a charge is called the region of electric field.

Interaction of electric field between two charged particles :

Two charged particles always interact with each other due to their electric field. There may be force of repulsion or attraction between two charged particles.
This force of attraction exists between unlike charges and force of repulsion exist between like charges.
The force between two point charges q_1 and q_2 separated by distance 'r' is given by Coulomb's law.

Coulomb's law :

In 1785, Coulomb gave two laws for the force of attraction or repulsion between two electrically charged bodies separated from each other by a definite distance. The laws are stated as follows

(i) *"The force of attraction or repulsion between two electric charges is directly proportional to the product of two charges."*

(ii) *"The force of attraction or repulsion between two electric charges is inversely proportional to the square of the distance between them. This is known as inverse square law."*

$$F \propto q_1 q_2$$

$$\propto \frac{1}{r^2}$$

$$F \propto \frac{q_1 q_2}{r^2}$$

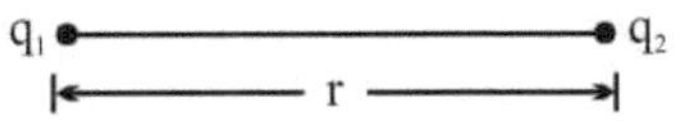

$$F = k\frac{q_1 q_2}{r^2}$$

where K is proportionality constant (or Electrostatic Force constant or Coulomb's constant). Its value depends upon the medium between charges and units used for charge, distance and force.

The value of $K = \frac{1}{4\pi\varepsilon_o} = 9 \times 10^9 \frac{Nm^2}{C^2}$

The constant ε_0 is called the **permittivity of free space**. Its value is $\mathbf{8.9 \times 10^{-12}\ C^2/N\text{-}m^2}$.

$$\Rightarrow \quad \boxed{F = \frac{1}{4\pi\varepsilon_0} \cdot \frac{q_1 q_2}{r^2}}$$

Force is a vector quantity.

Vector Form of coulomb's law $\vec{F} = \frac{kq_1q_2}{r^2}\hat{r}$; $\hat{r} = \frac{\vec{r}}{|r|}$ $\Rightarrow \vec{F} = \frac{kq_1q_2}{|r|^3}\vec{r}$

Intensity of electric field ($\vec{E}$) :

The intensity of electric field at a point in the electric field is defined as the force experienced by a unit positive charge placed at that point

$$\boxed{\vec{E} = \frac{\vec{F}}{q_0}} \quad \text{where } q_0 = 1$$

$$F = K\frac{q \times 1}{r^2}$$

In terms of magnitude, $E = \frac{F}{1} = K\frac{q}{r^2}$ where $K = \frac{1}{4\pi\varepsilon_0}$

Electric field is vector quantity and SI unit of electric field is N/C

1.4 ELECTRIC POTENTIAL AND POTENTIAL DIFFERENCE :

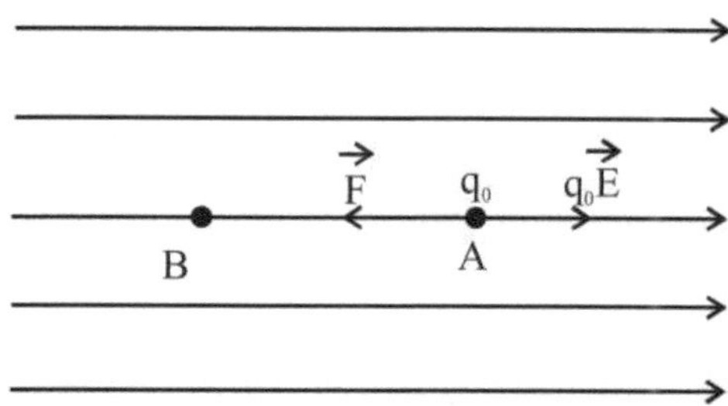

If a positive test charge q_0 is placed at a point A in an uniform electric field (see figure), a force $q_0\vec{E}$ will act on this charge along the direction of electric field. Now if test charge q_0 is displaced from A to B, by applying a force $F = q_0\vec{E}$ in opposite direction to electric field intensity, then we have to do some work. Let this work be W_{AB}.

In this way, work done in carrying a unit positive charge from point A to B is defined as potential difference between points B and A. i.e. potential difference between point B and A–

$$\boxed{V_B - V_A = \frac{W_{AB}}{q_0}}$$

The electrons (negative charges) in a conductor or a wire flow from one end to another end of the conductor if there is electric pressure difference called electric potential difference between the ends of the conductor.

If point A is considered as a reference point (initial point where potential is zero) at infinity, then–

$$V_B = V_B - 0 = \frac{W_{\infty B}}{q_0}$$

Electric potential at point B is defined by above equation. That is, work done in carrying a unit positive charge from infinity (V = 0) to the point under consideration in electric field, without change of its kinetic energy, is called the electric potential of that point.

The S.I. unit for electric potential and potential difference is **joule/coulomb**, which is also known as **Volt**. "*One volt potential at a point means that work done in carrying one coulomb charge from infinity to this point would be one joule.*" Electric potential and potential difference are scalar quantity. It is to be noted that "*positive charge always moves from high potential to low potential, similarly negative charge moves from low potential to high potential.*" From reference point of view, the electric potential of earth is considered as zero.

Smaller units of electric potential
1 mili volt (mV) = 10^{-3} V
1 micro volt (μV) = 10^{-6} V
Larger units of electric potential
1 kilovolt (kV) = 10^{3} V

1 megavolt (MV) = 10^6 V

The electrons move only if there is a difference of electric pressure (i.e. the potential difference) along the conductor. This difference of potential may be produced by a battery, consisting of one or more electric cells.

The potential difference is measured by means of an instrument called the **voltmeter**.

Note : The voltmeter is always connected in parallel across the points between which the potential difference is to be measured.

"A continuous and closed path of an electric current is called an electric circuit."

Concept of Electric Potential Difference

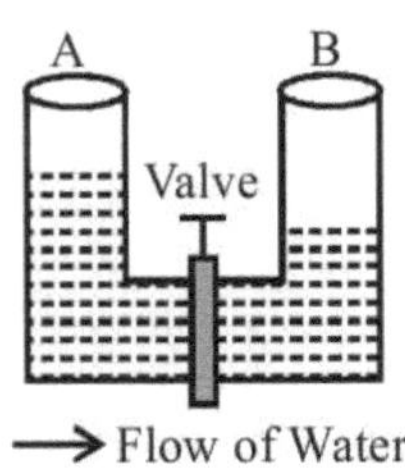

To understand the concept of electric potential take a vessel consisting of two arms A and B as shown in Figure. The water level in arm A is higher than the level in arm B, when valve is closed. We know that pressure exerted by a liquid in a vessel at the bottom of the vessel is directly proportional to the height of the liquid in the vessel.

Therefore, pressure exerted by water in arm A is greater than the pressure exerted by water in arm B. It means that there is pressure difference between the arms A and B. When the valve is opened, the water flows from arm A to arm B of the vessel due to pressure difference. This flow of water continues till the water level in both the arms of the vessel becomes equal or there is no pressure difference between the two arms. This activity shows that the water flows from higher pressure to lower pressure. In other words, water flow from one region to another region only if there is a pressure difference between the two regions.

The electric potential difference across the ends of a conductor is maintained by a dry cell or a battery. The chemical reaction taking place in a cell makes one electrode of the cell as positive and the other electrode of the cell as negative. When, a conductor is connected across these electrodes of the cell, then one end of the conductor is at positive potential and the other end of the conductor is at negative potential. Thus, there exists an electric potential difference across the ends of the conductor. This electric potential difference moves the electrons (negative charges) in the conductor from one end to the other end.

Illustration

Five joule of work is done in moving 12.5×10^{18} electrons from one end to other end of a conductor. What is the potential difference between the two ends of conductor ?

Sol. The charge on 6.25×10^{18} electrons is 1 C.

$\therefore$ When 12.5×10^{18} electrons move, the net charge transferred is 2 C.

$\therefore$ Q = 2C.

Work done (W) in moving 2C charge = 5 J. (given)

The potential difference (V) between the ends of conductor is

$$V = \frac{\text{Work done}}{\text{charge}} = \frac{5\,J}{2\,C} = 2.5\,J\,C^{-1}.$$

$$V = 2.5 \text{ volts}$$

Drift Velocity

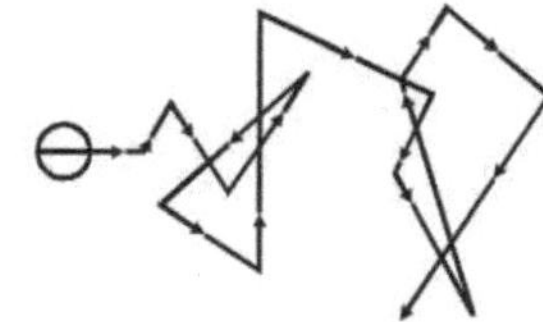

In a conductor or a wire, negatively charged particles called electrons have random or zig-zag motion as show in figure. Therefore, the net flow of electrons (or net flow of charge) across any cross-section of the conductor is zero. This is because number of electrons flowing through the given cross-section to the right side is equal to the number of electrons flowing to the left side through the given cross section.

Hence, there is no electric current in the conductor. However, when the ends of the conductor are connected across a dry cell, there is a potential difference across the conductor. Now, the electrons move from one end to another end of the conductor. But the motion of these electrons is not in straight lines. These electrons collide with the ions of the conductor while moving from one end to another end of the conductor. As a result of these collision, electrons drift from one end to another end with an average speed known as drift velocity. The drift velocity of electrons in a conductor is very small. Typical value of the drift velocity of an electron in a conductor is about 2.22×10^{-4} m s^{-1}. It means, electrons will take time about 2.5 hours to travel 5 metre long conductor.

Illustration Electric potential at a point in an electric field is 0.5 V when charge of 3C was brought from infinity to that point. Calculate the work done.

Sol. Electric potential (V) = 0.5 volts

Charge (Q) = 3C; Work done (W) = ?

$$V = \frac{W}{Q}$$

$$\therefore \quad W = VQ = 0.5\,V \times 3\,C = 1.5\,V\,C = 1.5\,J \text{ Ans.}$$

1.5 FLOW OF CHARGE (ELECTRIC CURRENT) :

Electric current is defined as continuous rate of flow of electric charge. Consider flow of charges through a conductor as shown in figure. If ΔQ charge flows in Δt time through the cross section of conductor under consideration then the current over this time interval is defined as $I = \frac{\Delta Q}{\Delta t}$

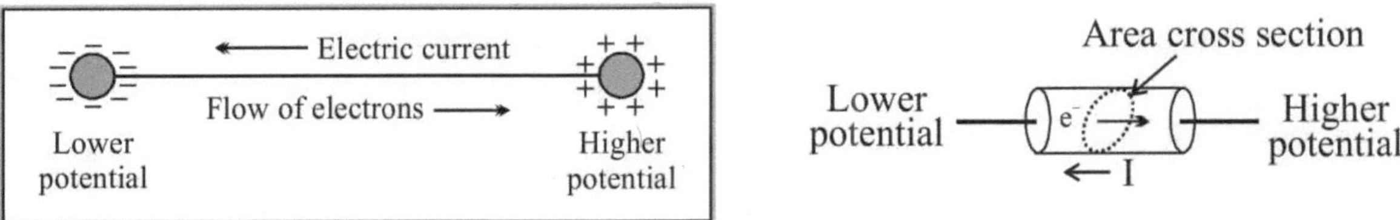

The S. I. unit of current is the **ampere** symbolically represented as **A**. Therefore also,

$$\text{Current (I)} = \frac{\text{Charge (Q)}}{\text{Time (t)}} = \frac{Q}{t}$$

$$\boxed{1\,mA = 10^{-3}A, 1\,\mu A = 10^{-6}A}$$

Knowledge Enhancer

In a metallic conductor, when an atom loses one or more electrons, then atom becomes a positive ion, which remains fixed at one place in the conductor. The electrons detached from an atom become free and capable of moving from one part to another part of the conductor. The electric current in a metallic conductor is due to the flow of electrons (i.e., negative charge carriers).

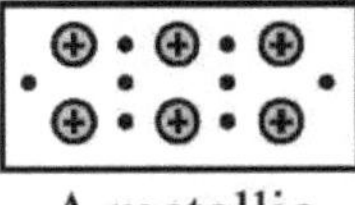
A metallic conductor

⊕ Positive ions which are fixed at one place • Free electrons

Note : 1 A of current is equivalent to one coulomb of charge passing through conductor in 1 second.
Conventionally, we define the direction of the current in the direction of flow of negative charge. Whereas, the direction of current is considered opposite to the direction of flow of electrons.
An instrument called **ammeter** measures electric current in a circuit. It is always connected in series in a circuit.

A conductor or a wire carrying current is neutral. That is, it has net charge on it equal to zero.

Types of electrical Materials :

(1) Insulators (2) Semiconductors (3) Conductors

Charge flow or conduction of electric current takes place only if free charge carriers are present. Since protons are bounded and present in the nucleus so the conduction takes place only due to electrons.

(1) Insulators do not conduct electricity because of the absence of free electrons in them, Rubber is an excellent insulator.
(2) Conductors conduct electricity due to presence of free electrons in them for example wire made of Cu, Al. are good conductors.
(3) Semiconductors behave as insulators at low temperature whereas they behave as conductors at high temperatures.

POINTS TO REMEMBER

However, because we tend to associate the word "positive" with "surplus" and "negative" with "deficiency." The standard label for electron charge

does seem backward. Because of this, many engineers decide to retain the old concept of electricity with "positive" referring to a surplus of charge and "negative" referring to a deficiency of charge, and label charge flow (current) accordingly.
This is know as conventional flow notation.

Conventional flow notation

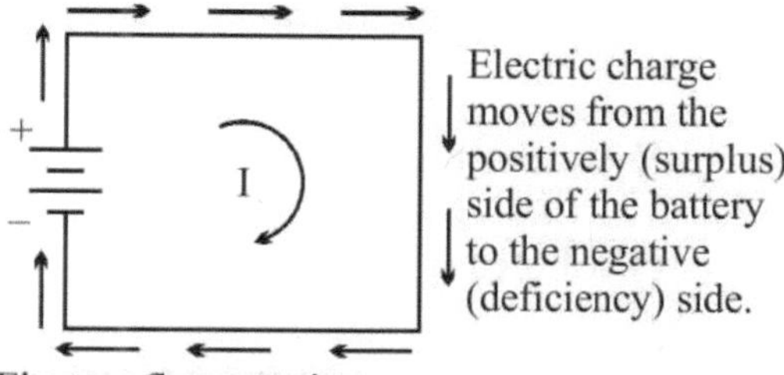

Electron flow notation

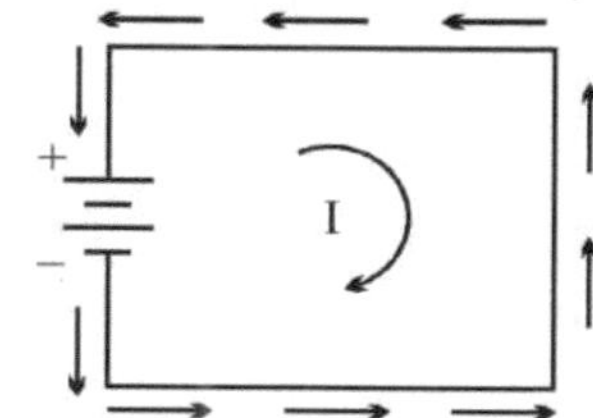

Electric (–)ve charge moves from the negative (surplus) side of the battery to the positive (deficiency) side.

Others chose to designate charge flow according to the actual motion of electrons in a circuit. This form of symbology is known as electron flow notation:
In conventional flow notation, we show the motion of charge according to the (technically incorrect) labels of + and –. In this way or method the labels are kept same, but the direction of charge flow is incorrect. In electron flow notation, we follow the actual motion of electrons in the circuit, but the + and – labels are same as before. Does it matter, really, how we designate charge flow in a circuit ? Not really, so long as we're consistent in the use of our symbols. You may follow an imagined direction of current (conventional flow) or the actual (electron flow) as far circuit analysis is concerned.
Conventionally positive charge is at higher potential than negative charge flow always takes place from higher potential to lower potential. The flow of current takes place from positive charge to negative charge. The direction of electric current is from negative charge to positive charge i.e. the flow of electrons.

Symbols of some commonly used components in circuit diagrams.

(1) An electric cell

(2) A battery or a combination of cells

(3) Plug key or switch (open)

(4) Plug key or switch (closed)

(5) A wire joint or junction

(6) Galvanometer — or

(7) Wires crossing without joining

(8) Heater

(9) Electric bulb — or

(10) A resistor of resistance R

(11) Tapping key

(12) Variable resistance or rheostat

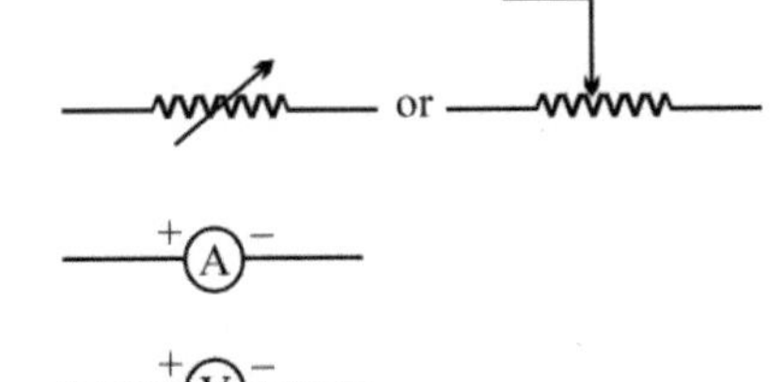

(13) Ammeter

(14) Voltmeter

1.6 ELECTRIC RESISTANCE

Electric Circuit :

An electric circuit is a closed conducting path containing a source of electric energy (i.e., a cell or a battery) and
a device or element or load utilizing the electric energy.

For example, an electric bulb or lamp connected with a cell with the help of connecting wires form simple electric circuit. In this circuit, a cell is a source of electric energy and an electric lamp is the load.

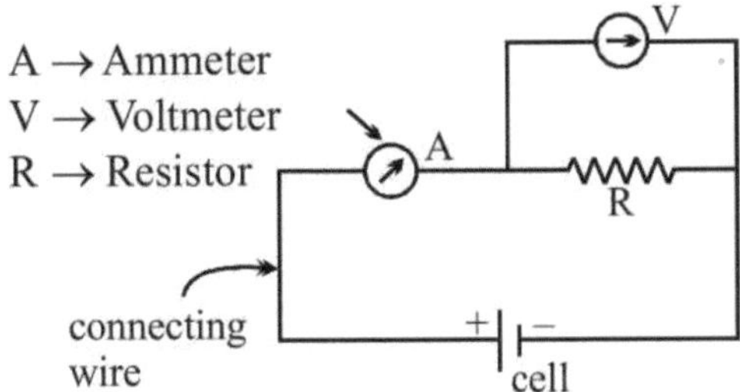

In fact, electric current is a means of transferring electric energy from the source to the load. Thus, "a closed conducting path containing the source of electric energy and the load through which electric current flows is known as electric circuit".

A simple electric circuit is shown in figure.

Open and Closed Electric Circuits

Open electric circuit : An electric circuit through which no electric current flows is known as open electric circuit.

The electric circuit shown in figure will be open circuit if the plug of the key is taken out or if the connecting wire breaks from any point.

Closed circuit : An electric circuit through which electric current flows continuously is known as closed circuit.

(1) **Electric Cell :** An electric cell is a device which maintains a continuous flow of charge in a circuit. The Cell changes Chemical energy into electrical energy.

(2) **Electro Motive Force (E.M.F.) of a cell :** The work done by the cell in forcing unit positive charge to flow in the whole circuit once, is called the electromotive force (e.m.f.) of the cell.

$$E = \frac{w}{q}\left(J/C\right)$$

The unit of emf is called **'volt'(V)**. If in the flow of 1C of charge in a circuit the energy given by the cell by 1J, then the emf of the cell is 1V.

(3) **Internal Resistance of a cell :** When we connect the plates of a cell by a wire, an electric current flows in the wire from the positive plate of the cell towards the negative plates, and in the electrolyte (inside the cell) it flows from the negative plate towards the positive plate. The resistance offered by the electrolyte of the cell to the flow of current (ions) through it is called the 'internal Resistance' of the cell.

(4) **Terminal Potential Difference :** The potential difference across the terminals of a cell or battery when the cell is in charging or discharging mode is called terminal potential difference.

Electrical Resistance :

In a conductor whenever current flow takes place the motion of electrons takes place. During motion they are opposed to flow and this is known as electrical resistance. **The SI unit of electrical resistance is Ohm denoted by Ω.**

Factors which determine the electric resistance of a conductor :

(1) The resistance of a conductor is directly proportional to its length

$$R \propto l$$

(2) The resistance is inversely proportional to the area of cross-section of the conductor

$$R \propto \frac{1}{A}$$

(3) The resistance depends upon the nature of the material of the conductor

(4) Removing the proportionality sign we have

$$R = \rho\frac{l}{A}$$

(5) ρ - Resistivity of the conductor.

Resistivity : The resistance of a unit volume of a substance is known as its resistivity.

Resistivity is also known as specific resistance and its SI unit is ohm m.

(6) **Effect of temperature on resistance :**

The resistance of conductors increases with increase in temperature. Let the resistance of a conductor at 0°C be R_0.

Let the resistance of the conductor at t° C be R_t.

Then, $R_t = R_0(1 + \alpha t)$, where 'α' is known as the **temperature coefficient of resistance**.

Pure metals have positive temperature coefficient of resistance. The resistance of metals increases with an increase in temperature.

Alloys have a very less temperature coefficient of resistance. So the resistance of alloy like Manganin and Constantan vary very little with an increase in temperature. Because of this property they are used in making standard resistances.

Semiconductors like germanium, silicon and bad conductors like glass, pure water etc., have negative temperature coefficient. The resistance of these materials decreases with an increase in temperature.

Reason for variation of resistance with temperature :

Resistance offered by a metallic conductor is due to the collisions between drifting electrons, and the ions present in the metallic conductor. When the temperature of the conductor increases, the amplitude of vibration of ions in the lattice increases and hence the collisions between electrons and the ions become more frequent. Therefore, the opposition to the flow of electrons (constituting the electric current) increases. In other words, resistance of the metallic conductor increases or decreases with the increase or decrease of the temperature respectively.

Then, $R_t = R_0 [1 + \alpha(t_2 - t_1)]$

Where, α is the temperature coefficient of the resistance.

$$\alpha = \frac{(R_t - R_0)}{R_0(t_2 - t_1)}$$

Thus, temperature coefficient of resistance (α) is defined as the change in resistance per unit original resistance per degree rise in temperature.

S.I. unit of α is $\frac{\text{ohm}}{\text{ohm kelvin}}$ or kelvin^{-1} or K^{-1}

α is positive for metallic conductors i.e. their resistance increases with the rise of temperature (i.e. $R_t > R_0$).

α is negative for insulators and semi - conductors i.e., their resistance decreases with the rise of temperature (i.e., $R_t < R_0$).

α is very - very small for high resistivity alloys like manganin ($\approx 10^{-5}\,°C^{-1}$). i.e. their resistance does not change appreciably with change in temperature. It is for this reason that manganin and constantan are used in making standard resistance coils.

Illustration :

The length of copper wire is 100 m and its radius is 1 mm. Calculate its resistance if resistivity of copper is $1.72 \times 10^{-8}\,\Omega$m.

Sol. Length of copper wire (l) = 100 m.

Area of cross section (a) = $\pi r^2 = 3.14 \times 10^{-6}\,m^2$

Resistivity (ρ) of copper = $1.72 \times 10^{-8}\,\Omega\,m$

Resistance offered by a conductor is given by

$$R = \rho\frac{l}{A}$$

$$= \frac{1.72\times10^{-8}\times100}{3.14\times10^{-6}} = 0.55\ \Omega.$$

In this numerical, length of copper wire is 100 m. If the length is 1000 m i.e., 1 km, the resistance offered by it would be 5.5 Ω which is very less. Thus copper is a good conductor of electricity.

Illustration :

The resistance of 1 m of nichrome wire is 6 Ω. Calculate its resistance if its length is 70 cm.

Sol. Given

1st case

Length of nichrome wire (l_1) = 1 m = 100 cm

Resistance of nichrome wire (R_1) = 6Ω

2nd case

l_2 = 70 cm

$R_2 = ?$

By 1st law of resistance

$$\frac{R_1}{R_2} = \frac{l_1}{l_2}$$

$$\frac{6\,\Omega}{R_2} = \frac{100\text{ cm}}{70\text{ cm}}$$

$\therefore\ R_2 = 4.2\ \Omega.$

Illustration :

Two wires made of German-silver are taken such that the length and area of cross-section of the second wire are twice and thrice respectively those of the first wire. If the resistance of the second wire is 12 r, find the resistance of the first wire.

Sol.

1st case

Silver is the best conductor of electricity.

l_1 = length of German silver wire;
a_1 = area of cross section;
R_1 = resistance

$$R_1 = \rho\frac{l_1}{a_1} \qquad .....(i)$$

2nd case

l_2 = length of wire = $2l_1$ $\qquad$ a_2 = area of cross section of wire = $3a_1$.
R_2 = resistance of wire = 12Ω.

$$R_2 = \rho\frac{l_2}{a_2}$$

$$\therefore \quad 12 = \rho\frac{2l_1}{3a_1} \qquad .....(ii)$$

dividing (i) by (ii)

$$\frac{R_1}{12} = \frac{pl}{a_1} \times \frac{3a_1}{\rho(2l_1)} = \frac{3}{2} \qquad \therefore \quad R_1 = 18\Omega.$$

Knowledge Enhancer

1. The connecting wires in an electric circuit are made of copper and aluminium. The resistivity of pure metals is very low. So, electric current passes easily through them. Out of metals, silver is the best conductor of electricity because its resistivity is the lowest among all metals. Thus, connecting wires in an electric circuit must be made of silver. However, the silver metal is costly as compared to other metals like aluminium and copper. The resistivity of copper and aluminium are also low and these metals are cheaper than silver. Therefore, connecting wires are made of copper and aluminium metals.
2. Filament of an electric bulb is made of tungsten metal. Tungsten being a metal has high resistivity. Moreover, it does not burn (or oxidise) even at higher temperatures. The melting point of tungsten is

very high i.e., about 3380°C. For these reasons, filament of an electric bulb (incandescent lamp) is made of tungsten.

3. Heating elements of electrical appliances like electric iron, electric heater, electric toaster, room heater, immersion rod are made of nichrome (an alloy of nickel, iron, chromium and manganese). Nichrome is an alloy of metals. The resistivity of nichrome is more than the resistivity of the metals used to make it. Moreover, nichrome does not burn (or oxidise) even at higher temperature. The melting point of nichrome is 1500°C. That is why, heating elements of electrical appliances are made of nichrome i.e. an alloy.

4. Insulators are used to protect ourselves from the severe shock of electric current.

1.7 OHM'S LAW :

"When physical conditions (temperature, length, cross section) remains the same, the current flowing through a conductor is directly proportional to the potential difference across the ends of a conductor".

i.e. $I \propto V$

So we can also write

$\therefore V \propto I$

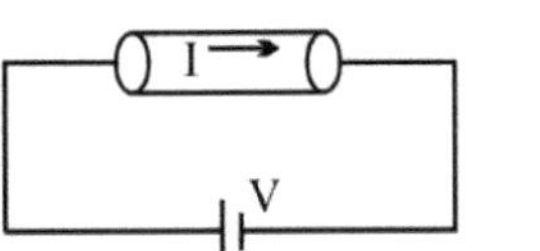

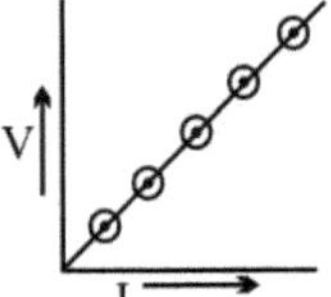

$$\boxed{V = IR}$$

$R = \dfrac{V}{I}$ = Constant, provided length, cross section and temperature of the conductor remains same.

Bigger units of resistance.

1 kilo ohm (KΩ) = 10^3 Ω

1 Mega ohm (MΩ) = 10^6 Ω

$$\boxed{\Rightarrow 1\,ohm = \frac{1\,Volt}{1\,Ampere}}$$

1 ohm is the resistance of a conductor is defined as when 1V of potential difference is applied across the conductor and then a current of 1A flows through it.

Exception of Ohm's law– In general almost all metal conductors obey the Ohm's law V = IR for which graph between V and I is a straight line as shown in figure. The conductors (or devices) obeying the ohm's law are called ohmic. However, there are some exceptions such as vacuum tube, semiconductor diode, transistor, liquid electrolytes etc. in which relation V = IR does not hold good. These devices are called **non-ohmic**.

Figure (a) shows V – I curve for a bulb. This appears from the figure that this device do not obey the relation V = IR.

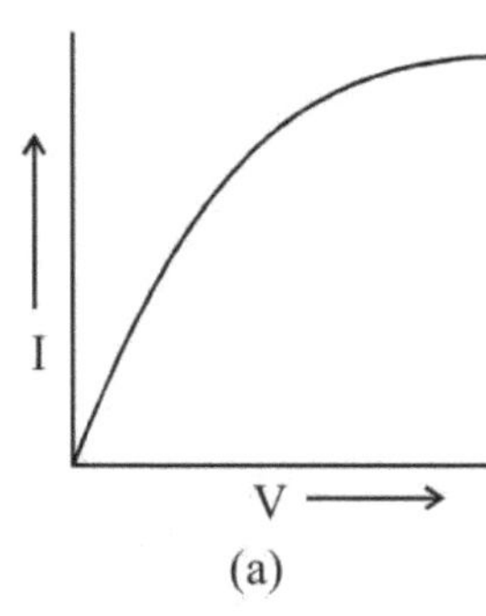

(a)

Figure (b) shows V – I curve for a semiconductor device such as diode or transistor. Again this graph is not fitted in the form of standard Ohm's law. Hence such devices are non-ohmic.

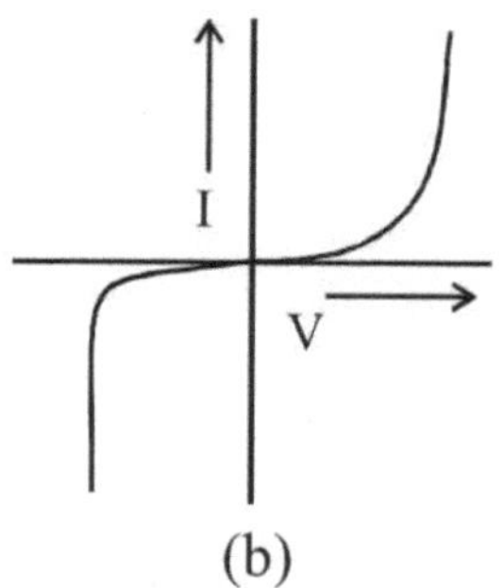

(b)

Knowledge Enhancer

The reciprocal of resistance is called conductance G = 1/R.
Its SI unit is ohm^{-1} or mho or siemen(s).
The substances which obey Ohm's law are called Ohmic or linear conductors. The resistance of such conductors is independent of magnitude and polarity of applied potential difference. Here the graph between I and V is a straight line passing through the origin. The reciprocal of slope of straight line gives resistance

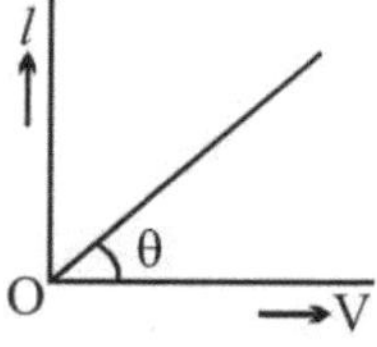

$$R = \frac{V}{I} = \frac{1}{\tan\theta} = \text{constant.}$$

Examples silver, copper, mercury, carbon, mica etc.
The substances which do not obey Ohm's law are called non-ohmic or non linear conductors. The I – V curve is not a straight line.
i.e. p-n diode, transistor, thermionic valves, rectifiers etc.

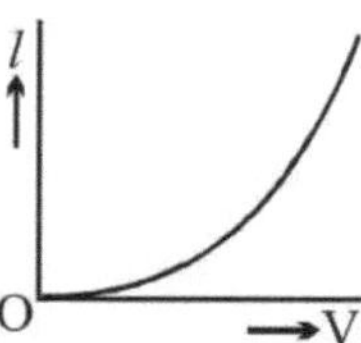

Check Point

Choose the correct alternative :

(a) **Alloys of metals usually have (greater/less) resistivity than that of their constituent metals.**

(b) **Alloys usually have much (lower/higher) temperature coefficients of resistance than pure metals.**

(c) **The resistance of graphite and most non-metals increases/decreases with increase in temperature.**

(d) **The resistivity of a semiconductor increases/decreases rapidly with increasing temperature.**

(e) **The resistivity of the alloy manganin is nearly independent of / increases rapidly with increases of temperatures.**

(f) **The resistivity of a typical insulator (e.g, amber) is greater than that of a metal by a factor of the order of (10^{22} /10^{23}).**

Solution

(a) Alloys of metals usually have greater resistivity than that of their constituent metals.

(b) Alloys usually have much lower temperature coefficients of resistance than pure metals.

(c) The resistance of graphite and most non metals decreases with increase in temperature.

(d) The resistivity of a semiconductor decreases rapidly with increasing temperature.

(e) The resistivity of the alloy manganin is nearly independent of increasing temperature.

(f) The resistivity of a typical insulator (e.g. amber) is greater than that of a metal by factor of the order of 10^{22}.

Important terms :

Resistor : A component in an electric circuit which offers resistance (i.e. opposition) to the flow of electrons constituting electric current is known as a resistor. For example, a metallic wire or a conductor used in an electric circuit is known as resistor.

Variable resistance : In an electric circuit, sometimes current has to be increased or decreased. A component used in an electric circuit to change the current without changing the potential difference across the circuit is called variable resistance.

Rheostat is a device used in an electric circuit to change the resistance and hence current in the circuit. It means, rheostat acts as a variable resistance of unknown value in the circuit.

1.8 COMBINATION OF RESISTANCES (OR RESISTORS):

Series Combination :

In this combination, the resistances are joined end to end. In series combination the current across each resistance is same but the potential difference across each R_1, R_2 and R_3 are V_1, V_2 and V_3. To replace R_1, R_2 and R_3 by an equivalent resistance the potential difference across equivalent should be equal to the sum of the potential difference across the three resistances.

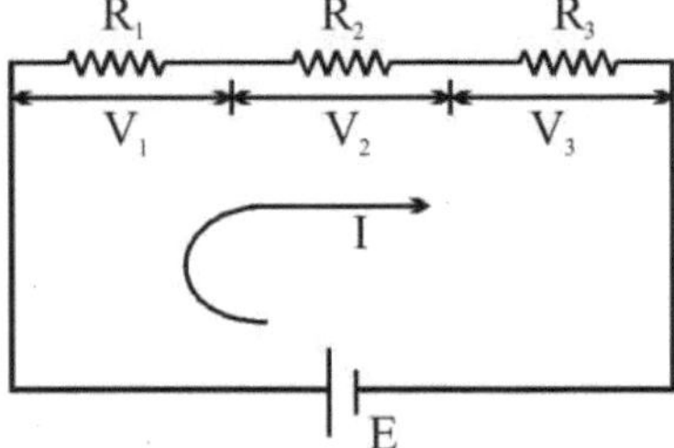

$V_1 = IR_1$

$V_2 = IR_2$

$V_3 = IR_3$

$E = V_1 + V_2 + V_3$

$IR_{eq} = IR_1 + IR_2 + IR_3$

$$\boxed{R_{eq} = R_1 + R_2 + R_3}$$

Characteristics of series circuit :

(i) Same current is flowing through all the resistances.

(ii) The effective resistance is the sum of the individual resistances. Effective resistance $R_{eff} = R_1 + R_2 + R_3$.

(iii) The applied voltage $V = V_1 + V_2 + V_3$.

(iv) The maximum power is consumed by the resistor having the highest resistance, or the voltage drop is maximum across the highest resistance.

Disadvantage of a series arrangement of resistors :

(i) Suppose all electric appliances like bulbs and electric tubes are connected in series in a circuit. If any one of them fuses (i.e., breaks), then all the other appliances will also not work. This is because series arrangement is not used in domestic electric circuits.

(ii) Different electric appliances like bulbs, electric tubes, electric heaters, toaster etc. have different resistance and hence they require different amount of electric current for their operations. If they all are connected in series, they will not operate properly.

Illustration : Calculate (a) the equivalent resistance, (b) the electric current, and (c) the potential difference across each resistor in the circuit shown in figure

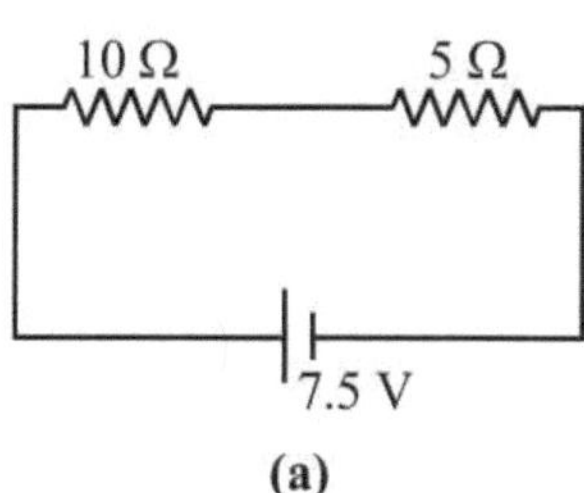

(a)

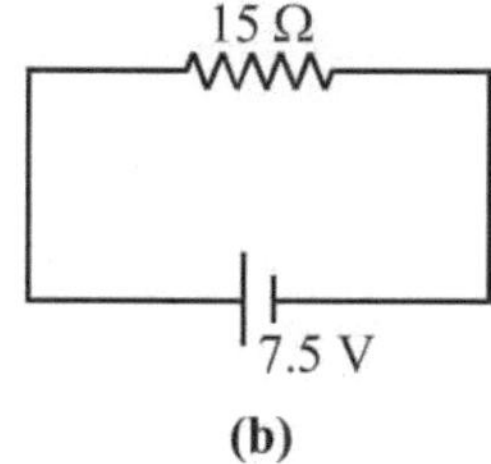

(b)

Sol.

(a) Any current that passes through the resistor of 10Ω also passes through the resistor of 5Ω. So, the 10Ω and 5Ω resistors are connected in series. Their equivalent resistance is

$$R = 10\Omega + 5\Omega = 15\ \Omega$$

(b) The circuit is equivalent to that shown in figure (b). The current is

$$i = \frac{V}{R} = \frac{7.5V}{15\,\Omega} = 0.5\text{ A.}$$

This is the current through both the resistors.

(c) The potential difference across the 10 Ω resistor is

$$V_1 = iR_1 = (0.5\text{ A}) \times (10\ \Omega) = 5V$$

The potential difference across the 5Ω resistor is

$$V_2 = iR_2 = (0.5\text{ A}) \times (5\Omega) = 2.5\text{ V.}$$

Parallel Combination :

When two or more resistances are combined in such a way that their first ends are connected to one point and the second ends to another point then this combination is in parallel. In this combination the potential difference between the ends of all the resistances is same but the current in different resistances are different.

$$I = I_1 + I_2 + I_3$$

$$I = \frac{V}{R_1} + \frac{V}{R_2} + \frac{V}{R_3}$$

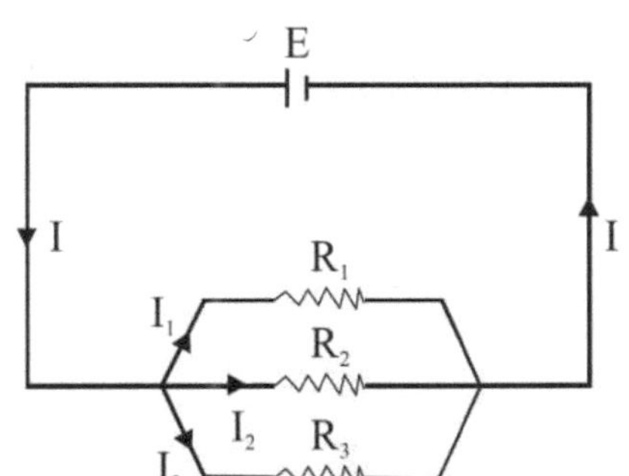

$$\frac{V}{R_{eq}} = \frac{V}{R_1} + \frac{V}{R_2} + \frac{V}{R_3}$$

$$\Rightarrow \boxed{\frac{1}{R_{eq}} = \frac{1}{R_1} + \frac{1}{R_2} + \frac{1}{R_3}}$$

The reciprocal of the equivalent resistance of the resistances connected in parallel is equal to the sum of the reciprocal of those resistances.

Advantages of connecting electrical devices in parallel :

1. In a series circuit the current is constant throughout the electric circuit. Thus it is obviously impracticable to connect an electric bulb and an electric heater in series, because they need currents of widely different values to operate properly.
2. Another major disadvantage of a series circuit is that when one component fails the circuit is broken and none of the components works.
3. On the other hand, a parallel circuit divides the current through the electrical gadgets. The total resistance in a parallel circuit is decreased. This is helpful particularly when each gadget has different resistance and requires different current to operate properly.

If 'n' number of resistors each of same value connected in parallel, then the equivalent resistance of the parallel combination of 'n' resistors is given by

$$\mathbf{R_{eq.}} = \frac{R}{n}$$

Illustration :

Determine the equivalent resistance between points A and B in the following circuits

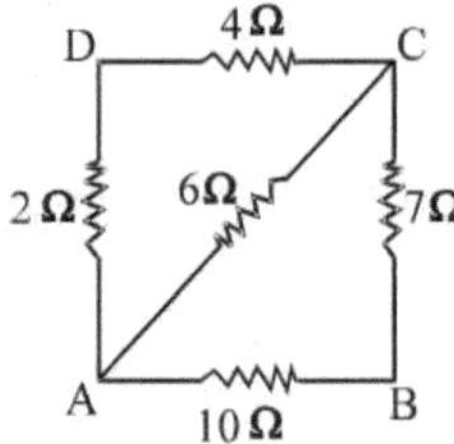

Solution

1Ω and 2Ω in series

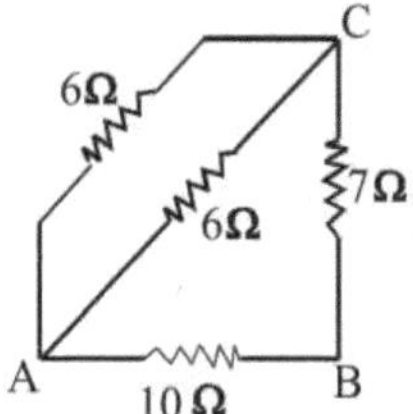

$R_{eq_1} = 4 + 2 = 6\Omega$

6Ω and 6Ω in parallel reduces to

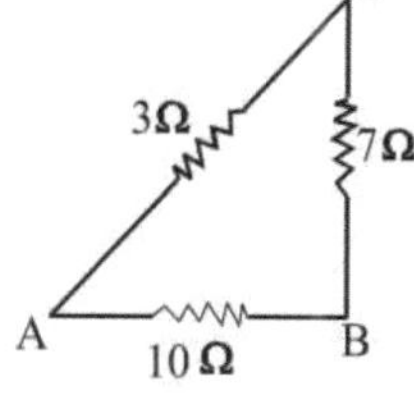

$$\frac{1}{R_{eq_2}} = \frac{1}{6} + \frac{1}{6} = 3\Omega$$

3Ω and 7Ω in series

10 Ω
A 10 Ω B

$$R_{eq_3} = 3 + 7 = 10\Omega$$

10Ω and 10Ω in parallel

A 5Ω B

$$\frac{1}{R_{eq}} = \frac{1}{10} + \frac{1}{10} = 5\Omega$$

Check Point

Q. Given n resistors each of resistance R, how will you combine them to get the (i) maximum (ii) Minimum effective resistance? What is the ratio of the maximum to minimum resistance?

Solution

(i) For maximum effective resistance, all the resitors should be joined in series.

$$R_{max} = R + R + R + \text{........ n or } R_{max} = nR$$

(ii) For minimum effective resistance all the resistors should be joined in parallel.

$$\frac{1}{R_{min}} = \frac{1}{R} + \frac{1}{R} + \frac{1}{R} + \text{........n} \quad \text{or} \quad \frac{1}{R_{min}} = \frac{n}{R}$$

so, $R_{min} = \frac{R}{n}$

Now, $\frac{R_{max}}{R_{min}} = n^2$.

Try yourself :

1. Determine the value of current in the 2Ω resistance and the potential difference between A and B in the circuit diagram given

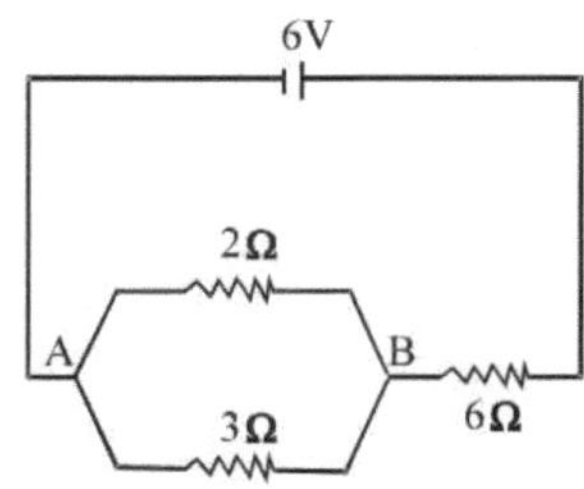

2. Find the equivalent resistance between the points A and D of the adjoining circuit diagram.

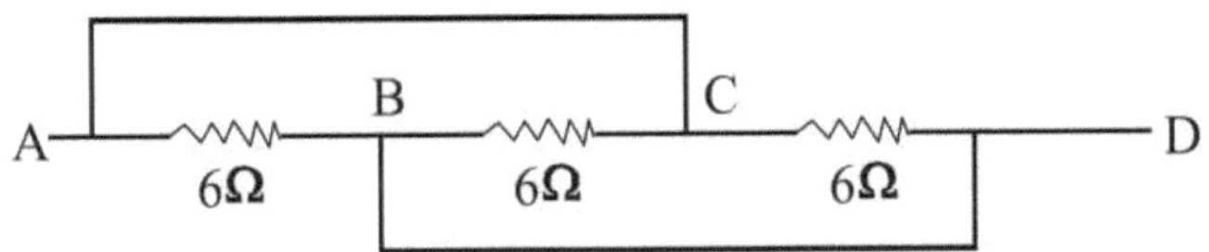

Distribution of Current in Two Resistors in Parallel :

Consider the circuit in Figure. The resistance R_1 and R_2 are connected in parallel. The current i gets distributed in the two resistors.

We have $i = i_1 + i_2$ ....(i)

Applying Ohm's law to the resistor R_1,

$$V_A - V_B = R_1 i_1. \qquad \text{........(ii)}$$

And applying Ohm's law to the resistor R_2,

$$V_A - V_B = R_2 i_2. \qquad \text{........(iii)}$$

From (ii) and (iii), $R_1 i_1 = R_2 i_2$ or $i_2 = \frac{R_1}{R_2} i_1$.

Substituting for i_2 in (i), we have

$$i = i_1 + \frac{R_1}{R_2} i_1 = i_1 \left(1 + \frac{R_1}{R_2}\right) = i_1 = \frac{R_1 + R_2}{R_2} \qquad \text{or} \qquad \boxed{i_1 = \frac{R_2}{R_1 + R_2} i}$$

Similarly, $\boxed{i_2 = \frac{R_1}{R_1 + R_2} i}$

Thus, $\frac{i_1}{i_2} = \frac{R_2}{R_1}$.

The current through each branch in a parallel combination of resistors is inversely proportional to its resistance.

Illustration : Two resistors of resistance 10 Ω and 20 Ω are connected in parallel. A battery supplies 6 A of current to the combination, as shown in figure. Calculate the current in each resistor.

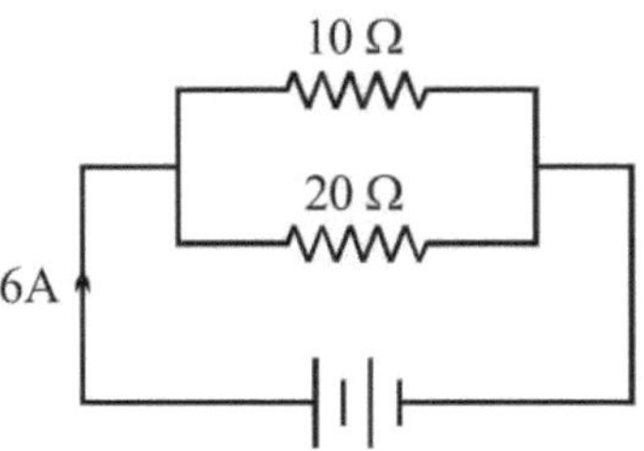

Sol. The current in the 10 Ω resistors is

$$i_1 = \frac{R_2}{R_1 + R_2} i = \frac{(20\,\Omega) \times (6A)}{(10\,\Omega) + (20\,\Omega)} = 4A.$$

The current in the 20 Ω resistor is

$$i_2 = \frac{R_1}{R_1 + R_2} i = \frac{(10\,\Omega)\times(6A)}{(10\,\Omega)+(20\,\Omega)} = 2A.$$

1.9 KIRCHHOFF'S LAW :

Kirchhoff's First law or Junction Rule :

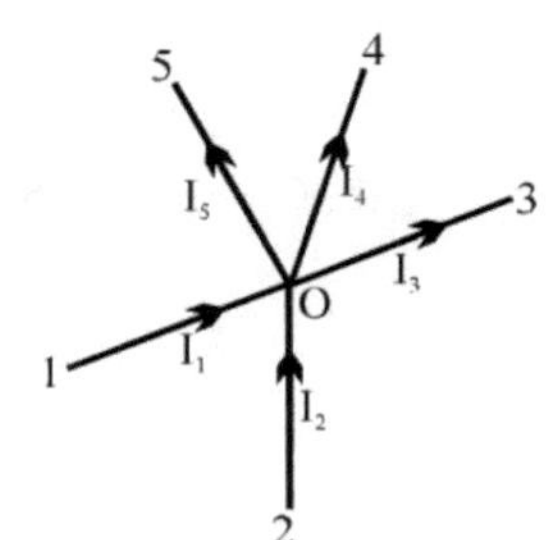

In an electric circuit, the 'algebraic' sum of the currents meeting at any junction in the circuit is Zero, that is

$$\sum i = 0$$

$I_1 + I_2 - I_3 - I_4 - I_5 = 0$

$I_1 + I_2 = I_3 + I_4 + I_5$

Kirchhoff's First law is a statement of the conservation of charge.

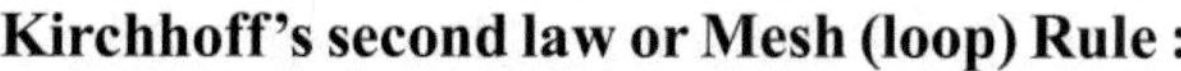

Kirchhoff's second law or Mesh (loop) Rule :

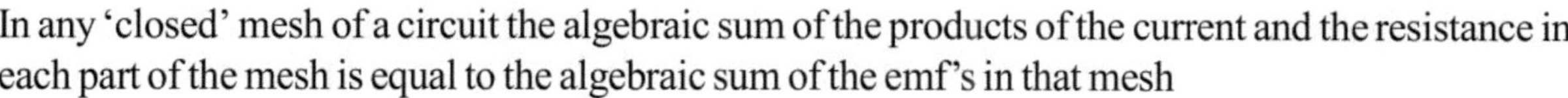

In any 'closed' mesh of a circuit the algebraic sum of the products of the current and the resistance in each part of the mesh is equal to the algebraic sum of the emf's in that mesh

$$\sum E = 0$$

Kirchoff's second law is simply a statement of the conservation of energy.

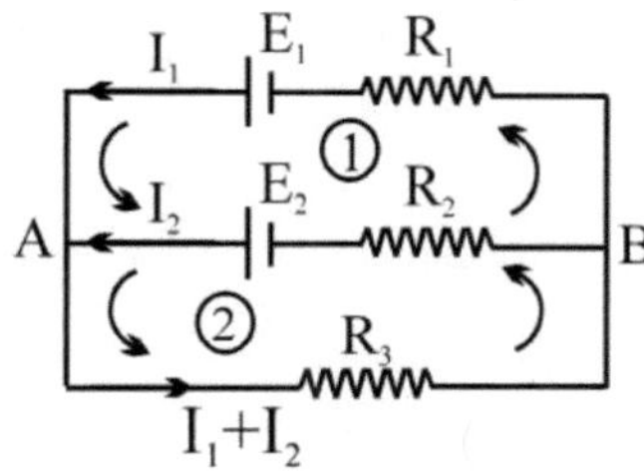

Kirchhoff's second law for mesh 1, we have

$-I_1R_1 + E_1 - E_2 + I_2R_2 = 0$ (1)

Kirchoff's second law for mesh 2, we have

$-I_2R_2 + E_2 - (I_1 + I_2)R_3 = 0$ (2)

Illustration :

Apply Kirchhoff's Voltage law to the adjoining circuit and obtain two equations for I_1 and I_2.

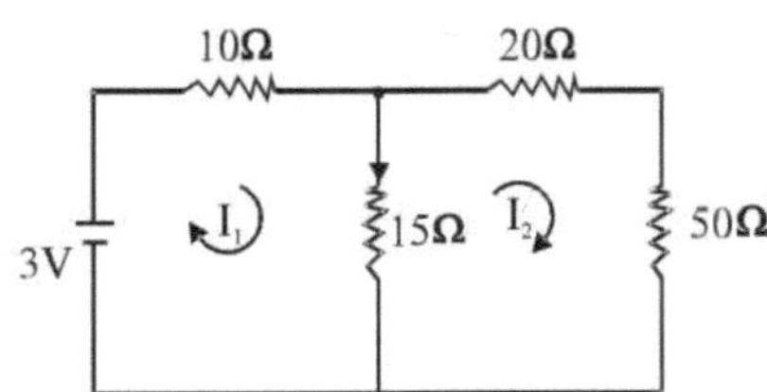

Solution

Mark the current distribution for the circuit.

Apply Kirchoff's law for the first closed mesh, we have

$$I_1 \times 10 + (I_1 - I_2) \times 15 - 3 = 0$$

$$25I_1 - 15I_2 = 3 \qquad ..(1)$$

Applying Kirchoff's voltage law for the second closed mesh, we have

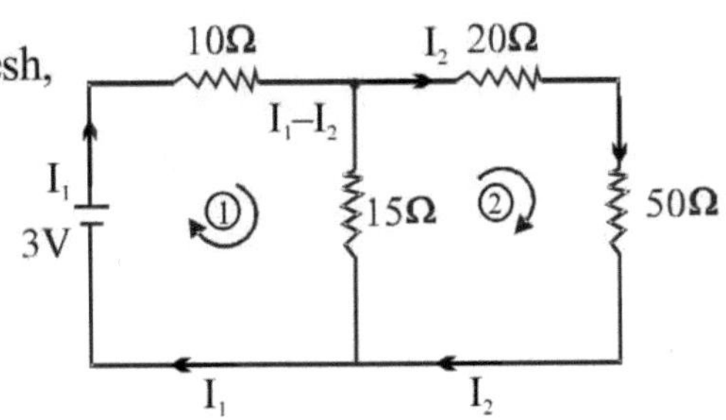

$$I_2 \times 20 + I_2 \times 50 - (I_1 - I_2)15 = 0$$

$$17I_2 - 3I_1 = 0 \qquad ..(2)$$

Solving equation (1) and (2), we get

$$I_1 = \frac{51}{380} = 0.134\,A$$

and $$I_2 = \frac{9}{380} = 0.024\,A$$

Relation among Terminal Potential Difference, EMF and Internal Resistance of a cell :

Let

E = Emf of cell

V = Terminal Potential difference

r = Internal resistance of cell

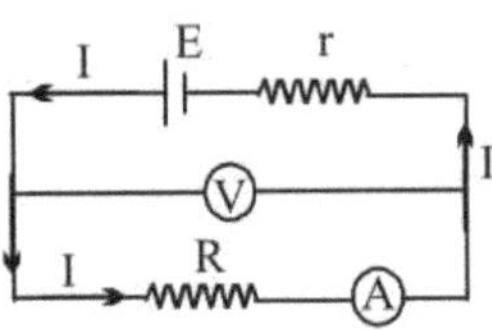

During discharging Mode

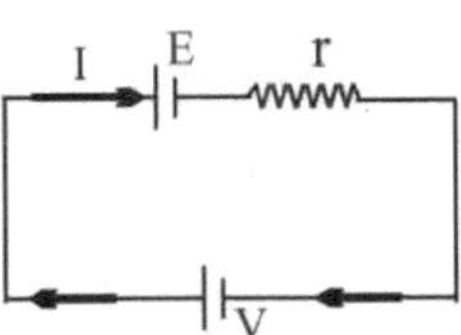

$\boxed{V = E - Ir}$ Where, $I = \dfrac{E}{R + r}$

During charging Mode

$\boxed{V = E + Ir}$

1.10 HEATING EFFECT OF ELECTRIC CURRENT :

When conductor is connected to a source of electricity like cell or batteries, an electric field is developed across its ends and due to this field the free electrons of the conductor get moving in a definite direction. During their motion these free electrons experience the resistance due to the collisions with the ions or atoms already present in that conductor. Therefore, some energy of the electrons gets lost in this process which appears in the form of heat energy. This effect of electric current is known as **heating effect of electric current**. The electric appliances like electric kettle, heater, press etc. operate their functioning based on the heating effect of electric current.

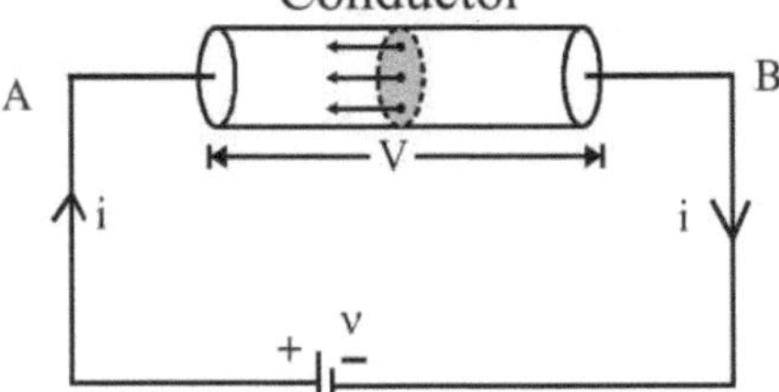

Passing of an electric current of strength 'i' through a conductor of resistance 'R' for time-interval Δt produces a potential difference 'V' across its ends then the total charge passing

through the conductor in time-interval Δt will be

$$q = \text{Strength of Current} \times \text{time-interval or } q = i \times \Delta t$$

In this process the work done in carrying q coulomb of charge from one end to the other at potential difference V will be

$$W = q.V \text{ or } W = (i \times \Delta t) \times V = i \times \Delta t \times (i \times R) = i^2 \times R\,\Delta t$$

If this entire work is converted into heat then heat produced is;

$$H = \frac{W}{J} = \frac{Vi\,\Delta t}{J}$$

Here J is a conversion constant and known as the **Mechanical equivalent of heat**. Its value is 4.18 joule/calorie (1 cal = 4.18 J)

Hence the heat produced due to flow of current through a conductor.

$$H = \frac{Vi.\Delta t}{4.18} = 0.239\ Vi\ .\ \Delta t = 0.239\ i^2\ R\Delta t \quad \text{(in calorie)}$$

The production of heat in a conductor due to flow of electric current through it is called heating effect of electric current.

1.11 JOULE'S LAW :

These are as follows :–

(i) The amount of heat (H) produced in a conductor in a definite time interval Δt is directly proportional to the square of the strength of current passing through it.

Hence $H \propto I^2$

It is also known as law of current.

(ii) If the current of definite strength i passes through a conductor of resistance R for a definite time interval Δt then the amount of heat (H) produced in the conductor is directly proportional to its resistance R.

Hence $H \propto R$

It is also known as the law of resistance.

(iii) If the current of definite strength i passes through a conductor of resistance R then the amount of heat (H) produced in the conductor is directly proportional to the time interval Δt for which the current flows in it.

Hence $H \propto \Delta t$

It is also known as the law of time.

Therefore the amount of heat produced (H) when a current of strength i passes through a conductor of resistance R for a time interval Δt is given by

$$H \propto I^2 R \Delta t$$

$$H = I^2 Rt \text{ Joule}$$

or

$$\boxed{H = \frac{1}{J} I^2 R\Delta t = 0.239 I^2 R\Delta t \text{ calorie}}$$

This equation is a mathematical **expression of Joule's law.**

Check Point

Specimen Numerical :– An electric heater of resistance 500 ohm is connected to a main supply for 30 minutes. If 5 A current flows through the filament of the heater, calculate the heat energy produced in the heater.

Solution : Here, $I = 5$ A; $R = 500$ ohm

$t = 30$ minute $= 30 \times 60$ s $= 1800$ s.

Using, $H = I^2Rt$, we get

$H = (5)^2 \times 500 \times 1800 = 22500000\ J = 2.25 \times 10^7\ J$

Thus, heat energy produced $= 2.25 \times 10^7$ J

1.12 PRACTICAL APPLICATIONS OF HEATING EFFECT OF ELECTRIC CURRENT

1. **Electric heater, electric iron and water heater etc. work on the heating effect of current.**

   When electric appliances like electric heater, electric iron and water heater etc. are connected to the main supply of electricity, these appliances become hot but the connecting wires remain cold.

   The element of electric heater is made of nichrome. Nichrome has high value of resistivity and hence high resistance. We know, heat produced is directly proportional to the resistance of the material through which current flows. Since, resistance of nichrome is high, so a large amount of heat is produced in the element of the electric heater. Thus, filament of electric heater becomes red hot. On the other hand, connecting wires are made of copper or aluminium is very small, so a very small heat is produced in the connecting wires made of copper or aluminium.

2. **Electric bulb glows when electric current flows through the filament of the bulb.**

   Filament of an electric bulb is made of a thin wire of tungsten. The melting point of filament is high i.e., about 3380°C. The filament of the bulb is enclosed in a glass envelope fixed over an insulated support. The glass envelope of electric bulb is filled with inactive gases like nitrogen and argon.

   Since resistance of thin filament is very high, so a large heat is produced as the electric current flows through the filament of the bulb becomes white hot. Hence, the filament of the bulb emits light and heat.

3. **Electric fuse in the electric circuit melts when large current flows in the circuit.**

   Electric fuse is a safety device connected in series with the electric circuit. Electric fuse is a wire made of a material whose melting point is very low. Examples of the materials for making fuse wire are copper or tin-lead alloy. When large current flows through a circuit and hence through a fuse wire, a large amount of heat is produced. Due to this large amount of heat, the fuse wire melts and the circuit is broken so that current stops flowing in the circuit. This saves the electric circuit from burning.

Electric fuses used in electrical circuits are rated as 1A, 2A, 3A, 5A, 10A etc. When we say, electric fuse is rated as 1A, it means the maximum current that can flow through the fuse wire without melting it is 1A. If an electric current flows through the electric circuit is more than 1A, then the fuse rated as 1A will melt and the circuit breaks. For such electric circuit, fuse rated as 2A is used.

1.13 ELECTRIC POWER :

The rate of doing work, in an electric device due to flow of current in it, is defined as the power of that electric device.

If, in a circuit with an electric source, the potential difference V is developed across the two ends of a conductor of resistance R as current of strength i passes through it for a time-interval Δt then work done in carrying a charge q through a potential difference V in the circuit will be–

$$W = q \times V = i \times \Delta t \times V$$

So the rate of work done, i.e., Power of the electric device (P);

$$P = \frac{W}{\Delta t} = \frac{i \times \Delta t \times V}{\Delta t} = i \times V$$

or $$P = V \times i = \frac{V^2}{R} = i^2 R$$

P = VI, when either V or I or both V and I change.

$P = I^2R$ is applied when current I is constant in the electric circuit.

$P = \frac{V^2}{R}$ is applied when potential difference is constant in the electric circuit.

1 VA = 1 W

1 kVA = 10^3 W

1 h.p. = 746 W

* Equivalent power in series and parallel combination.

- In series combination

$$\frac{1}{P_{eq}} = \frac{1}{P_1} + \frac{1}{P_2} + \frac{1}{P_3}$$

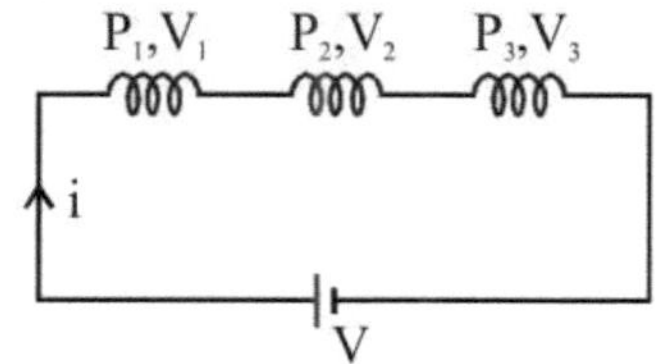

- In parallel combination

$$P_{eq} = P_1 + P_2 + P_3$$

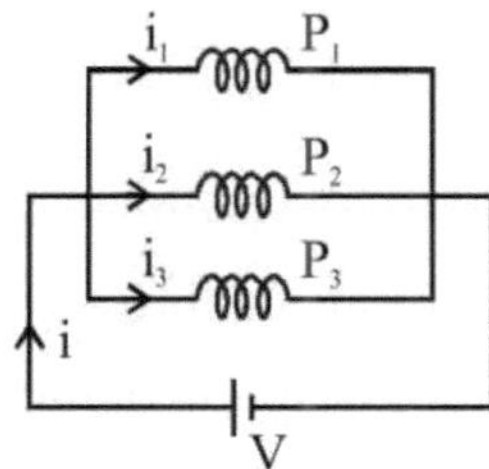

The S.I. unit of electric power is **watt**. Therefore in an electric circuit if 1 ampere current flows for a time-interval of 1 second through a potential difference of 1 Volt then the power of the electric device is termed as 1 watt.

In general kilowatt & Megawatt are used for measurement of electric power, Hence –

1 Kilowatt = 1000 watt = 10^3 watt

and 1 Megawatt = 1000 kilowatt = 10^6 watt

In practice, Horse Power (H.P.) is also used for the measurement of electric power. The value of 1 Horse Power is 746 Watt.

1.14 ELECTRIC ENERGY :

The work done in moving an electric charge through a circuit is electric energy.

The work done by an electric source for the flow of current for a certain time interval is known as electric energy of the circuit. If electric power P is given for a small time Δt in a electric circuit then electric energy of the circuit will be $W = P \times \Delta t$ so the electric energy of the electric circuit is–

$$W = P \times \Delta t = Vi\ \Delta t = i^2 R\Delta t$$

The unit for the measurement of electric energy is **watt × sec** or **joule**. In practice **kilo-watt** hour is used for the measurement of Electric Energy. It is also known as Board of Trade Unit (B.O.T.U.) or simply Electric Unit i.e.,

1 Electric Unit = 1 k.w.h. = 1 kilo watt × 1 hour = 1000 watt × 3600 second

or 1 Electric Unit = 3.6×10^6 watt × second or joule. The rate of doing work, in an electric device due to flow of current in it, is defined as the power of that.

How to calculate electricity bill?

Suppose electric appliances of a house have consumed 100 kWh of electric energy in a month and the cost of one unit is 50 paise. Then the total bill for month = 100 × 50 = 5000 paise = Rs. 50.00. Here 1 kWh = 1 unit.

LET US RECAPITULATE

- Electric current : An electric current is defined as the amount of charge flowing through any cross-section of a conductor per unit time, $I = \frac{Q}{t}$. Electric current is a scalar quantity.
- Electric current in terms of number of electrons (n) in a conductor, $I = \frac{ne}{t}$,

  e = charge on an electron = -1.6×10^{-19} C.
- In a metallic wire or conductor, the flow of electric current is due to the flow of electrons from one end to the other end of the wire.
- Charge carrier in a metallic wire are conduction elements.
- 6.25×10^{18} electrons make one coulomb of charge.
- S.I. unit of electric current is ampere (A).
- Ampere (A) : Electric current through a conductor is said to be 1 ampere if one coulomb charge flows through any cross-section of the conductor in one second.
- Ammeter is used to measure electric current.
- Ammeter is always connected in series in an electric circuit.
- Electric potential is defined as work done per unit charge.

$$V = \frac{W}{q}$$

- Electric potential is a scalar quantity.
- Electric potential difference is defined as the work done in moving a unit positive charge from one point to another point.

$$dV = \frac{W}{q}$$

- SI unit of electric potential is volt (V).
- Voltmeter is used to measure the potential difference between two points in an electric circuit.
- Voltmeter is always connected in parallel in an electric circuit.
- **Ohm's Law :** This law states that, "the electric current flowing in a conductor is directly proportional to the potential difference across the ends of the conductor, provided the temperature and other physical conditions of the conductor remain the same".
- **Resistance (R) :** Resistance of a conductor is the ability of the conductor to oppose the flow of charge through it.
- Unit of resistance is ohm.
- 1 Ohm : Resistance of a conductor is said to be 1 ohm if a potential difference of 1 volt across the ends of the conductor produces a current of 1 ampere through it.
- Resistor is a component (say a metallic wire) in an electric circuit which offers resistance to the flow of electrons constituting the electric current in the electric circuit.
- Law of Resistance :

  (i) Resistance of a conductor depends upon the nature of the material of the conductor.

  (ii) Resistance of a conductor is directly proportional to the length of the conductor.

  (iii) Resistance of a conductor is inversely proportional to the each of cross-section of the conductor.

  (iv) Resistance of metallic conductor increases with the increase of temperature and decreases with the decrease of the temperature.

- $R = \frac{\rho l}{A}$
- Resistivity or Specific Resistance (ρ) : Resistivity is defined as the resistance of the conductor of unit length and unit area of cross-section.
- Unit of Resistivity :

  In CGS system, unit if resistivity is ohm-cm.

  In SI system, unit of resistivity is ohm-metre.
- Two or more resistors are said to be connected in series if same amount of current flows through these resistors.
- The effective resistance of series combination of resistors is the algebraic sum of the individual resistances of the resistors in the combination.
- An electric bulb or a heater or a metallic wire acts as a resistor.
- If one of the electric bulbs connected in a series is fused, then no electric bulb will glow inspite of the fact that the combination is connected with a source of electric current.
- Two or more resistors are said to be connected in parallel if the potential difference across each resistor is equal to the applied potential difference across the combination of the resistors.
- The effective resistance of the resistors connected in parallel is less than the minimum resistance of a resistor in the combination.

- Resistors are connected in series if the resistance of the electric circuit is to be increased.
- Resistors are connected in parallel if the resistance of the electric circuit is to be decreased.
- Joule's Law of Heating :

  The amount of heat produced in a conductor is

  (i) Directly proportional to the square of the electric current flowing through it.

  (ii) Directly proportional to the resistance of the conductor.

  (iii) Directly proportional to the time for which the electric current flows through the conductor.

  $$H = I^2Rt \quad \text{(joule)}$$
- Electric fuse is a safety device used to save the electric appliances from burning.
- Electric fuse is a wire made of a material having low melting point.
- Electric fuse wire is made of copper or tin-lead alloy.
- Electric energy : The work done by a source of electricity to maintain a current in an electric circuit is known as electric energy.

  $$E = VIt$$
- Electric power : Electric power is defined as the amount of electric work done in one second.

  $$P = VI = I^2R = \frac{V^2}{R}$$
- SI unit of power is watt.
- Practical unit of power is horse power (h.p.)

  $$1 \text{ h.p.} = 746 \text{ W}$$
- Electric energy = Electric power × time
- Commercial unit of Energy : kilowatt-hour (kWh)
- $1 \text{ kWh} = 3.6 \times 10^6 \text{ J}$

Electric Current	$i = \frac{Q}{t}$
Ohm's Law	$V = iR$
	$R = \rho \frac{l}{A}$
Resistors in series	$R_{eq} = R_1 + R_2 + R_3 + ...$
Resistors in parallel	$\frac{1}{R_{eq}} = \frac{1}{R_1} + \frac{1}{R_2} + \frac{1}{R_3} + ...$
Heat produced by electric current	$U = i^2 Rt = \frac{V^2}{R} t = Vit$
Electric power	$P = \frac{U}{t} = i^2 R = \frac{V^2}{R} = Vi$

CONCEPT APPLICATION LEVEL - I [NCERT Questions]

Q.1 A piece of wire of resistance R is cut into five equal parts. These parts are then connected in parallel. If the equivalent resistance of this combination is R', then the ratio R/R' is :

(A) 1/ 25 (B) 1/5 (C) 5 (D) 25

Ans. Resistance of each one of the five parts $= \frac{R}{5}$

$$\frac{1}{R'} = \frac{1}{R/5} + \frac{1}{R/5} + \frac{1}{R/5} + \frac{1}{R/5} + \frac{1}{R/5}$$

or $$\frac{1}{R'} = \frac{5}{R} + \frac{5}{R} + \frac{5}{R} + \frac{5}{R} + \frac{5}{R} = \frac{25}{R}$$

or $$\frac{R}{R'} = 25$$

Thus, (D) is the correct answer.

Q.2 Which of the following terms does not represent electrical power in a circuit :

(A) I^2R (B) IR^2 (C) VI (D) V^2/R

Ans. Electrical power,

$$P = VI = (IR)R = I^2R = V\left(\frac{V}{R}\right) = \frac{V^2}{R}$$

Obviously, IR^2 does not represent electrical power in a circuit.

Thus, (B) is the current an answer .

Q.3 An electric bulb is rated 220 V and 100 W. When it is operated on 110 V, the power consumed will be

(A) 100W (B) 75 W (C) 50W (D) 25W

Ans. Resistance of the electric bulbs,

$$R = \frac{V^2}{P} \qquad (P = V^2/R)$$

or $$R = \frac{(220)^2}{100} = 484\Omega$$

power consumed by the bulb when it is operated at 110 V is given by

$$P' = \frac{V'^2}{R} = \frac{(110)^2}{484} = \frac{110 \times 110}{484} = 25W$$

(V' = 110 V)

Thus, (D) is the correct answer .

Q.4 Two conducting wires of the same material and of equal lengths and equal diameters are first connected in series and then in parallel in electric circuit. The ratio of the heat produced in series and parallel combinations would be :

(A) 1 : 2 (B) 2 : 1 (C) 1 : 4 (D) 4 : 1

Ans. Since both the wires are made of the same material and have equal lengths and equal diameters, these have the same resistance. Let it be R.

When connected in series, their equivalent resistance is given by

$$R_s = R + R = 2R$$

When connected in parallel, their equivalent resistance is given by

$$\frac{1}{R_p} = \frac{1}{R} + \frac{1}{R} = \frac{2}{R} \text{ or } R_p = \frac{R}{2}$$

Further, electrical power is given by $P = \frac{V^2}{R}$

Power (or heat produced) in series, $P^s = \frac{V^2}{R_s}$

Power (or heat produced) in parallel, $P_p = \frac{V^2}{R_p}$

Thus, $\frac{P_s}{P_p} = \frac{V^2/R_s}{V^2/R_p} = \frac{R_p}{R_s} = \frac{R/2}{2R} = \frac{1}{4}$ or $P_s : P_p :: 1:4$

thus, (C) is the correct answer

Q.5 How is voltmeter connected in the circuit to measure potential difference between two points?

Ans. A voltmeter is always connected in parallel across the points between which the P.D. is to be determined.

Q.6 A copper wire has a diameter of 0.5 mm and a resistivity of 1.6×10^{-6} ohm cm. How much of this wire would be required to make a 10 ohm coil ? How much does the resistance change if the diameter is doubled ?

Ans. We are given that, Diameter of the wire, $D = 0.5 \text{ mm} = 0.5 \times 10^{-3}$ m

resistivity of copper (ρ), $= 1.6 \times 10^{-6}$ ohm cm $= 1.6 \times 10^{-8}$ ohm m

required resistance, R = 10 ohm

As $R = \frac{\rho\ell}{A}, \ell = \frac{RA}{\rho} = \frac{R(\pi D^2/4)}{\rho} = \frac{\pi R D^2}{4\rho} [A = \pi r^2 = \pi(D/2)^2 = \pi D^2/4]$

or $\ell = \frac{3.14 \times 10 \times (0.5 \times 10^{-3})^2}{4 \times 1.6 \times 10^{-8}} \text{m} = 112.7 \text{ m}$

Since, $R = \frac{\rho\ell}{\pi D^2/4} = \frac{4\rho\ell}{\pi D^2} . (R \propto 1/D^2)$. When D is doubled, R becomes $\frac{1}{4}$ times.

Q.7 The value of current, I, flowing in a given resistor for the corresponding value of potential difference, V, across the resistor are given below :

I (ampere)	:	0.5	1.0	2.0	3.0	4.0
V (volt)	:	1.6	3.4	6.7	10.2	13.2

Plot a graph between V and I and calculate the resistance of resistor.

Ans. The V-I graph is as shown in fig.

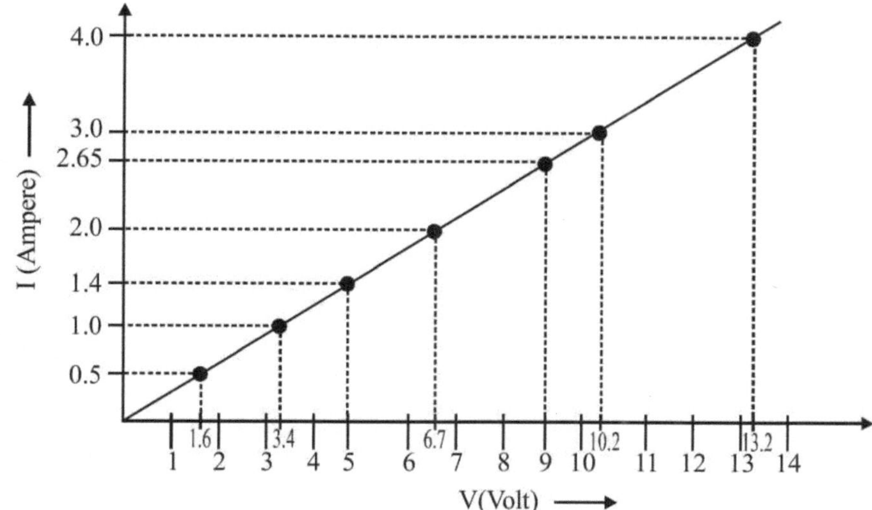

For V = 4V (i.e., 9V - 5V), I = 1.25 A (i.e., 2.65 A - 1.40 A). Therefore,

$$R = \frac{V}{I} = \frac{4V}{1.25A} = 3.2\ \Omega$$

The value of R obtained from the graph depends upon the accuracy with which the graph is plotted.

Q.8 When a 12 V battery is connected across an unknown resistor, there is a current of 2.5 mA in the circuit. Find the value of the resistance of the resistor.

Ans. Here, V = 12V, I = 2.5 mA = 2.5×10^{-3} A

Resistance of the resistor

$$R = \frac{V}{I} = \frac{12V}{2.5 \times 10^{-3} A} = 4800\ \Omega = 4.8\ k\Omega$$

Q.9 A battery of 9 V is connected in series with resistors of 0.2 , 0.3 , 0.4 , 0.5 and 12 . How much current would flow through the 12 resistor ?

Ans. Since all the resistors are in series, equivalent resistance.

$R_s = 0.2 + 0.3 + 0.4 + 0.5 + 12 = 13.4$

Current through the circuit,

$$I = \frac{V}{R_s} = \frac{9V}{13.4\Omega} = 0.67A$$

In series, same current (I) flows through all the resistors.

Thus, current flowing through 12 Ω resistor = 0.67 A

Q.10 How many 176 Ω resistors (in parallel) are required to carry 5 A in 220 V line ?

Ans. Here, I = 5A, V = 220 V.

Resistance required in the circuit, $R = \frac{V}{I} = \frac{220V}{5A} = 44\Omega$, resistance of each resistor, r = 176 Ω.

If n resistors, each of resistance r, are connected in parallel to get the required resistance R,

then $R = \frac{r}{n}$ or $44 = \frac{176}{n}$ or $n = \frac{176}{44} = 4$

Q.11 Show how you would connect three resistors, each of resistance 6 Ω, so that the combination has a resistance of (i) 9 Ω (ii) 2 Ω.

Ans. (i) In order to get a resistance of 9 Ω from three resistors, each of resistance 6, we connect two resistors in Parallel combination (or resistance 3 Ω) in series with the third resistor as shown in fig.

(ii) In order to get a resistance of 2 Ωfrom three resistors, each of resistance 6 Ω, we connect all the three resistors in parallel as shown in fig (b) as equivalent resistance in parallel combination,

i.e., R_p is given by $R_p = \frac{6\Omega}{3} = 2\Omega$

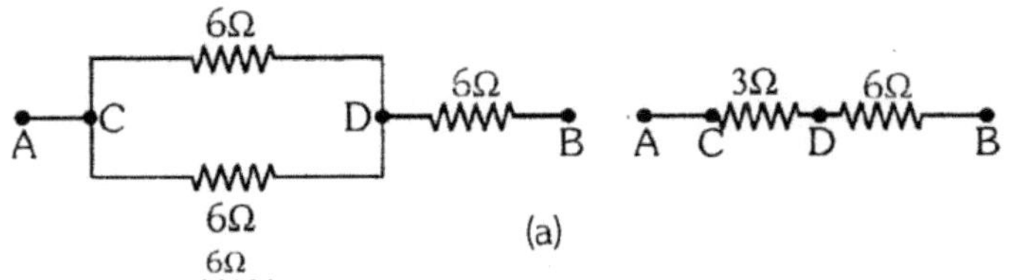

6Ω 6Ω 6Ω 3Ω 6Ω
A C D B A C D B
(a)

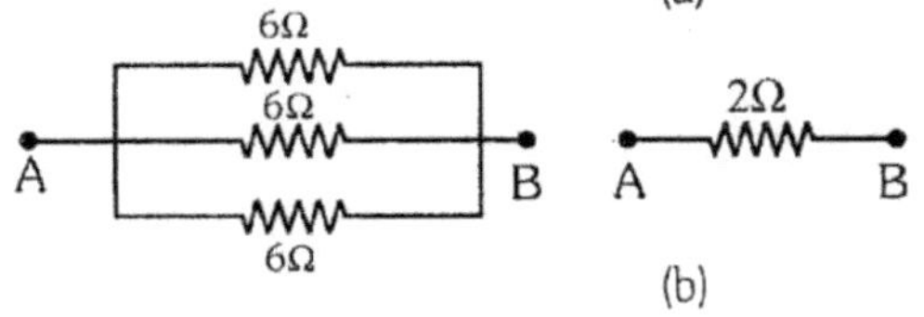

6Ω 6Ω 6Ω 2Ω
A B A B
(b)

Q.12 Several electric bulbs designed to be used on a 220 V electric supply line, are rated 10 W. How many lamps can be connected in parallel with each other across the two wires of 220 V line if the maximum allowable current is 5 A ?

Ans. Resistance of each bulb, $r = \frac{V^2}{P} = \frac{(220)^2}{10} = 4840\Omega$

Total resistance in the circuit, $R = \frac{220V}{5A} = 44\Omega$

Let n be the number of bulbs (each of resistance r) to be connected in parallel to obtain a resistance R.

Clearly, $R = \frac{r}{n}$ or $n = \frac{r}{R} = \frac{4840\Omega}{44\Omega} = 110$

Q.13 A hot plate of an electric oven connected to a 220 V line has two resistance coils A and B, each of 24 Ω resistance, which may be used separately, in series, or in parallel. What are the currents in the three cases ?

Ans. Here, potential difference, V = 220 V.

Resistance of each coil, r = 24 Ω.

(i) When each of the coils A or B is connected separately, current through each coil, i.e.,

$I = \frac{V}{r} = \frac{220V}{24\Omega} = 9.2A$

(ii) When coils A and B are connected in series, equivalent resistance in the circuit,

$$R_s = r + r = 48\ \Omega$$

Current through are series combination , ie.e, $I_s = \frac{V}{R_s} = \frac{220V}{48\Omega} = 4.6A$

(iii) When the coils A and B are connected in parallel, equivalent resistance in the circuit,

$$R_p = \frac{r}{2} = \frac{24\Omega}{2} = 12\Omega$$

Current through the parallel combination, i.e, $I_p = \frac{V}{R_p} = \frac{220V}{12\Omega} = 18.3A$

Q.14 Compare the power used in the 2 Ω resistor in each of the following circuits :

(i) a 6V battery in series with 1Ω and 2Ω resistors, and

(ii) a 4 V battery in parallel with 12Ω and 2Ω resistors.

Ans.

(i) Since 6V battery is in series with 1 Ω and 2 Ω resistors, current in the circuit.

$$I = \frac{6V}{1\Omega + 2\Omega} = \frac{6V}{3\Omega} = 2A$$

Power used in 2Ω resistor, $P_1 = i^2 R = (2A)^2 \times 2\ \Omega = 8W$

(ii) Since 4 V battery is in parallel with 12 Ω and 2 Ω resistors, pd across 2Ω resistor, V = 4V.

Power used in 2Ω resistor, $P_2 = \frac{V^2}{R} = \frac{(4V)^2}{(2\Omega)} = 8W$

Clearly, $\frac{P_1}{P_2} = \frac{8W}{8W} = 1$

Q.15 Two lamps, one rated 100 W at 220 V, and the other 60 W at 220 V, are connected in parallel to the electric mains supply. What current is drawn from the line if the supply voltage is 220 V?

Ans. Resistance of first lamp , $r_1 = \frac{V^2}{P} = \frac{(220)^2}{100} = 484\Omega$

Resistance of the second lamp, $r_2 = \frac{V^2}{P} = \frac{(220)^2}{60} = 806.7\Omega$

Since the two lamps are connected in parallel , the equivalent resistance is given by

$$\frac{1}{R_p} = \frac{1}{r_1} + \frac{1}{r_2} = \frac{r_2 + r_1}{r_1 r_2}$$

or $$R_p = \frac{r_2 r_1}{r_1 + r_2} = \frac{484 \times 806.7}{484 + 806.7} = \frac{390442.8}{1290.7} = 302.5\Omega$$

Current drawn from the line, i.e., $I = \frac{V}{R_p} = \frac{220V}{302.6\Omega} = 0.73A$

Alternate Method

Given $P_1 = 100$ Watt $V_1 = 220$ volt

$P_2 = 100$ Watt $V_2 = 220$ volt

Both lamp are connected in parallel the

$P_{eq} = P_1 + P_2 = 100 + 60$

$P_{eq} = 160$ Watt

Voltage supply in electric line V = 220 Volt

than P = VI

$$I = \frac{V}{P_{eq}} = \frac{P_{eq}}{V} = \frac{2160}{220}$$

I = 0.727 Ampere

Q.16 Which uses more energy, a 250 W TV set in 1 h, or 1200 W toaster in 10 minutes ?

Ans. Energy used by 250 W TV set in 1 h = 250 W × 1h = 250 Wh

Energy used by 1200 W toaster in 10 min. (i.e., 1/6 h) = 1200 W ×(1/6) h = 200 Wh

Thus, a 250 W TV set uses more power in 1h than a 1200 W toaster in 10 minutes.

Q.17 An electric heater of resistance 8 Ω draws 15 A from the service mains for 2 hour. Calculate the rate at which heat is developed in the heater

Ans. Here, I = 15A, R = 8 Ω, t = 2h

Rate at which heat is developed , i.e, electric power , $P = I^2 R = (15)^2 \times 8 = 1800$ W or J/s

Q.18 Explain the following :

(a) Why is tungsten used almost exclusively for filament of incandescent lamps ?

(b) Why are the conductors of electric heating devices, such as toasters and electric irons, made of an alloy rather than a pure metal ?

(c) Why is the series arrangement not used for domestic circuits ?

(d) How does the resistance of a wire vary with its cross-sectional area ?

(e) Why are copper and aluminium wires usually employed for electricity transmission.

Ans. (a) Tungsten has a high milting point (3380°C) and becomes incandescent (i.e., emits light at a high temperature) at 2400 K.

(b) The resistivity of an alloy is generally higher than that of pure metals of which it is made of.

(c) In series arrangement, if any one of the appliances fails or is switched off, all the other appliances stop working because the same current is passing through all the appliances.

(d) The resistance of wire (R) varies inversely with its cross-sectional area (A) as $R \propto 1/A$.

(e) Copper and Aluminium wires possess low resistivity and are economic so they are generally used for electricity transmission.

CONCEPT APPLICATION LEVEL - II

SECTION–A

Q.1 What does an electric circuit mean?

Ans. An electric circuit is a closed conducting path containing a source of potential difference or electric energy (i.e. a cell or battery) and a device or element utilizing the electric energy.

Q.2 Define the unit of current.

Ans. Unit of electric current is ampere. Electric current in a conductor is said to be 1 A if 1 coulomb charge flows through the cross-section of the conductor in 1 second.

Q.3 Calculate the number of electrons consisting one coulomb of charge.

Ans. $q = 1\ C$

Let n = number of electrons consisting 1 C of charge.

Using $q = ne$, we have

$$n = \frac{q}{e} = \frac{1C}{1.6\times10^{-19}C} = 6.25 \times 10^{18} \text{ electrons.}$$

Q.4 Name a device that helps to maximize a potential difference across a conductor.

Ans. A cell or battery.

Q.5 What is meant by saying that a potential difference between two points is 1 V?

Ans. Potential difference between two points is 1 V if 1 joule work is done in moving 1 coulomb charge from one point to another point.

Q.6 How much energy is given to each coulomb of charge passing through a 6 V battery?

Ans. Energy = Charge × Potential difference = 1 C × 6 V = 6 Joule.

Q.7 On what factors does the resistance of a conductor depend?

Ans. Resistance of a conductor depends on (i) length (l) of the conductor, (ii) area of cross-section of the conductor, (iii) nature of the material of the conductor and (iv) temperature of the conductor.

Q.8 Will current flow more easily through a thick wire or a thin wire of the same material, when connected to the same source? Why?

Ans. $$I = \frac{V}{R}. \text{ Since } R \propto \frac{1}{\text{Area of cross} - \text{section}}$$

Therefore, resistance of thin wire is more than the resistance of thick wire. Hence, current in thick wire flows easily than in thin wire.

Q.9 Let the resistance of an electrical component remains constant while the potential difference across the ends of the component decreases to half of its former value. What change will occur with current through it?

Ans. $I = \frac{V}{R}$. When $V' = \frac{V}{2}$

$I' = \frac{V}{2R} = \frac{I}{2}$.

Thus, current in the component become half of it former value.

Q.10 Why are coil of electric toasters and electric irons made of an alloy rather than a pure metal?

Ans. It is because (i) alloy does not oxidize (i.e. do not burn easily at high temperature), whereas pure metal burns easily at high temperature, (ii) resistivity of an alloy is more than the resistivity of pure metal, so large heat is produced due to the flow of current in an alloy.

Q.11 (a) Which among, iron and mercury is better conductor?
(resistivity of iron = $10.0 \times 10^{-8}\ \Omega$ m and resistivity of mercury = $94 \times 10^{-8}\ \Omega$ m)

(b) Which material is the best conductor?

Ans. (a) A material whose resistivity is low is a good conductor of electricity. Therefore, iron is better conductor than mercury.

(b) Silver is the best conductor of electricity.

Q.12 Draw a schematic diagram of a circuit consisting of three batteries of 2 V each, a 5 Ω resistor, 8 Ω resistor and a 12 Ω resistor and a plug key, all connected in series.

Ans.

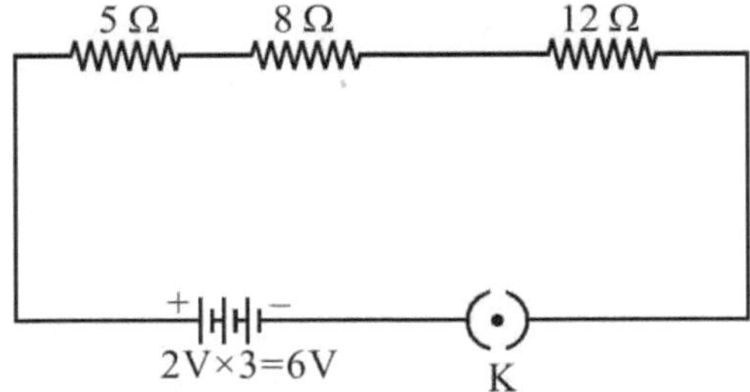

Q.13 Redraw the circuit of question 12, putting an ammeter to measure the current through the resistor and a voltmeter to measure the potential difference across 12 Ω resistor. What would be the reading in the ammeter?

Ans. Total resistance of the circuit,

$R = 5\ \Omega + 8\ \Omega + 12\ \Omega = 25\ \Omega$

$V = 6$ V

$I = \frac{V}{R} = \frac{6}{25} = 0.24$ A

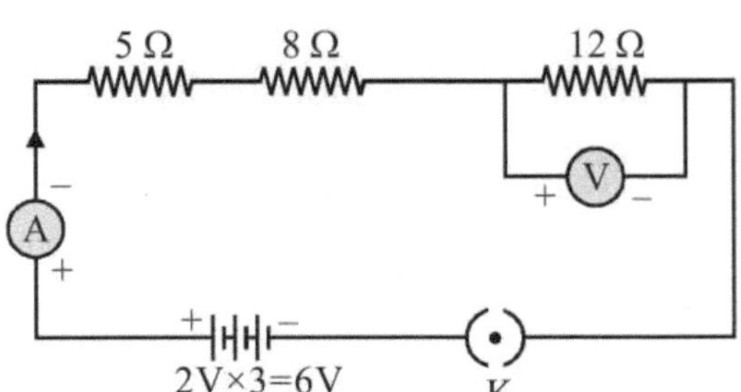

Therefore, reading of ammeter = 0.24 A

Reading of voltmeter = IR = 0.24 A × 12 Ω = 2.88 V.

Q.14 Judge the equivalent resistance when the following are connected in parallel :
(a) 1 Ω and 10^6 Ω (b) 1 Ω and 10^3 Ω and 10^6 Ω.

Ans. (a) When resistors are connected in parallel, then equivalent resistance of the combination is less than the least resistance in the combination. Therefore, equivalent resistance of 1 Ω and 10^6 Ω connected in parallel is approximately 1 Ω but less than 1 Ω.

(b) The equivalent resistance is approximately 1 Ω but less than 1 Ω.

Q.15 An electric lamp of 100 W, a toaster of resistance 50 Ω, and a water filter of resistance 500 Ω are connected in parallel to 220 V source. What is the resistance of an electric iron connected to the same source that takes as much current as all three appliances and what in the current through it?

Ans. Resistance of electric lamp, $R_1 = \frac{V^2}{P} = 220 \times \frac{220}{100} = 484\ \Omega$

Net resistance when all appliances are connected in parallel

$$\frac{1}{R} = \frac{1}{R_1} + \frac{1}{R_2} + \frac{1}{R_3} = \frac{1}{484} + \frac{1}{50} + \frac{1}{500} = \frac{2912}{121000}$$

Therefore $R = 41.55\ \Omega$

Therefore $I = \frac{V}{R} = \frac{220}{41.55} = 5.3\text{ A.}$

Q.16 What is (a) highest (b) lowest resistance that can be secured by combining four coils of resistances 4 Ω, 8 Ω, 12 Ω, 24 Ω?

Ans. (a) Highest resistance is obtained when coils are connected in series.

Therefore $R = 4 + 8 + 12 + 24 = 48\ \Omega$

(b) Lowest resistance is obtained when coils are connected in parallel.

Therefore $\frac{1}{R} = \frac{1}{4} + \frac{1}{8} + \frac{1}{12} + \frac{1}{24} = \frac{12}{24}$

Therefore $R = \frac{24}{12} = 2\ \Omega.$

Q.17 Why does the connecting cord of an electric heater does not glow while the heating element does?

Ans. This is because resistance of cord of electric heater is less than the resistance of heating element. So more heat is produced in the heating element and less heat is produced in the cord. Due to more heat, heating element glows.

Q.18 Compute the heat generated while transferring 96000 coulomb of charge in one hour through a potential difference of 50 V.

Ans. $H = VIt$

$H = V \times \frac{Q}{t} \times t \qquad \left(\because I = \frac{Q}{t}\right)$

$= VQ$

$= 50 \times 96000 = 4.8 \times 10^6$ J.

Q.19 An electric iron of resistance 20 Ω takes a current of 5 A. Calculate the heat developed in 30 seconds.

Ans. $H = I^2Rt$

$= (25)^2 \times 20 \times 30$

$= 15000$ J.

Q.20 What are the advantage of connecting electrical devices in parallel with a battery instead of connecting them in series?

Ans. (i) If any one of the electric devices in parallel fuses, then the working of other devices will not be affected.

(ii) When different devices are connected in parallel, they draw the current as per their requirement and hence they work properly.

Q.21 How can three resistors of resistance 2 Ω, 3 Ω and 6 Ω be connected to give a total resistance of (a) 4 Ω, (b) 1 Ω ?

Ans. (a) We get 4 Ω resistance if 3 Ω and 6 Ω resistors are connected in parallel and this parallel combination is connected in series with 2 Ω as shown in figure.

Equivalent resistance of 3 Ω and 6 Ω is given by

$$\frac{1}{R} = \frac{1}{R_1} + \frac{1}{R_2} = \frac{1}{3} + \frac{1}{6} = \frac{3}{6} = \frac{1}{2}$$

Or $R = 2\ \Omega$

Now 2 Ω and 2 Ω are in series,

So net resistance = 2 Ω + 2 Ω = 4 Ω

(b) We get 1 Ω resistance if all three resistors are connected in parallel.

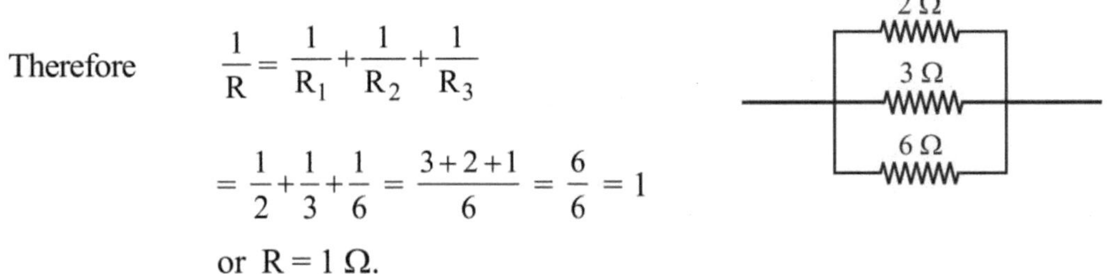

Therefore $\frac{1}{R} = \frac{1}{R_1} + \frac{1}{R_2} + \frac{1}{R_3}$

$$= \frac{1}{2} + \frac{1}{3} + \frac{1}{6} = \frac{3+2+1}{6} = \frac{6}{6} = 1$$

or $R = 1\ \Omega$.

Q.22 What determine the rate at which energy is delivered by an electric current?

Ans. Electric power determines the rate at which energy is delivered by an electric current.

Q.23 An electric motor takes 5 A from a 220 V line. Determine the power of the motor and energy consumed in 2 h.

Ans. Power, $P = VI = 220 \times 5 = 1100$ W

Energy consumed = Power × Time

= 1100 W × 2 h

= 2200 Wh

= 2.2 kWh.

SECTION – B

Conceptual Problems :

Q.1 Electrical resistivity of some substances at 20°C are given below :

Silver	$1.60 \times 10^{-8}\ \Omega$-m
Copper	$1.62 \times 10^{-8}\ \Omega$-m
Tungsten	$5.2 \times 10^{-8}\ \Omega$-m
Iron	$10.0 \times 10^{-8}\ \Omega$-m
Mercury	$94.0 \times 10^{-8}\ \Omega$-m
Nichrome	$10.0 \times 10^{-8}\ \Omega$-m

Answer the following question in relation to them :

(i) Among silver and copper, which one is a better conductor? Why?

(ii) Which material would you advise to be used in electrical heating devices? Why?

Ans.

(i) A material whose electrical resistivity is low is a good conductor of electricity. Since the electrical resistivity of silver is less than that of the copper, so silver is a better conductor than the copper.

(ii) For making the elements of heating devices, alloy is used instead of a pure metal. This is because the resistivity of an alloy is more than that of a metal and alloy does not burn (or oxidise) even at higher temperature. Out of the given substance, nichrome is an alloy, so nichrome is used in electrical heating devices.

Q.2 The length of different metallic wires but of same area of cross-section and made of the same materical are given below.

Wire	Length
A	1 m
B	1.5 m
C	2.0 m

(i) Out of these wires, which wire has higher resistance.

(ii) Which wire has the highest electrical resistivity? Justify your answer.

Ans. (i) Resistance of a metallic wire $\propto$ lenght of the wire.

Since, length of wire C is more than the lengths of wire A and B, therefore the wire C has the higher resistance than that of wire A and B.

(ii) Electrical resistivity of a wire depends on the nature of the material of the wire and independent of the length of the wire. Since all wires are made of same material, so the electrical resistivity of all wires is same.

Q.3 Two metallic wires A and B of same material are connected in parallel. Wire A has length l and radius r and wire B has length 2 l and radius 2r. Compute the ratio of the total resistance of parallel combination and the resistance of wire A.

Ans. Resistance of wire A, $R_1 = \frac{\rho l}{A_1} = \frac{\rho l}{\pi r^2}$ Resistance of wire B, $R_2 = \frac{\rho \times 2l}{\pi (2r)^2} = \frac{\rho l}{2\pi r^2}$

Total resistance of the parallel combination,

$$\frac{1}{R} = \frac{1}{R_1} + \frac{1}{R_2} \quad \text{or} \quad \frac{1}{R} = \frac{\pi r^2}{\rho l} + \frac{2\pi r^2}{\rho l} = \frac{3\pi r^2}{\rho l}$$

$$R = \frac{\rho l}{3\pi r^2} \quad \therefore \quad \frac{R}{R_1} = \frac{\rho l}{3\pi r^2} \times \frac{\pi r^2}{\rho l} = \frac{1}{3}$$

SECTION – C

Numerical Ability :

Q.1 How much work will be done in bringing a charge of 5.0 millicoulombs from infinity to a point P at which the potential is 12 V ?

Sol. The potential at infinity is usually taken as zero. So, the work done is

$$W = QV = (5.0\times 10^{-3}\ C) \times (12\ V) = 60 \times 10^{-3}\ J = 0.06\ J.$$

Q.2 A particle with a charge of 1.5 coulombs is taken from a point A at a potential of 50 V to another point B at a potential of 120 V. Calculate the work done.

Sol. We have

$$W = Q(V_B - V_A)$$
$$= (1.5\ C) \times (120\ V - 50\ V) = (1.5 \times 70)\ J = 105\ J.$$

Q.3 How many electrons are required to get 1 C of negative charge ?

Sol. Each electron has a negative charge of 1.6×10^{-19} C.

So, the number of electrons for 1 C of negative charge is

$$n = \frac{1\ C}{1.6\times 10^{-19}\ C} = 6.25 \times 10^{18}.$$

Q.4 Calculate the current in a wire if 900 C of charge passes through it in 10 minutes.

Sol. $i = \frac{Q}{t} = \frac{900\ C}{10\times 60\ s} = \frac{9}{6} = 1.5\ A$

Q.5 How much current will flow through a resistor of resistance 12 Ω if a battery of 18 V is connected across it ?

Sol. From Ohm's law,

$$i = \frac{V}{R} = \frac{18\ V}{12\ \Omega} = 1.5\ A.$$

Q.6 Calculate the resistance of a copper wire of length 1 m and area of cross section 2 mm^2. Resistivity of copper is $1.7 \times 10^{-8}\ \Omega$ m.

Sol. From Ohm's law

$$R = \rho\frac{l}{A} = (1.7 \times 10^{-8}\ \Omega\ m) \times \frac{1\ m}{2\times 10^{-6} m^2} = 8.5 \times 10^{-3}\ \Omega.$$

Q.7 A copper wire has a resistance of 0.6 Ω. Another copper wire of the same mass as the first one is double in length of the first. Find the resistance of the second wire.

Sol. For the first wire, let

l = length and A_1 = cross-sectional area.

For the second wire,

$2l$ = length and A_2 = cross-sectional area.

Now, density = mass/volume.

The two wires have the same mass and they have the same density (being made of the same material). So, their volumes are equal.

$\therefore \quad lA_1 = 2lA_2 \qquad$ or $\qquad A_1 = 2A_2$.

Let the resistivity of copper be ρ.

Resistance of the first wire is $0.6\,\Omega = \rho \frac{l}{A_1}$ ....(i)

Resistance of the second wire is $R = \rho \frac{2l}{A_2}$ ....(ii)

Dividing (ii) by (i),

$$\frac{R}{0.6\,\Omega} = \frac{2lA_1}{lA_2} = \frac{2(2A_2)}{A_2} = 4$$

$\therefore \quad R = 0.6\,\Omega \times 4 = 2.4\,\Omega$.

Q.8 In an experiment to verify Ohm's law, the current through a resistor and the potential difference across it are measured. From the values given below, plot a graph of i versus V. Show that the data confirms Ohm's law, and find the resistance of the resistor.

Current (A)	0.1	0.2	0.3	0.4
Potential difference (V)	1.2	2.4	3.6	4.8

Sol. The graph is shown in figure. Scales are chosen to cover the given maximum values. We see that the graph is a straight line passing through the origin.

Thus, $i \propto V$, which is Ohm's law. The resistance is

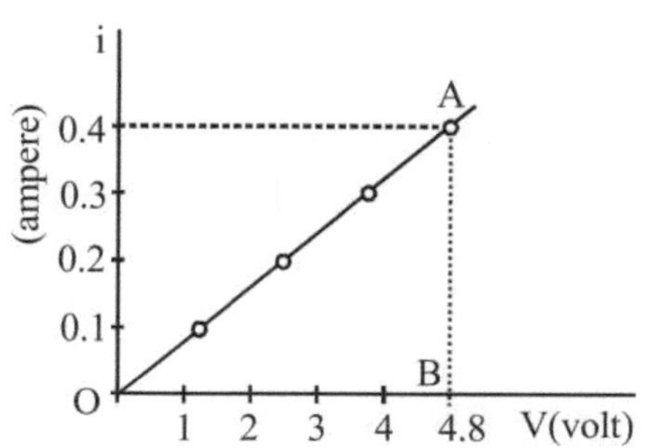

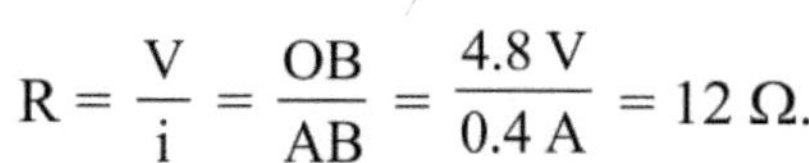

$$R = \frac{V}{i} = \frac{OB}{AB} = \frac{4.8\text{ V}}{0.4\text{ A}} = 12\,\Omega.$$

Q.9 When a potential difference of 20 V is applied across a resistor, it draws a current of 3A. If 30 V is applied across the same resistor, what will be the current ?

Sol. The resistance of the resistor is

$$R = \frac{V}{i} = \frac{20\text{ V}}{3\text{ A}} = \frac{20}{3}\Omega$$

When 30 V is applied across the resistor,

$$i = \frac{V}{R} = \frac{30\text{ V}}{20/3\,\Omega} = 4.5\text{ A}.$$

Q.10 How will the resistance of a wire change if its diameter (d) is doubled, its length remaining the same ?

Sol. the cross-sectional area of the wire is $A_1 = \pi r^2 = \pi\left(\frac{d}{2}\right)^2 = \frac{\pi d^2}{4}$.

Its resistance $= R_1 = \rho\frac{l}{A_1} = \rho\frac{l}{\frac{\pi d^2}{4}} = \frac{4\rho l}{\pi d^2}$.

When the diameter is doubled, cross-sectional area $A_2 = \pi\left(\frac{2d}{2}\right)^2 = \pi d^2$.

Its resistance $= R_2 = \rho\frac{l}{A_2} = \rho\frac{l}{\pi d^2}$.

Thus $\frac{R_2}{R_1} = \frac{\frac{\rho l}{\pi d^2}}{\frac{4\rho l}{\pi d^2}} = \frac{1}{4}$

or $R_2 = \frac{1}{4} R_1$.

So, on doubling the diameter, the area of cross section becomes 4 times and the resistance becomes one-fourth of the initial value.

Q.11 Calculate the potential difference across each resistor in the circuit shown in figure.

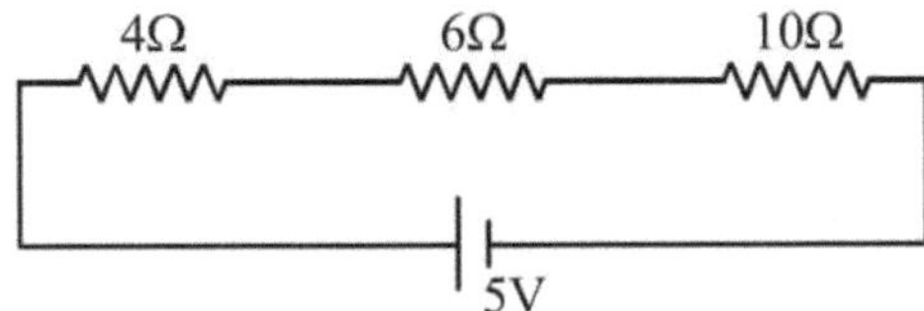

Sol. The three resistors are joined in series. Their equivalent resistance is ⇒ 20Ω

The current through the cell is $i = \frac{5\text{ V}}{20\ \Omega} = 0.25\text{ A}$.

The same current passes through each resistor Using Ohm's law, the potential difference across the 4Ω resistor = 0.25 A × 4Ω = 1V,
across the 6 Ω resistor = 0.25 A × 6 Ω = 1.5 V, and
across the 10 Ω resistor = 0.25 A × 10 Ω = 2.5 V.

Q.12 Three identical bulbs are connected in parallel with a battery. The current drawn from the battery is 6A. If one of the bulbs gets fused, what will be the total current drawn from the battery?

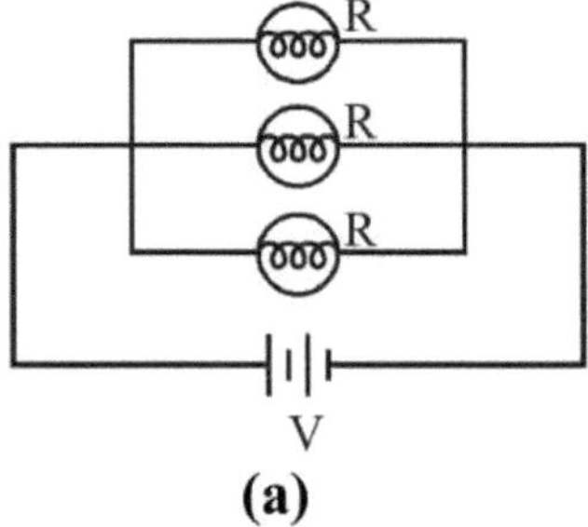

(a)

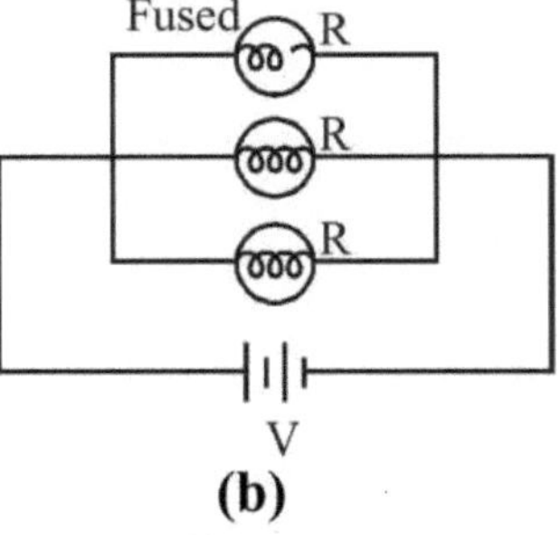

(b)

Sol. Let the potential difference maintained by the battery be V, and let the resistance of each bulb be R (Figure). If the equivalent resistance of the circuit is r,

$$\frac{1}{r} = \frac{1}{R} + \frac{1}{R} + \frac{1}{R} \text{ or } r = \frac{R}{3}.$$

The current is $i = \frac{V}{r} = \frac{3V}{R}$. It is given that this current is 6A.

So, $6\text{A} = \frac{3V}{R}$ or $\frac{V}{R} = 2\text{A}$.

If one of the bubls gets fused (figure), only two bulbs remain connected in parallel. The equivalent resistance r' in that case is given by

$$\frac{1}{r'} = \frac{1}{R} + \frac{1}{R} \text{ or } r' = \frac{R}{2}.$$

The current in the battery will be

$$i' = \frac{V}{r'} = \frac{2V}{R} = 2 \times (2\,A) = 4\,A.$$

Alternative :

As the three bulbs are identical, they will draw equal currents. As the total current is 6 A, each bulb will draw 2 A of current. When one bulb gets fused, there is no current through it. Each of the remaining bulbs remains connected to the battery as before. So current through each is still 2 A, giving a total current of 4 A through the battery.

Q.13 A uniform wire of resistance R is cut into three equal pieces, and these pieces are joined in parallel. What is the resistance of the combination ?

Sol. Resistance of the wire is $R = \rho\frac{l}{A}$.

Resistance of a piece of length $\frac{l}{3}$ is $R' = \rho\frac{l}{3A}$.

or $R' = \frac{R}{3}$.

Let the equivalent resistance of the three wires in parallel be R_p. Then

$$\frac{1}{R_P} = \frac{1}{R/3} + \frac{1}{R/3} + \frac{1}{R/3} = \frac{3}{R} + \frac{3}{R} + \frac{3}{R} = \frac{9}{R}.$$

$\therefore$ $R_p = \frac{R}{9}$.

Q.14 Consider the circuit shown in figure. The voltmeter on the left reads 10 V and that one the right reads 8 V. Find (a) the current through the resistance R, (b) the value of R, and (c) the potential difference across the battery.

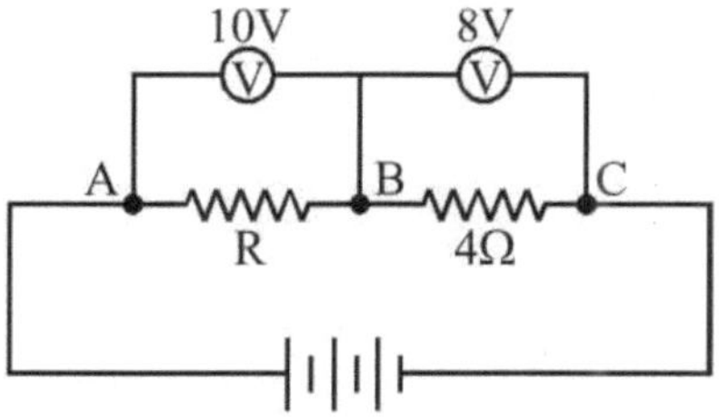

Sol. (a) Apply Ohm's law to the 4Ω resistor. The current through this resistor is

$$i = \frac{8\,V}{4\,\Omega} = 2A.$$

As the two resistors are connected in series, the same current passes through the two resistors (the voltmeters draw only a negligible current). Hence, the current through R is 2A.

(b) Applying Ohm's law to the resistance R,

$$10\text{ V} = R \times (2\text{ A}) \qquad \text{or} \qquad R = \frac{10\text{ V}}{2\text{ A}} = 5\Omega.$$

(c) The potential difference across the battery is

$$V_A - V_C = (V_A - V_B) + (V_B - V_C) = 10\text{ V} + 8\text{ V} = 18\text{ V}.$$

Q.15 Three resistors of resistances 10 Ω, 20 Ω and 30 Ω are connected in parallel with a 6 V cell. Find (a) the current through each resistor, (b) the current supplied by the cell, and (c) the equivalent resistance of the circuit.

Sol.

(a) Let the current through the 10 Ω, 20 Ω and 30 Ω resistors be i_1, i_2 and i_3 respectively. The potential difference across each of them is 6 V. Thus,

$$i_1 = \frac{6\text{ V}}{10\,\Omega} = 0.6\text{ A},\ i_2 = \frac{6\text{ V}}{20\,\Omega} = 0.3\text{ A},\ i_3 = \frac{6\text{ V}}{30} = 0.2\text{ A}.$$

(b) The current supplied by the cell is

$$i = i_1 + i_2 + i_3 = 0.6\text{ A} + 0.3\text{ A} + 0.2\text{ A} = 1.1\text{ A}.$$

(c) The equivalent resistance of the circuit is

$$R = \frac{V}{i} = \frac{6\text{ V}}{1.1\text{ A}} \approx 5.5\ \Omega.$$

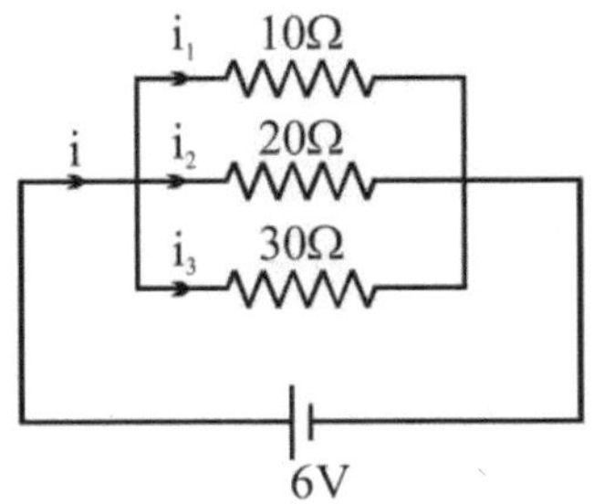

Alternative :

$$\frac{1}{R} = \frac{1}{10\,\Omega} + \frac{1}{20\,\Omega} + \frac{1}{30\,\Omega} = \frac{11}{60\,\Omega}.$$

$$\therefore \qquad R = \frac{60\,\Omega}{11} \approx 5.5\ \Omega.$$

Q.16 Consider the circuit shown in figure. Calculate the current through the 3Ω resistor.

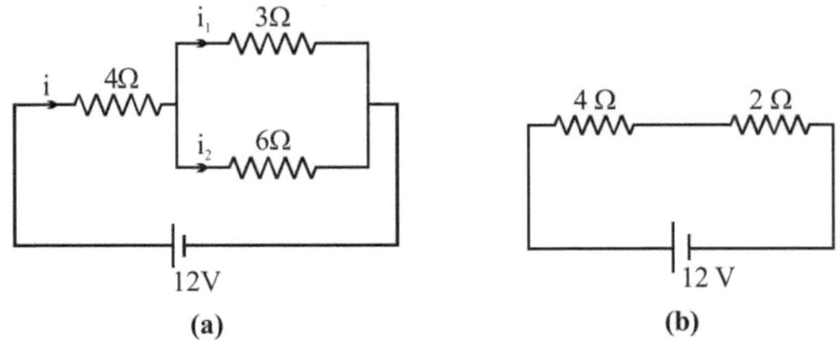

Sol. The 3 Ω resistor and the 6 Ω resistor are joined in parallel. Their equivalent resistance is

$$R = \frac{(3\Omega) \times (6\Omega)}{(3\Omega) + (6\Omega)} = 2\Omega.$$

Thus, the two resistors may be replaced by a single resistor of resistance 2Ω. The circuit can be redrawn as shown in figure. The two resistors in the figure are joined in series. The equivalent resistance is $4\Omega + 2\Omega = 6\Omega$.

The current through the battery is $i = \frac{12\text{ V}}{6\,\Omega} = 2\text{A}$.

Now look at Figure (a). The current through the battery and the 4 Ω resistor is 2 A. This current is divided in the two resistors (3Ω and 6Ω) which are joined in parallel.

Using $i_1 = \frac{R_2 i}{R_1 + R_2}$, the current through the 3 Ω resistors is

$$i_1 = \frac{(6\Omega)\times(2\text{A})}{(3\Omega)+(6\Omega)} = \frac{12\,\Omega\,\text{A}}{9\,\Omega} = 1.33\text{ A.}$$

Q.17 (a) How will you join three resistors of resistances 4Ω, 6Ω and 12 Ω to get an equivalent resistance of 8 Ω?

(b) What would be the highest and the lowest equivalent resistances possible by joining these resistors?

Sol.

(a) As the equivalent resistance is 8 Ω, the 12 Ω resistor cannot be in series. So it must be in parallel with some other resistors.

In parallel connection, the equivalent resistance (8Ω) has to be less than all the resistances. So, the resistors of 4Ω and 6Ω cannot be in parallel at one time with 12Ω.

So, the resistors have to be in a mixed combination. Let us try the combination shown in figure.

The equivalent resistance of the resistors in parallel between B and C is

$$\frac{(6\,\Omega)\times(12\,\Omega)}{(6\,\Omega)+(12\Omega)} = 4\,\Omega.$$

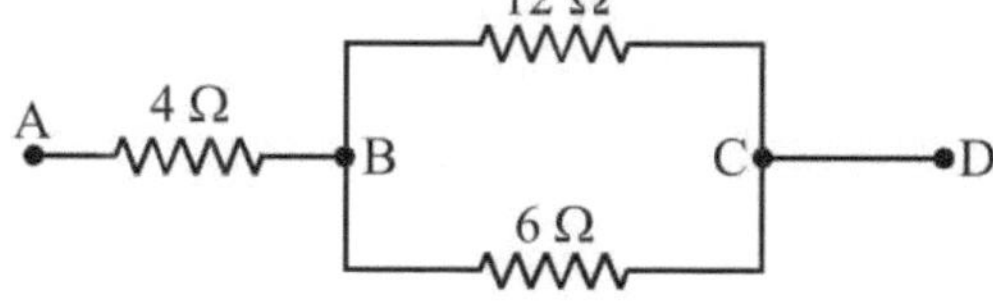

So, the resistance between A and D is

$$4\Omega + 4\Omega = 8\,\Omega.$$

Thus, the combination shown in the figure is correct.

(b) The highest resistance would be from a series combination, and is equal to

$$4\Omega + 6\Omega + 12\,\Omega = 22\,\Omega$$

A parallel combination will give the lowest resistance, which is given by

$$\frac{1}{R} = \frac{1}{4\,\Omega} + \frac{1}{6\,\Omega} + \frac{1}{12\,\Omega} = \frac{3+2+1}{12\,\Omega} = \frac{6}{12\,\Omega}.$$

$\therefore\ R = 2\Omega.$

Q.18 How many bulbs of resistance 6 ohms should be joined in parallel to draw a current of 2 amperes from a battery of 3 volts ?

Sol. The equivalent resistance of the circuit $= R = \frac{V}{i} = \frac{3\text{ V}}{2\text{ A}} = 1.5\,\Omega.$

Let n bulbs be joined in parallel to achieve this resistance, Then

$$\frac{1}{1.5\,\Omega} = \frac{1}{r_1} + \frac{1}{r_2} + \ldots\ldots + \frac{1}{r_n} = \frac{n}{6\Omega} \quad \text{(as all resistances} = 6\Omega)$$

$$\therefore \quad n = \frac{6\,\Omega}{1.5\,\Omega} = 4.$$

So, 4 bulbs should be connected in parallel.

Q.19 A current of 4 A passes through a resistance of 100 Ω for 15 minutes. Calculate the heat produced in calories.

Sol. The heat produced is $U = i^2Rt$

$$= (4A)^2 \times (100\ \Omega) \times (15 \times 60\ s) = 1.44 \times 10^6\ J.$$

Now 4.186 J = 1 cal.

Thus, $1.44 \times 10^6 = \dfrac{1.44 \times 10^6}{4.186}$ cal $= 3.4 \times 10^5$ cal.

Q.20 A 12 volt battery is connected to a bulb. The battery sends a current of 2.5 A through it. Calculate

(a) The power delivered to the bulb, and

(b) The energy transferred to the bulb in 5 minutes.

Sol. (a) The power delivered is

$$P = Vi = (12\ V) \times (2.5\ A) = 30\ W.$$

(b) Energy transferred in 5 minutes is

$$U = P \times t = (30\ W) \times (5 \times 60\ s) = 9000\ J.$$

Q.21 A current passes through a resistor for some time. It produced 400 cal of heat in this period. If the current is doubled, how much heat will be produced for the same durations?

Sol. The heat produced is $U = i^2 Rt$ ......(i)

or $400\ cal = i^2Rt$ ......(ii)

If the heat produced is U_1 when the current is doubled, $U_1 = (2i)^2 Rt$

From (i) and (ii), we have

$$\frac{U_1}{400\ cal} = \frac{(2i)^2\ Rt}{i^2\ Rt} = 4.$$

or $U_1 = 1600$ cal.

Q.22 Calculate the wattage of an electric heater which draws 5 A current when connected to a 220 V power supply.

Sol. The wattage is $P = V \times I = (220\ V) \times (5\ A) = 1100\ W.$

Q.23 A bulb draws 24 W when connected to a 12 V supply. Find the power if it is connected to a 6 V supply. (Neglect resistance change due to unequal heating in the two cases.).

Sol. We have $P = \dfrac{V^2}{R}$

or $24\ W = \dfrac{(12\ V^2)}{R}.$ ....(i)

Suppose the bulb draws power P_1 when connected to the 6 V battery. Then,

$P_1 = \dfrac{(6\ V^2)}{R}.$ ....(ii)

From (i) and (ii), we have

$$\frac{P_1}{24\ W} = \frac{(6\ V)^2}{(12\ V)^2} = \frac{1}{4}.$$

or $P_1 = \dfrac{24\ W}{4} = 6\ W.$

Q.24 Two identical resistors of resistance R are connected in series with a battery of potential difference V for time t. The resistors are later connected in parallel and the same battery is connected across the combination for time t. Compare the heat produced in the two cases.

Sol. The equivalent resistance of the series combination = $R_1 = R + R = 2R$.

The heat produced in time t is, $H_1 = \frac{V^2}{2R} t$.

The equivalent resistance of the parallel combination is, $R_2 = \frac{(R)(R)}{R+R} = \frac{R^2}{2R} = \frac{R}{2}$.

The heat produced in time t is $H_2 = \frac{V^2}{R/2} t = \frac{2V^2}{R} t \Rightarrow \frac{H_1}{H_2} = \frac{1}{4} \Rightarrow H_2 = 4H_1$

The heat produced with the parallel combination is four times that with the series combination.

Q.25 A bulb is rated 40 W, 220 V. Find the current drawn by it when it is connected to a 220 - V supply.

Sol. Since the bulb is rated at 220 V and it is connected to a 220 V supply, the power consumed will be 40 W. The current drawn by it is, $i = \frac{P}{V} = \frac{40 W}{220 V} = \frac{2}{11}$ A.

Q.26 A bulb is rated 60 W, 240 V. Calculate its resistance when it is on. If the voltage drops to 192 V, what will be the power consumed and the current drawn?

Sol. Power, $P = \frac{V^2}{R}$.

$$\therefore \quad R = \frac{V^2}{P} = \frac{(240 V)^2}{60 W} = 960 \Omega.$$

When the voltage drops to 192 V, the power consumed will be

$$P = \frac{V^2}{R} = \frac{(192 V)^2}{960 \Omega} = 38.4 W.$$

The current drawn will be $i = \frac{V}{R} = \frac{192 V}{960 \Omega} = 0.2$ A.

Q.27 A room has two tube lights, a fan and a TV. Each tube light draws 40 W, the fan draws 80 W, and the TV draws 60 W. On the average, the tube lights are kept on for five hours, the fan for twelve hours and the TV for eight hours every day. The rate for electrical energy is Rs. 3.10 per kWh. Calculate the cost of electricity used in this room in a 30 day month.

Sol. For each tube light, power $P = 40 W = \frac{40}{1000}$ kW. So, the energy consumed by each tube light in a day is $U = P \times t = \left(\frac{40}{1000} kW\right) \times (5 h) = 0.2$ kWh.

Energy consumed by the fan in a day is, $U = P \times t = (80 W) \times (12 h) = 0.96$ kWh.

Energy consumed by the TV in a day is, $U = P \times t = (60 W) \times (8 h) = 0.48$ kWh.

Total energy consumed in a day is, 2×0.2 kWh + 0.96 kWh + 0.48 kWh = 1.84 kWh

Energy consumed in a month is, (1.84 kWh) $\times$ 30 = 55.2 kWh.

The cost of electricity = Rs 55.2 $\times$ 3.1) = Rs. 171.12.

SECTION-D [PREVIOUS YEARS QUESTIONS, (1 MARK)]

Q.1 A bulb cannot be used in place of a resistor to verify Ohm's law. Justify this statement with reason. **[SAI-2012]**

Ans. It is because Ohm's law holds good at constant temperature only.

Q.2 Name the instrument/device used to measure electric current in a circuit. **[SAI-2010, 2011, 2012]**

Ans. Ammeter.

Q.3 How is an ammeter connected in a circuit to measure current flowing through it? **[SAI-2011,2012]**

Ans. In series.

Q.4 In an electric circuit, state the relationship between the direction of conventional current and the direction of flow of electrons. **[SAI-2011, 2012]**

Ans. The direction of conventional current is opposite to the direction of flow of electrons.

Q.5 Name the device/instrument used to measure potential difference. How is it connected in electric circuit? **[SAI-2010, 2011, 2012]**

Ans. Voltmeter, in parallel.

Q.6 What is the resistance of an ideal voltmeter? **[SAI-2013]**

Ans. Infinity.

Q.7 Write SI unit of resistivity. **[SAI-2013]**

Ans. Ohm-metre.

Q.8 State a difference between the wire used in the element of an electric heater and in a fuse wire. **[SAI-2013]**

Ans. The wire used in the element of an electric heater has very high resistance while that in a fuse wire has a low resistance.

Q.9 What is meant by the statement that the rating of a fuse in a circuit is 5 A? **[SAI-2013]**

Ans. It means that the fuse wire melts when more than 5 A current flows through it.

Q.10 Why tungsten is used almost exclusively for filament of electric lamps? **[SAI-2014]**

Ans. Tungsten is an alloy as such it has a high resistivity and high melting point. Therefore, it is used exclusively in filaments of electric lamps ..

Q.11 Define one watt. **[SAI-2014]**

Ans. The power expended by a source is said to be 1 watt if one ampere of current flows through it under a potential difference of 1 volt.

Q.12 Two students perform the experiments on series and parallel combinations of two given resistors R_1 and R_2 and plot the following V-I graphs.

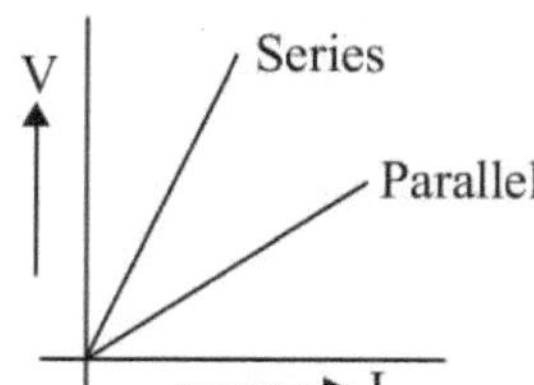

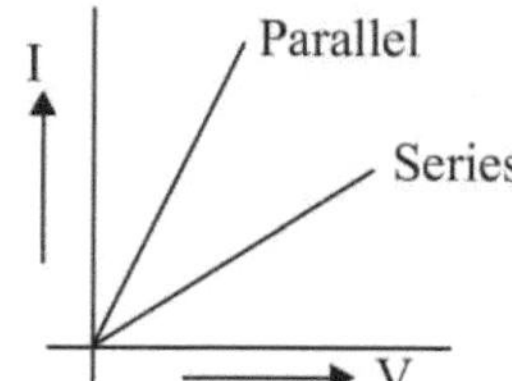

Which of the graphs is (are) correctly labelled in terms of the words 'series' and 'parallel'. Justify your answer **[SAI-2014,2015]**

Ans. In series combination, for a given voltage current is less as compared to that in parallel combination. Therefore, both the graphs are labelled correctly.

SECTION - E [PREVIOUS YEARS QUESTIONS, (2 MARKS)]

Q.1 Name a device that you can use to measure a potential difference between the ends of a conductor. Explain the process by which this device does so. **[SAI-2003]**

Ans. A voltmeter is used to measure potential difference between the ends of a conductor. It is always connected in parallel across the points between which the potential difference is to be measured.

Q.2 Define '1 volt'. State the relation between work, charge and potential difference for an electric circuit. Calculate the potential difference between two terminals of the battery if 100 J of work is required to transfer 20 C of charge from one terminal of the battery to the other. **[SAI-2013]**

Ans. The potential difference between two points is said to be 1 V if one joule of work is done in moving a charge of 1 C between the two points.

$$\text{Work} = Q \times V$$
$$100 = 20 \times V$$
or $$V = 5 \text{ V}$$

Q.3 State the factors on which the heat produced in a current carrying conductor depends. Give one practical application of this effect. **[SAI-2012, 2013]**

Ans. Heat produced in a current carrying conductor depends upon: (i) Square of the current (ii) Resistance of the given conductor. (iii) Time for which the current flows. Electric iron, heater.

Q.4 List in a tabular form two differences in between a voltmeter and an ammeter. **[SAI-2012, 2013]**

Ans.

Voltmeter	Ammeter
(a) Used to measure Potential difference.	(a) Used to measure current
(b) Connected in parallel in the electric circuit	(b) Connected in series in the electric circuit
(c) Has high resistance	(c) Has low resistance

Q.5 A large number of free electrons are present in metals yet no current flows in the absence of electric potential across it. Explain the statement with reason. **[SAI-2013]**

Ans. A large number of free electrons are present in metals; yet no current flows. It is because the electrons move in a random way such that there is no net flow of electrons in anyone direction. When a potential difference is applied across the conductor all electrons move in the same direction, thereby constituting current.

Q.6 Explain the term resistance. Give its SI unit of measurement. **[SAI-2014]**

Ans. The word resistance means resist or opposition that a conductor offers to the flow of charges through it. When a potential difference is applied across the conductor, the free electrons get accelerated. These moving electrons collide with other electrons and atoms due to which the electrons are slowed down. In other words, the motion of the electrons is opposed. This opposition is called resistance of the conductor. Resistance is measured in ohm (Ω).

Q.7 On what factors does the resistance of a conductor depend? **[SAI-2014,2015]**

Ans. The resistance (R) of a conductor depends upon :

(i) its length (L), where $R \propto L$

(ii) its cross-sectional area (A), where

$$R \propto \frac{1}{A}$$

(iii) resistivity (ρ) of its material, where $R \propto \rho$.

Q.8 Draw a schematic diagram of a circuit consisting of a battery of three cells of 2 V each, a 5 Ω resistor, 8 Ω resistor and a 12 Ω resistor and a plug key all connected in series. **[SAI-2015]**

Ans. The schematic diagram of the above mentioned circuit is given below :

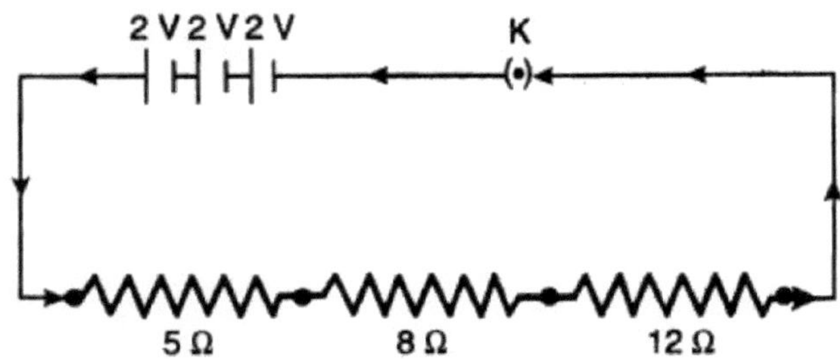

Q.9 What are the conditions under which Ohm's law is not obeyed? **[SAI-2015]**

Ans. Ohm's law is not obeyed under the following conditions :

(i) Potential difference depends upon current non-linearly.

(ii) For the same value of V, I changes sign with V.

(iii) V and I have non-unique relation.

(iv) If temperature and pressure varies then ohm's law is not obeyed.

SECTION - F [PREVIOUS YEARS QUESTIONS, (3 MARKS)]

Q.1 (a) State with the help of a circuit diagram an activity to find the resistance 'R' of a given wire.

(b) A current of 0.2 A passes through a resistor of 20 Ω. Find the potential difference across its ends. **[SAI-2013]**

Ans. (a) (i) A circuit is set-up using the wire of resistance R, an ammeter, a voltmeter and four cells of 1.5 V each.

(ii) First one cell is used as source and the reading of ammeter and voltmeter is noted down to find the current (I) and potential difference (V).

(iii) The number of cells is increased one by one and the readings are noted down.

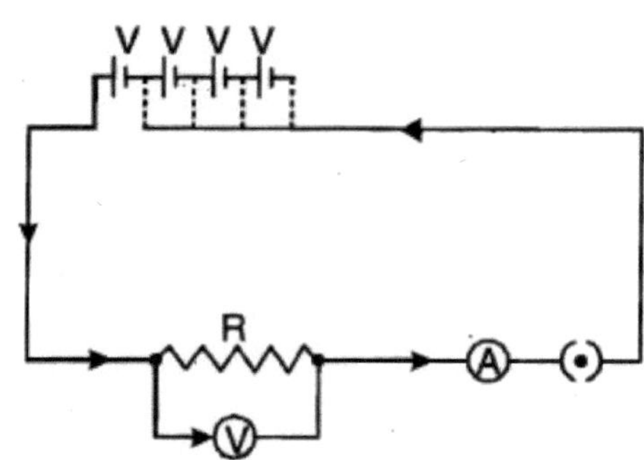

(iv) The average ratio of V to I gives the resistance R' of the wire.

(b) Given, $I = 0.2\ A, R = 20\ \Omega$

$V = I\,R = 0.2 \times 20 = 4\ V$

Q.2 Find the equivalent resistance of the following circuit. **[SAI-2012,2013]**

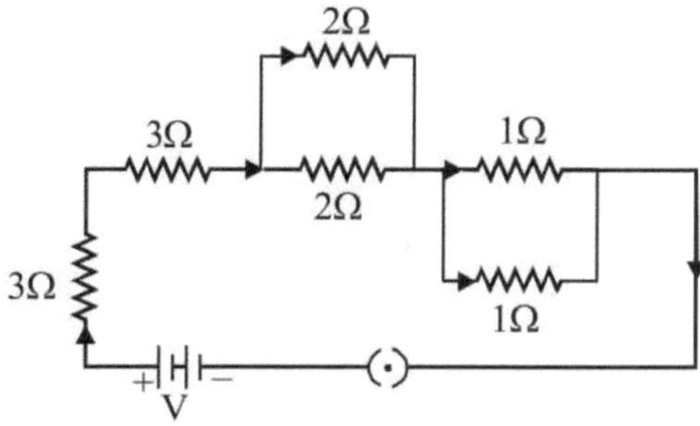

Ans. Resistance of 2Ω each are connected in parallel. Let their combined resistance by R_{P_1}.

So, $$\frac{1}{R_{P_1}} = \frac{1}{2} + \frac{1}{2} = 1$$

$$\Rightarrow \quad R_{P_1} = 1\ \Omega$$

Also, resistance of 1Ω each are connected in parallel. Let their combined resistance be R_{P_2}.

So $$\frac{1}{R_{P_2}} = 1 + 1 = 2\ \Omega$$

$$\Rightarrow \quad R_{P_2} = \frac{1}{2} = 0.5\ \Omega$$

Equivalent resistance (R) of the circuit is given by

$$R = 3 + R_{P_1} + R_{P_2} + 3 = 6 + 1 + 0.5 = 7.5\ \Omega$$

Q.3 State the formula co-relating the electric current flowing in a conductor and the voltage applied across it. Also, show this relationship by drawing a graph.

What would be the resistance of a conductor if the current flowing through it is 0.35 ampere when the potential difference across it is 1.4 volt ? **[SAI-2014]**

Ans. It states that "Physical conditions remaining same then the current flowing through a conductor is directly proportional to the potential applied across its two ends."

The graph is as shown below :

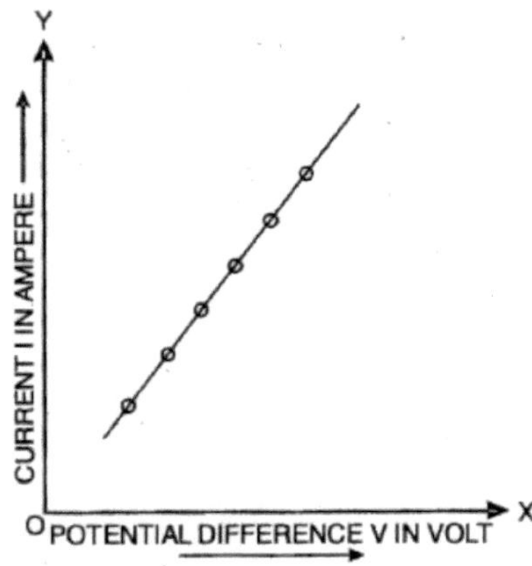

Given, V = 1.4 V, I = 0.35 A. Now resistance is given by the expression

$$R = \frac{V}{I} = \frac{1.4}{0.35} = 4\Omega$$

Q.4 What is meant by 'electrical resistance" of a conductor? State how resistance of a conductor is affected when (i) a low current passes through it for a .short duration; (ii) a heavy current passes through it for about 30 seconds. **[SAI-2015]**

Ans. It is the opposition offered to the flow of current by a conductor.

(i) No effect on resistance, low current, hence no appreciable rise in temperature, so no change in resistance.

(ii) Heavy current for about 30 seconds may increase the temperature of the conductor appreciably, so resistance will change/increase.

SECTION - G [PREVIOUS YEARS QUESTIONS, (5 MARKS)]

Q.1 (a) What is meant by saying that the potential difference between two points is 1 volt ?

(b) Why does the connecting cord of an electrical heater not glow while the heating element does ?

(c) Electrical resistivities of some substances at 20° C are given below :

Silver	$1.60 \times 10^{-8} \Omega m$
Copper	$1.62 \times 10^{-8} \Omega m$
Tungsten	$5.2 \times 10^{-8} \Omega m$
Iron	$10.0 \times 10^{-8} \Omega m$
Mercury	$94.0 \times 10^{-8} \Omega m$
Nichrome	$100 \times 10^{-6} \Omega m$

Answer the following questions in relation to them :

(i) Among silver and copper which one is better conductor ? Why ?

(ii) Which material would you advise to use in electrical heating device ? Why ?

[SAI-2010, 2012, 2014]

Ans. (a) Potential difference between two points is said to be one volt when one joule of work is done to move a charge of one coulomb between the two points.

(b) Heating element glows because its resistivity is much higher than the resistivity of the connecting cord.

(c) (i) Silver is a better conductor because it has the less resistivity.

(ii) Nichrome, because its resistivity is much higher in comparison to the others.

Q.2 (a) Explain how does a cell maintain current in a circuit.

(b) In the circuit given below the resistance of the path xTy = 2Ω and that of xzy = 6Ω.

(i) Find the equivalent resistance between x and y.

(ii) Find the current in the main circuit.

(iii) Calculate the current that flows through the path xTy and xzy. **[SAI-2014]**

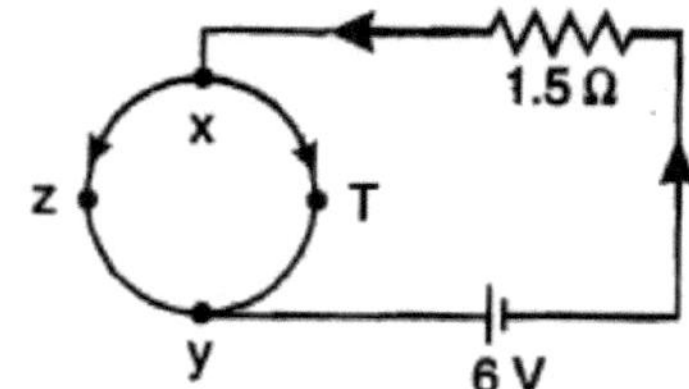

Ans. (a) The chemical action within a cell generates the potential difference across the terminals of the cell. This potential difference sets and maintain current in the circuit.

(b) (i) Equivalent resistance,

$$\frac{1}{R_e} = \frac{1}{2} + \frac{1}{6} = \frac{3+1}{6} = \frac{4}{6} = \frac{2}{3}$$

or $R_e = 1.5\ \Omega$

(ii) Total resistance of the circuit

$= R_e + 1.5\ \Omega$

$= 1.5\ \Omega + 1.5\ \Omega = 3\Omega$

$\therefore$ Current (I) $= \frac{6V}{3\Omega} = 2A$

(iii) Current flowing through path xTy (I_1)

$$I_1 = \frac{6}{6+2} \times 2 = 1.5\ A$$

Current flowing through path xZy (I_2)

$$I_2 = \frac{2}{6+2} \times 2 = 0.5\ A$$

Q.3 Draw a labelled circuit diagram showing three resistors R_1, R_2 and R_3 connected in series with a battery (E), a rheostat (Rh), a plug key (K) and an ammeter (A) using standard circuit symbols. Use this circuit to show that the same current flows through every part of the circuit. List two precautions you would observe while performing the experiment. **[SAI-2015]**

Ans. The circuit diagram is as shown: Join three resistors of different values in series. Connect them with a battery, an ammeter, a rheostat and a plug key, as shown in figure.

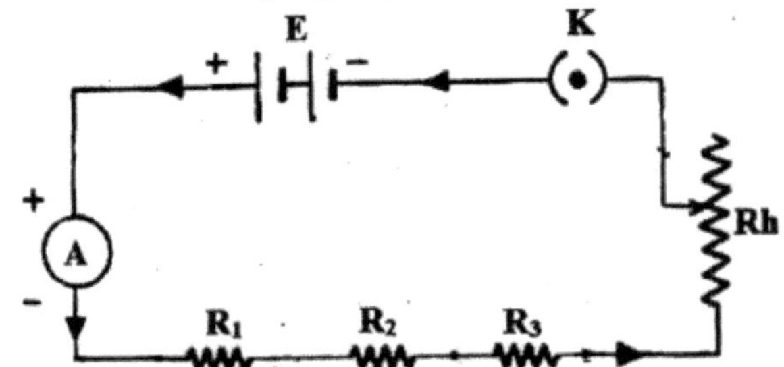

Plug the key. Note the ammeter reading. Change the position of ammeter to anywhere in between the resistors. Note the ammeter reading each time. We observe that the value of the current in the ammeter is the same, independent of its position in the electric circuit. It means that in a series combination of resistors the current is the same in every part of the circuit or the same current series through each resistor.

Precautions :

(i) The current should not be passed for a long time.

(ii) All the connections should be tight.

Q.4 (a) Derive the formula for the calculation of work done when current flows through a resistor.

(b) One electric bulb is rated 40 Wand 240 V and other 25 W and 240 V. Which bulb has higher resistance and how many times ? **[SAI-2015]**

Ans. (a) Suppose a current I is sent through a conductor of resistance R for time t under a potential difference of V volt as shown in figure.

Then charge flowing through the conductor is $Q = It$

The work done in taking Q coulomb charge from one end of the conductor to the other end at a potential difference V is

$W = VQ$

or $W = VIt$

(b) $P_1 = 40$ W, $V_1 = 240$ V

$$P_1 = \frac{V_1^2}{R_1} \quad \text{or} \quad R_1 = \frac{V_1^2}{P_1} = \frac{240 \times 240}{40}$$

$P_2 = 25$W, $V_2 = 240$ V

$$P_2 = \frac{V_2^2}{R_2} \text{ or } R_2 = \frac{V_2^2}{P_2}$$

$$\frac{240 \times 240}{25}$$

So $$\frac{R_1}{R_2} = \frac{\frac{240 \times 240}{40}}{\frac{240 \times 240}{25}} = \frac{25}{40} = \frac{5}{8} \quad \Rightarrow \quad \frac{R_1}{R_2} = \frac{5}{8}$$

25 W bulb has more resistance and $\frac{8}{5} R_1$ times.

CONCEPT APPLICATION LEVEL - III

SECTION-A

Direction for questions 1 to 5 : State whether the following statements are true or false.

1. Conventional current always flows from a body having high charge density to a body having low charge density.
2. At constant temperature, the resistance of a conductor changes according to the applied voltage.
3. In an electrolyte, the movement of ions is responsible for electric current.
4. Electric potential at a point in an electric field is defined as the work done in moving a unit positive charge from infinity to that point.
5. Earthing of electric appliances prevents electric shock.

SECTION-B

Directions for question 1 to 6. Fill in the blanks.

1. Power transmission is carried out at high ___________ and low ___________.
2. Switch is always connected to the ___________ wire.
3. Rate at which electric work is done is called ______________.
4. The process of depositing a thin layer of desired metal over another metal by passing an electric current through some electrolyte is called _______________.
5. Conductance is the reciprocal of ______________.
6. The amount of work done by the cell on a unit positive charge carrier to force it to go to the point of higher potential is called _______________.

SECTION-C

Direction for question : Match the entries in the column A with appropriate ones from column B.

Q.1

	Column I		Column II
(A)	Ohm	(p)	$\frac{\rho L}{A}$
(B)	Resistance	(q)	$\frac{1\,\text{volt}}{1\,\text{ampere}}$
(C)	Resistivity	(r)	zero resistance
(D)	Super conductor	(s)	ohm–meter

Q.2

	Column -A		Column-B
(A)	Electric potential	a.	Transistor
(B)	Commercial unit of electrical energy	b.	ohm-meter
(C)	Resistance	c.	$E = E_1 + E_2$
(D)	Superconductor	d.	$Q = I^2Rt$
(E)	1 ohm	e.	Black
(F)	Non-ohmic conductor	f.	$V = W/Q$
(G)	Resistivity	g.	kW h

(H)	Cells connected in series	h.	$\frac{\rho L}{A}$
(I)	Heat produced in a conductor	i.	zero resistance
(J)	Neutral wire	j.	1 volt/1 ampere

Q.3 Column II gives order of resistivity for materials in column I.

	Column I		Column II
(A)	Semi–conductor	(p)	$3 \times 10^3\ \Omega$-m
(B)	Conductor	(q)	$10^{-8}\ \Omega$-m
(C)	Insulator	(r)	$10^{16}\ \Omega$-m
(D)	Super conductor	(s)	$1\ \Omega$-m

Multiple Matching Type Questions (One to Many) :

Direction for question : Match the entries in the column A with appropriate more then ones from column B.

Q.4

	Column I		Column II
(A)	Ohm's Law	(p)	Materialistic property
(B)	Resistivity	(q)	Voltage α current
(C)	For Ohmic–conductor	(r)	$\frac{charge}{time}$
(D)	Electric current	(s)	V = IR

Q.5 **Column I** **Column II**

(A)

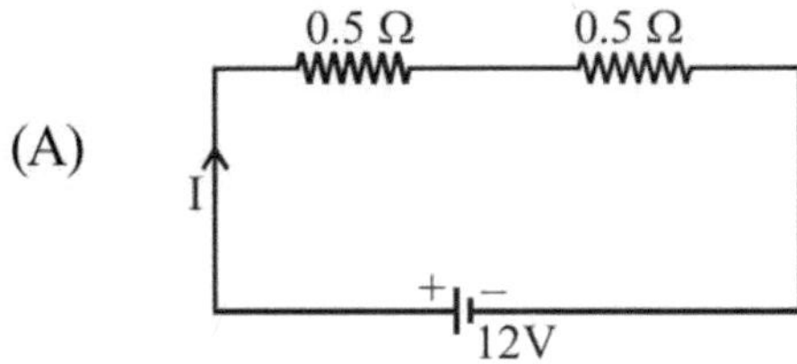

(p) $R_{eq} = 1\ \Omega, I = 12\ A$

(B)

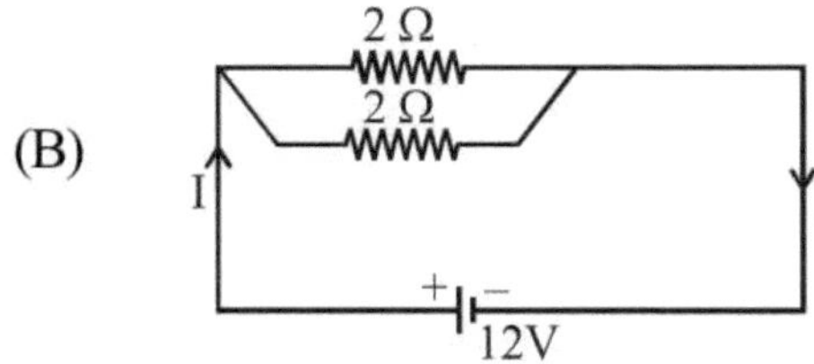

(q) α Length

(C) Resistance

(r) $R_{eq} = 1\Omega, I = 6A$

(D)

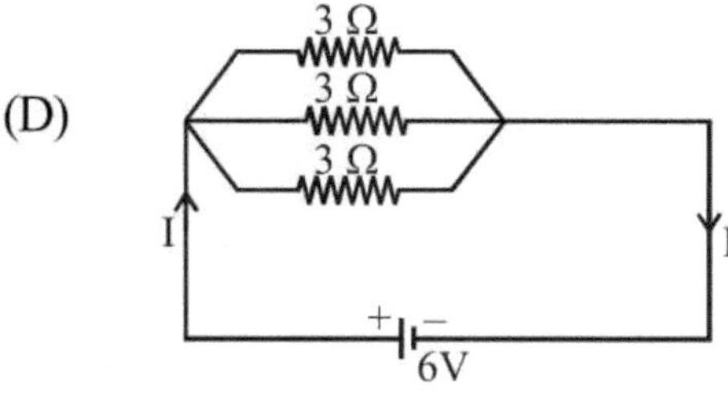

(s) $\alpha \frac{1}{\text{Area}}$

Q.6

	Column I		Column II
(A)	1 Ohm	(p)	1 Volt / 1 Amp
(B)	Current	(q)	Depends on matter of conductor
(C)	Resistivity	(r)	$\frac{charge}{time}$
(D)	Super conductor	(s)	Resistance = 0

Q.7

	Column I		Column II
(A)	Ohm's law	(p)	Nichrome wire
(B)	Heating effect	(q)	Battery
(C)	EMF	(r)	V = IR
(D)	Terminal potential difference	(s)	Ohmic resistance
		(t)	$v = \varepsilon \pm Ir$

SECTION-D

Multiple choice question with one correct answers :

Q.1 A cylindrical rod is reformed to twice its length with no change in its volume. If the resistance of the rod was R, the new resistance will be :

(A) R (B) 2 R (C) 4 R (D) 8 R

Q.2 A wire carries a steady current of 1.0 A over a period of 20s. What total charge passes through the wire in this time interval :

(A) 200 C (B) 20 C (C) 2.0 C (D) 0.20 C

Q.3 The length of a wire is doubled and the radius is doubled. By what factor does the resistance change :

(A) 4 times as large (B) twice as large (C) unchanged (D) half as large

Q.4 A 24 V potential difference is applied across a parallel combination of four 6 ohm resistor. The current in each resistor is :

(A) 1 A (B) 4 A (C) 16 A (D) 36 A

Q.5 Three resistances of 2, 3 and 5 Ω are connected in parallel to a 10 V battery of negligible internal resistance. The potential difference across the 3 Ω resistance will be :

(A) 2 V (B) 3 V (C) 5 V (D) 10 V

Q.6 You are given n identical wires, each of resistance R. When these are connected in parallel, the equivalent resistance is X. When these will be connected in series, then the equivalent resistance will be :

(A) X/n^2 (B) n^2X (C) X/n (D) nX

Q.7 Charge on an electron is 1.6×10^{-19} coulomb. Number of electrons passing through the wire per second on flowing of 1 ampere current through the wire will be :

(A) 0.625×10^{-19} (B) 1.6×10^{-19} (C) 1.6×10^{-19} (D) 0.625×10^{19}

Q.8 Three resistors of 4.0Ω, 6.0Ω and 10.0Ω are connected in series. What is their equivalent resistance :

(A) 20 Ω (B) 5 Ω (C) 6.0 Ω (D) 4.0 Ω

Q.9 Ampere-second stands for the unit of :
(A) Power (B) Charge (C) e.m.f. (D) Energy

Q.10 Three resistors are connected to form the sides of a triangle ABC as shown below.

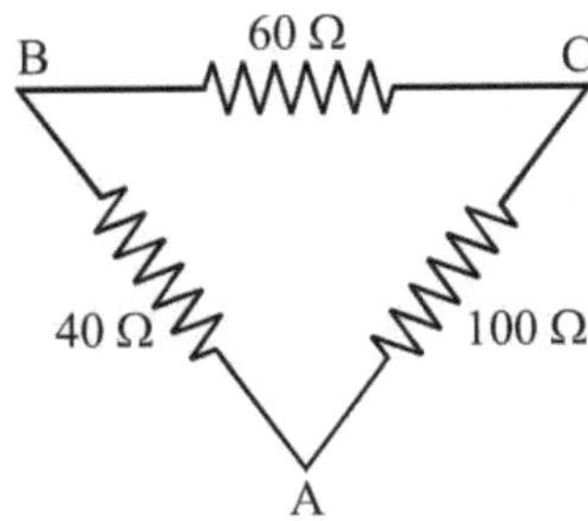

The resistance of side AB is 40 ohms, of side BC 60 ohms and of side CA 100 ohms. The effective resistance between A and B will be :
(A) 50Ω (B) 64Ω (C) 32Ω (D) 100Ω

Q.11 If one micro-amp. current is flowing in a wire, the number of electrons which pass from one end of the wire to the other end in one second is :
(A) 6.25×10^{12} (B) 6.25×10^{15} (C) 6.25×10^{18} (D) 6.25×10^{19}

Q.12 If the temperature of a conductor is increased, its resistance will :
(A) Not increase (B) Increase
(C) Decrease (D) Change according to the whether

Q.13 There are two wires of the same length and of the same material and radius r and 2r. The ratio of their specific resistance is :
(A) 1 : 2 (B) 1 : 1 (C) 1 : 4 (D) 4 : 1

Q.14 The resistance 4 R, 16 R, 64 R, ... ∞ are connected in series, their resultant will be :
(A) 0 (B) ∞ (C) 43 R (D) 34 R

Q.15 Resistance R, 2 R, 4 R, 8 R, ... ∞ are connected in parallel. Their resultant resistance will be :
(A) R (B) R/2 (C) 0 (D) ∞

Q.16 The equivalent resistance between points X & Y :

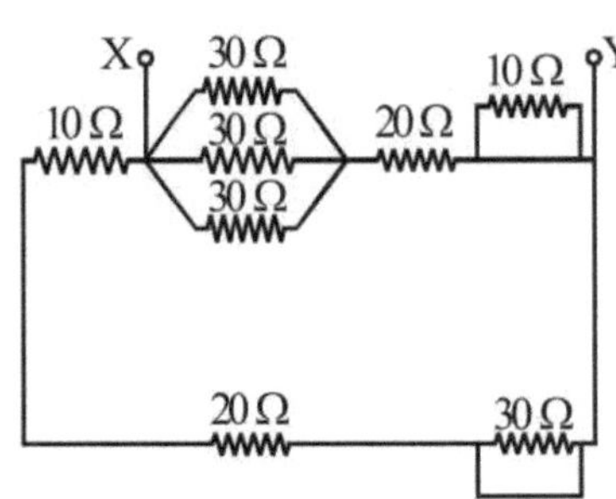

(A) 5 Ω (B) 10 Ω (C) 15 Ω (D) 60 Ω

Q.17 The equivalent resistance between points X & Y :

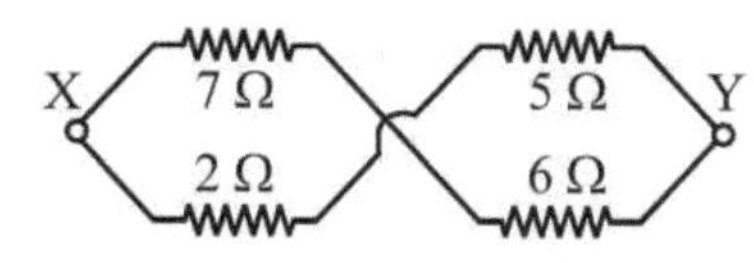

(A) 4 Ω (B) 4.5 Ω (C) 2 Ω (D) 20 Ω

Q.18 A certain wire has a resistance R. The resistance of another wire identical with the first except having twice its diameter is :

(A) 2 R (B) 0.25 R (C) 4 R (D) 0.5 R

Q.19 Masses of 3 wires of same metal are in the ratio 1 : 2 : 3 and their lengths are in the 3 : 2 : 1. The electrical resistances are in ratio :

(A) 1 : 4 : 9 (B) 9 : 4 : 1 (C) 1 : 2 : 3 (D) 27 : 6 : 1

Q.20 A solenoid is at potential difference 60 V and current flows through it is 15 ampere, then the resistance of coil will be :

(A) 4 Ω (B) 8 Ω (C) 0.25 Ω (D) 2 Ω

Q.21 In the circuit shown in the figure, the current through

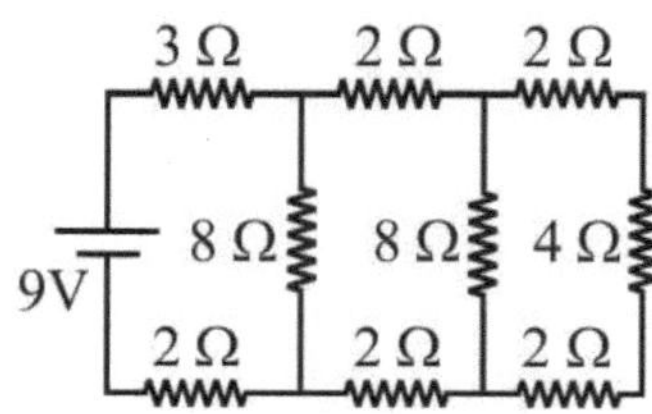

(A) The 3 Ω resistor is 0.50 A
(B) The 3 Ω resistor is 0.25 A
(C) The 4 Ω resistor is 0.50 A
(D) The 4 Ω resistor is 0.25 A

Q.22 Which of the following has a negative temperature coefficient?

(A) C (B) Fe (C) Mn (D) Ag

Q.23 Which two circuit components are connected in parallel in the following circuit diagram?

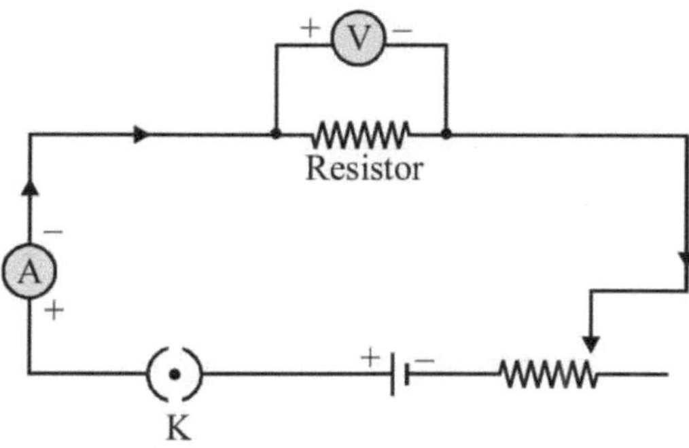

(A) Rheostat and voltmeter
(B) Voltmeter and resistor
(C) Voltmeter and ammeter
(D) Ammeter and resistor

Q.24 To determine the equivalent resistance of two resistors when connected in series, a student arranged the circuit components as shown in the diagram. But he did not succeed to achieve the objective.

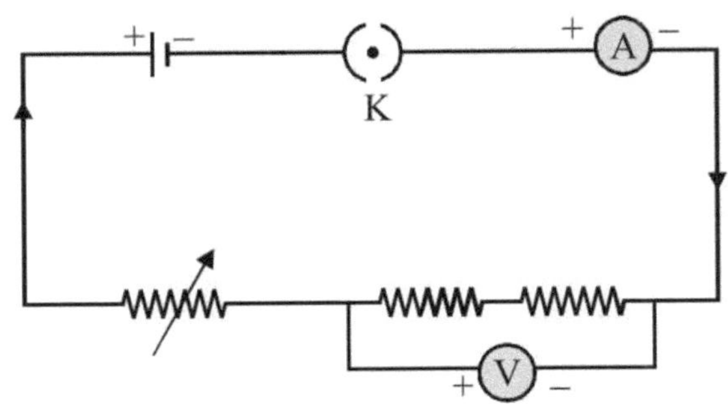

Which of the following mistakes has been committed by him in setting up the circuit?
(A) Position of ammeter is incorrect.
(B) Position of voltmeter is incorrect.
(C) Terminals of ammeter are wrongly connected.
(D) Terminals of voltmeter are wrongly connected.

Q.25 The following circuit diagram shows the experimental set-up for the study of dependence of current on potential difference. Which two circuit components are connected in series?

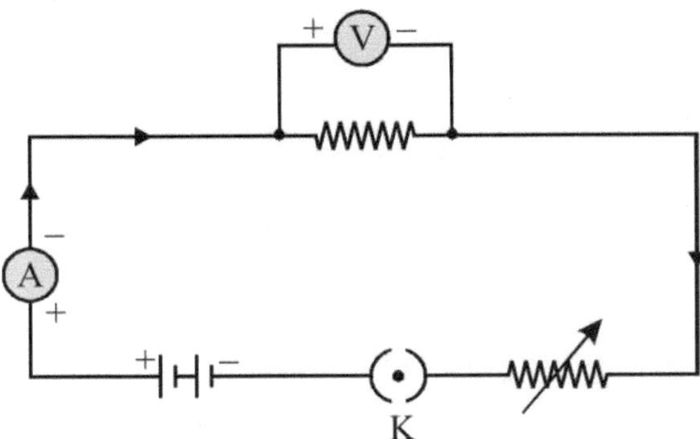

(A) Battery and voltmeter
(B) Ammeter and voltmeter
(C) Ammeter and Rheostat
(D) Resistor and voltmeter

Q.26 Which of the circuit components in the following circuit diagram and connected in parallel?

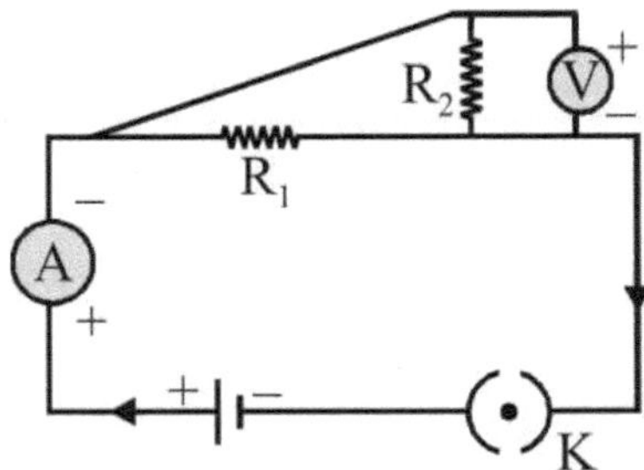

(A) R_1 and R_2 only (B) R_1, R_2 and V (C) R_2 and V only (D) R_1 and V only

SECTION-E

Multiple choice question with one or more than one correct answers :

Q.1 The terminal potential difference of a cell of EMF 'E' and internal resistance 'r' is given by the formula

(A) $V = E - Ir$ (B) $V = E$ (C) $V = 0$ (D) $V = E + Ir$

Q.2 The voltage across a conductor is directly proportional to the current flowing across it under constant conditions of

(A) Pressure (B) Humidity (C) Temperature (D) Density

Q.3 Choose all correct alternatives

(A) 1 volt × 1 coulomb = 1 joule

(B) 1 volt × 1 ampere = 1 J/s

(C) 1 volt × 1 watt = 1 HP

(D) Watt-hour can be measured in terms of electron-volt

Q.4 A current passes through a wire of non-uniform cross-section. Which of the following quantities are independent of the cross-section?

(A) The charge crossing in a given time interval

(B) Drift speed

(C) Current density

(D) Free-electron density

Q.5 Two conductors made of the same material have length L and 2L, but have equal resistances. The two are connected in series in a circuit in which current is flowing. Which of the following is / are correct?

(A) The potential difference across the two conductors is the same.

(B) The electron drift velocity is larger in the conductor of length 2L.

(C) The electric field in the first conductor is twice than that in the second.

(D) The electric field in the second conductor is twice than that in the first.

Q.6 Electric current arises from the flow of charged particles.

Now :

(A) In metals it is dominant due to flow of electrons.

(B) In semiconductor it is jointly due to flow of holes and electrons.

(C) In electrolytes it is due to flow of negative ions only.

(D) In discharged tubes containing gases at low pressure it is due to flow of positive ions only.

Q.7 Electric current is due to flow of charge carriers in the conductor. Which of the following is / are correct?

(A) The drift speed of charge carriers is a very small fraction of the mean thermal agitation speed of the same charge carriers.

(B) The number of charge carriers per unit volume is always the same as the number of atoms of the conductor per unit volume.

(C) The drift velocity is proportional to the electric field applied ordinarily.

(D) In an intrinsic semiconductor, the charge carriers are either electrons only or holes only; both of them may not participate in conduction.

Q.8 When some potential difference is maintained between A and B, current I enters the network at A and leaves at B.

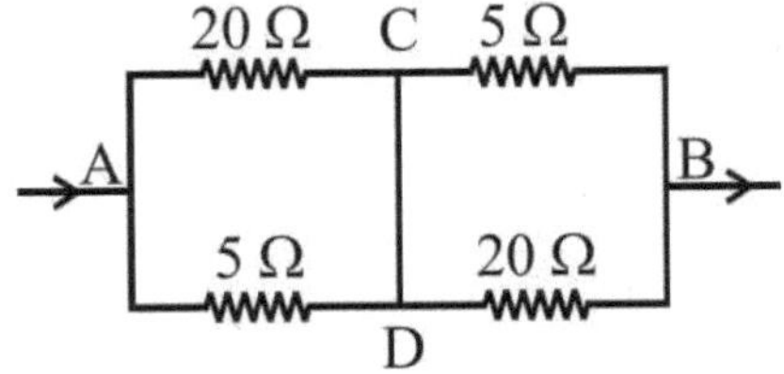

(A) The equivalent resistance between A and B is 8 Ω.
(B) C and D are at the same potential.
(C) No current flows between C and D.
(D) Current $(3I/5)$ flows D to C.

Q.9 Three voltmeters, all having different resistances, are joined as shown in the figure. When some potential difference is applied across A and B, their readings are V_1, V_2, V_3 :

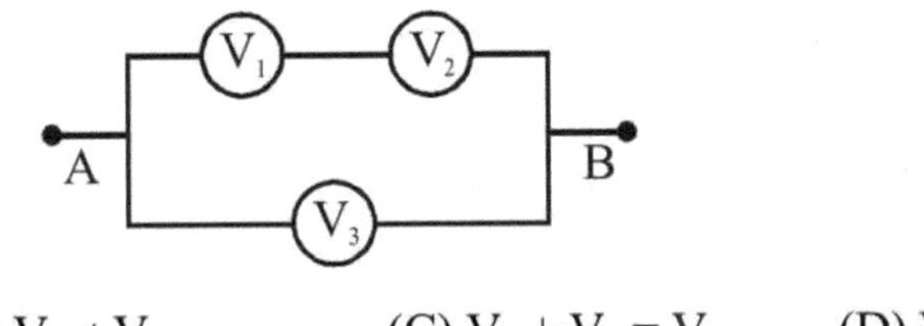

(A) $V_1 = V_2$ (B) $V_1 \neq V_2$ (C) $V_1 + V_2 = V_3$ (D) $V_1 + V_2 > V_3$

Q.10 In the circuit, the battery is ideal. A voltmeter of resistance 600 Ω is connected in turn across R_1 and R_2, giving readings V_1 and V_2 respectively :

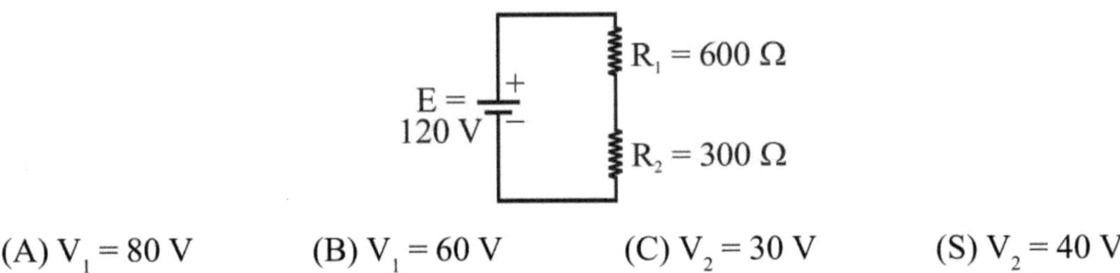

(A) $V_1 = 80$ V (B) $V_1 = 60$ V (C) $V_2 = 30$ V (S) $V_2 = 40$ V

SECTION-F

Comprehension – 1

A battery of EMF 10 V having internal resistance of 2Ω is connected to an external resistance of 3Ω. The battery is first in charging mode and then in discharging mode.

1. The current flowing through the external resistance is :
(A) 1A (B) 3A (C) 2A (D) 10A

2. The terminal potential difference during discharging mode of battery :
(A) 6V (B) 2V (C) 1V (D) 10V

3. The terminal potential difference during the charging mode of battery :
(A) 5V (B) 10V (C) 14V (D) 9V

Comprehension – 2

Answer the following questions based on the given circuit.

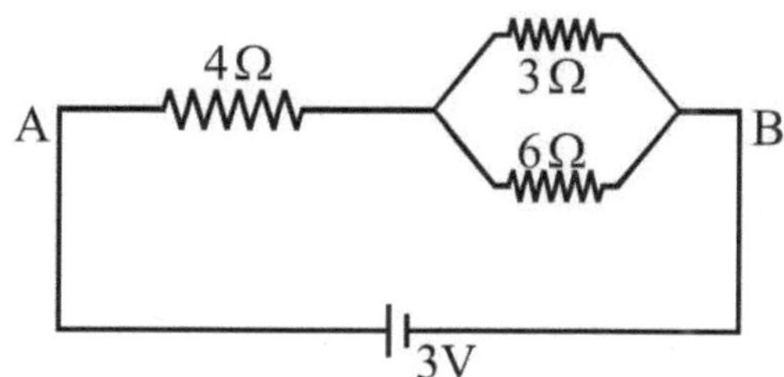

Q.1 The potential drop across the 3 Ω resistor is :
(A) 1 V (B) 1.5 V (C) 2 V (D) 3 V

Q.2 The equivalent resistance between points A and B is :
(A) 7 Ω (B) 6 Ω (C) 13 Ω (D) 5 Ω

Q.3 The current flowing through in the given circuit is :
(A) 0.5 A (B) 1.5 A (C) 6 A (D) 3 A

Comprehension – 3

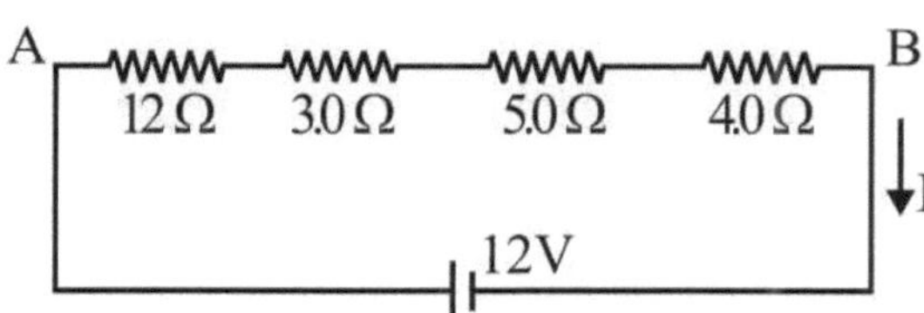

Q.1 The equivalent resistance between points A and B, is :
(A) 12 Ω (B) 36 Ω (C) 32 Ω (D) 24 Ω

Q.2 The current through each resistor is :
(A) 1 A (B) 2.3 A (C) 0.5 A (D) 0.75 A

Q.3 The potential drop across the 12 Ω resistor is :
(A) 12 V (B) 6 V (C) 8 V (D) 0.5 V

SECTION-G

Assertion & Reason

Instructions: In the following questions as Assertion (A) is given followed by a Reason (R). Mark your responses from the following options.

(A) Both Assertion and Reason are true and Reason is the correct explanation of 'Assertion'

(B) Both Assertion and Reason are true and Reason is not the correct explanation of 'Assertion'

(C) Assertion is true but Reason is false

(D) Assertion is false but Reason is true

Q.1 **Assertion :** Current is a vector quantity.

Reason : Current is charge flowing per unit time.

Q.2 **Assertion :** Current flows from positive to negative terminal of the battery.

Reason : This is the conventional direction of current.

Q.3 **Assertion :** The resistance of a conductor is proportional to the square of its length.

Reason : $R = \rho\frac{l}{A}$.

Q.4 **Assertion :** Resistivity changes when conductor is stretched or contracted.

Reason : Resitivity is a material property.

Q.5 **Assertion :** Kirchoff's current law states that the net current at a junction is zero.

Reason : This law is based on the conservation of charge principle.

ANSWER KEY

Try yourself :

1. Potential difference = 1 V & Current = 1/2 A. 2. 2 Ω.

CONCEPT APPLICATION LEVEL - III

SECTION-A

1.	False	2.	False	3.	True	4.	True	5.	True

SECTION-B

1.	Voltage, current	2.	Live	3.	Electric power
4.	Electroplating	5.	Resistance	6.	EMF

SECTION-C

Q.1 (A)-(q), (B)-(p), (C)-(s), (D)-(r)
Q.2 (A)-(f), (B)-(g), (C)-(h), (D)-(i), (E)-(j), (F)-(a), (G)-(b), (H)-(c), (I)-(d), (J)-(e)
Q.3 (A)-(p), (B)-(s), (C)-(r), (D)-(q)
Q.4 (A)-(q,s), (B)-(p), (C)-(q,s), (D)-(r)
Q.5 (A)-(p), (B)-(p), (C)-(q,s), (D)-(r)
Q.6 (A)-(p), (B)-(q,r), (C)-(q), (D)-(s)
Q.7 (A)-(r,s), (B)-(p), (C)-(q), (D)-(r,t)

SECTION-D

Q.1	C	Q.2	B	Q.3	D	Q.4	B	Q.5	D	Q.6	B	Q.7	D
Q.8	A	Q.9	B	Q.10	C	Q.11	A	Q.12	B	Q.13	B	Q.14	B
Q.15	B	Q.16	C	Q.17	B	Q.18	B	Q.19	D	Q.20	A	Q.21	D
Q.22	A	Q.23	B	Q.24	C	Q.25	C	Q.26	B				

SECTION-E

Q.1	AD	Q.2	AC	Q.3	ABD	Q.4	AD	Q.5	AC	Q.6	AD	Q.7	AC
Q.8	ABD	Q.9	BC	Q.10	BC								

SECTION-F

Comprehension – 1

Q.1 C Q.2 A Q.3 C

Comprehension – 2

Q.1 A Q.2 B Q.3 A

Comprehension – 3

Q.1 D Q.2 C Q.3 B

SECTION-G

Q.1 D Q.2 A Q.3 D Q.4 D Q.5 A

2 MAGNETIC EFFECTS OF ELECTRIC CURRENT

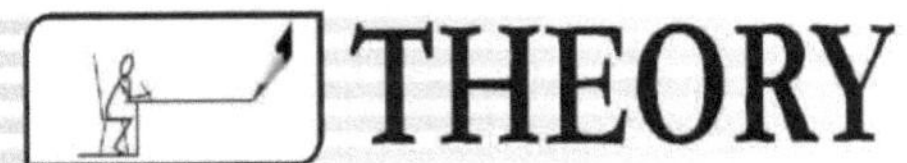

CONCEPT TREE :

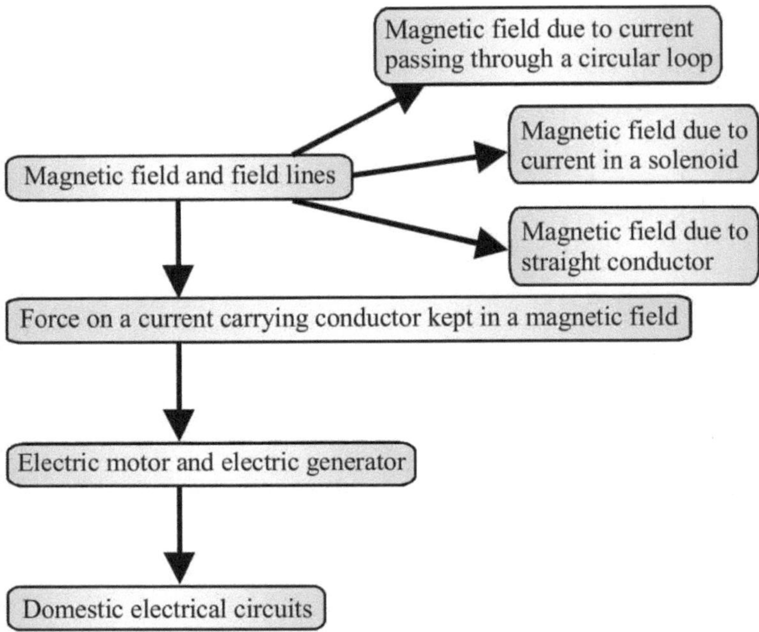

2.1 INTRODUCTION

It was found that magnetism and electricity are related to each other. This means that electricity can be used for the generation of electromagnetic effect and this effect is called electromagnetism. Similarly changing magnetic field can produce electricity, this is called electromagnetic induction.

Magnetism has been a source of curiosity for ages. Magnets are commonly found in science laboratories, toys and in the magnetic stickers that we stick to refrigerators and steel almirahs. The earth itself acts as a magnet. Actually, magnets are all around us, since each electron, proton and neutron behaves as a tiny magnet. Magnetism has many uses — from the simple magnetic sticker to magnetic resonance imaging (MRI). **MRI** is a diagnostic technique in which the magnetism of the protons inside the human body is used to form images of tissues.

Knowledge Based Questions:

1. A charge whenever in motion has
(A) only magnetic field linked with it
(B) only electric field linked with it
(C) both electric and magnetic field linked with it
(D) only gravitational field linked with it.

2. Magnetic forces
(A) are always attractive (B) are always repulsive
(C) may be attractive or repulsive (D) none of these

3. Magnetic field is generated by
(A) stone (B) mud (C) magnet (D) iron piece

4. A magnetic needle comes to rest in
(A) geographic East-west direction (B) geographic North-south direction
(C) vertical direction (D) in North-east direction

5. The device used for producing electric current is called
(A) generator (B) galvanometer (C) ammeter (D) motor

6. In an electric motor, conversion takes place of
(A) Chemical energy into electrical energy (B) Electrical energy into mechanical energy
(C) Electrical energy into light (D) Electrical energy into chemical energy

7. A magnet can be demagnetised by
(A) Hammering the magnet (B) Putting it in the water
(C) Cooling it (D) Putting in contact with iron

8. Which one of the following is the magnetic substance
(A) Mercury (B) Iron (C) Gold (D) Silver

9. Generally permanent magnets are prepared from
(A) Gold (B) Silver (C) Iron (D) Steel

10. If iron filings are sprinkled around a bar magnet then they arrange in a fixed pattern which is
(A) magnetic field lines pattern (B) Electric field lines pattern
(C) Faraday's electric field lines pattern. (D) None of these

2.2 MAGNET

A substance which attracts small pieces of iron, nickel, cobalt and steel and points in North-South direction when freely suspended (or hanged freely) is known as a magnet.

Natural magnets are irregular in shape, moreover they are weak magnets. An iron bar can be made a magnet by rubbing it with a natural magnet. Such a magnet is known as Man made or artificial magnet. Like magnetic poles (i.e. North and North or South and South) repel each other while unlike magnetic poles attract each other.

Magnetite is so called because it was found is magnesia in Asia Minor.

The Greek discovered the attractive property of the natural magnet, while the Chinese discovered the directive property of the natural magnet.

In 1600, Dr. William Gilbert, the English physicist concluded that the Earth behaves as a large permanet manget.

Artificial magnets are of different shapes. A bar magnet (i.e. rectangular in shape) and U-shaped magnet are common example of artificial magnets.

In the beginning, it was thought that electricity and magnetism have no relation with each other. However, in 1819, **Hans Christian Oersted**, a Danish physicist, discovered a relationship between electricity and magnetism. He found that a wire carrying current causes a deflection in the needle of a magnetic compass placed near the wire. Since needle of a magnetic compass is a tiny magnet, so it will be deflected from its equilibrium position if another magnet is brought close to it. As the magnetic compass is placed near the current carrying wire, so the current carrying wire behaves as a magnet. The effect of the electric current passing through a wire due to which the needle of magnetic compass deflects is known as **magnetic effect of electric current**.

Try yourself

1. What is a magnet?
2. Can the poles of a bar magnet be separated?

Important Properties of Magnets

- ***Property of attraction*** : Magnets attract small pieces of materials like iron, nickel, and cobalt. The property of a magnet to attract small pieces of iron seems to be concentrated in small regions at the ends of the magnet. These regions are called magnetic poles. The pole which points towards geographic north is called North pole of the magnet. The pole which points towards geographic south is called South pole of the magnet.
- ***Property of direction*** : A freely suspended magnet always aligns itself in the North-South direction.
- **Like-poles of magnets repel each other and unlike-poles attract each other,** just as like-charges repel and unlike-charges attract. Since a magnet can attract small pieces of iron and also the opposite pole of another magnet, property of attraction is not a sure test to find whether a given piece is a magnet or not. Repulsion is a sure test to confirm whether a given piece is a magnet or not.
- ***Property of induction*** : A magnet can induce magnetism in substances like soft iron, cobalt, nickel etc.
- Breaking a magnet successively into smaller pieces would still produce tiny magnets each with a north pole and south pole. The above phenomena is observed till we reach molecular stage.
- Magnetic poles always exist in opposite pairs. Single magnetic poles never exist.

2.3 MAGNETIC FIELD AND MAGNETIC FIELD LINES

When a bar magnet is suspended freely from its centre by a thread, one end of the magnet points towards the north of the earth and the other end of the magnet points towards the south of the earth. The end of the magnet pointing towards north of the earth is called **north seeking pole** or simply **north pole of the magnet.** On the other hand, the end of the magnet pointing towards sound of the earth is called **south seeking pole** or simply **south pole of the magnet.**

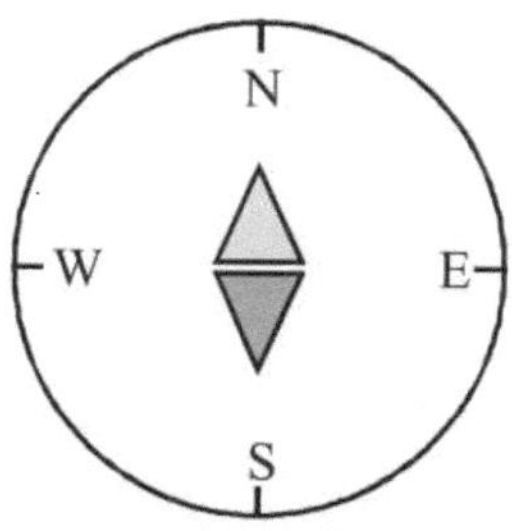

Magnetic compass

You must have seen a magnetic compass needle. The needle of a magnetic compass is, infact, a small bar magnet which is free to move in a horizontal plane on a pivot. One end of the compass needle pointing towards North is known as North Pole. The other end of the compass needle pointing towards South is known as South Pole.

When a north pole of a bar magnet is brought near the north pole of a magnetic compass needle, then the needle of the magnetic compass is deflected away from the north pole of the bar magnet. On the other hand, when a north pole of a bar magnet is brought near the south pole of a magnetic compass needle, then the needle of the magnetic compass is attracted towards the north pole of the bar magnet. Thus, we conclude :

Like magnetic poles repel each other while unlike magnetic potes attract each other.

The force with which a magnetic pole of a magnet attracts or repels another magnetic pole of another magnet is called **magnetic force.** The space or region around a magnet within which magnetic force is exerted on other magnet is called the **magnetic field** of the magnet.

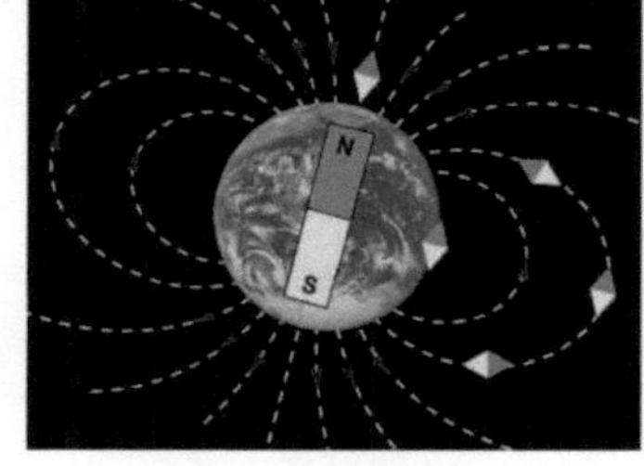

Definition of Magnetic Field : The space or region around a magnet (or a current carrying wire) within which its influence can be felt (or magnetic force is experienced) by another magnet is called magnetic field. It is denoted by $\vec{B}$.

To locate the magnetic field of a bar magnet, we use iron filings or a magnetic compass. When a magnetic compass is far away from a magnet, it is not deflected. However, when a magnetic compass is close to the magnet, it is deflected. So the space or region around a magnet within which a magnetic compass is deflected is known as the magnetic field of the bar magnet.

Magnetic Lines of Force (or Magnetic Field Lines) : A magnetic field is represented by a series of lines (or paths) around a magnet. These lines represent the paths of an imaginary independent north pole if it were allowed to move freely in the direction of the magnetic force.

Definition of magnetic field line : The path (straight or curved) along which unit north pole moves in a magnetic field (if free to do so) is called **magnetic line of force or magnetic field line.** Magnetic lines of force or magnetic field lines are helpful to show the direction and strength (or intensity) of a magnetic field.

The direction of the magnetic field at any particular place is the direction in which the north pole of a magnetic compass needle points if placed at that point. **The strength of the magnetic field is shown by how much close these lines are to each other**.

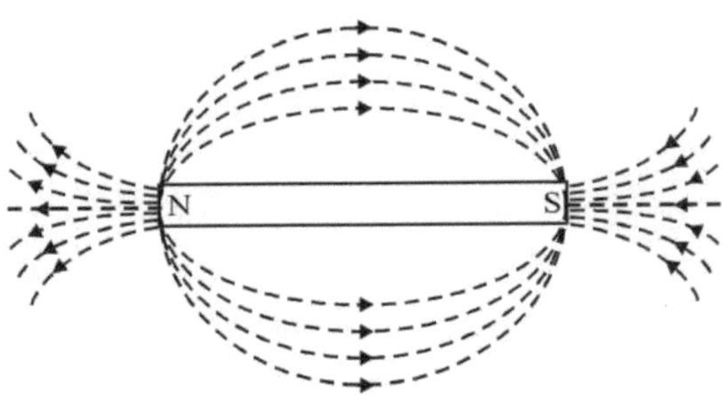

If magnetic field lines are very close to each other in a particular region, then the strength of the magnetic field in that region is very large. On the other hand, if the magnetic field lines are far from each other in a particular region, then the strength of the magnetic field in that region is very small.

The magnetic field lines around a bar magnet are shown in following figure.

PRACTICAL LEARNING

Magnetic field lines represent the magnetic field of a magnet pictorially.

1. Take a drawing board and paste a white sheet of paper on it.
2. Place the drawing board on the table.
3. Place a bar magnet at the centre of the paper.
4. Now sprinkle iron filings evenly around the magnet.
5. Tap the surface of the drawing board gently.

Observation : We will observe that the iron filings are arranged in a pattern as shown in figure. This pattern consists of a series of magnetic lines of force around the magnet.

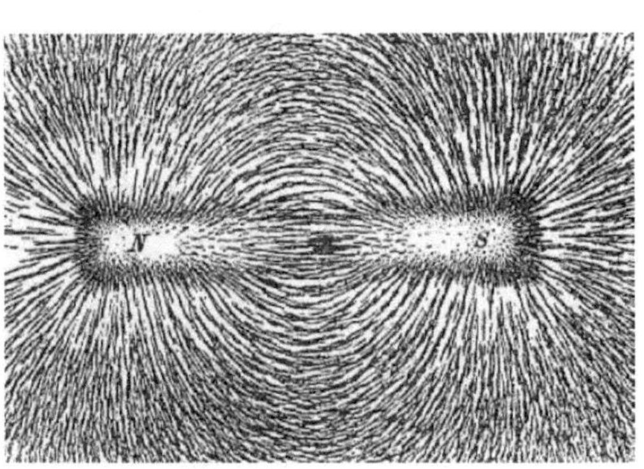

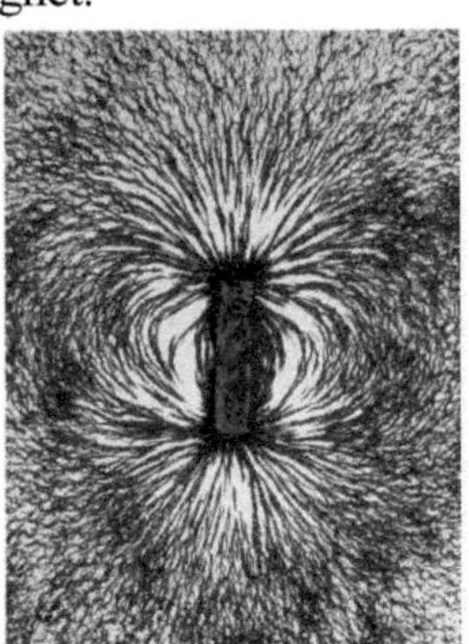

Plotting of magnetic field lines of a bar magnet

1. Describe an activity to draw a magnetic field lines outside a bar magnet from one pole to another pole.
   (i) Take a drawing board and fix a white sheet of paper on it with the help of drawing pins.
   (ii) Place a bar magnet at the centre of the paper and mark its boundary with a pencil.
   (iii) Place the magnetic compass needle close to any pole of the magnet, say North pole.
   (iv) Tap gently the surface of the drawing board so that the needle moves freely on the pivot.
   (v) Wait for sometime till the needle of the compass comes to rest. Mark the North and South positions of the compass needle as dots with a pencil on the paper as shown in figure.

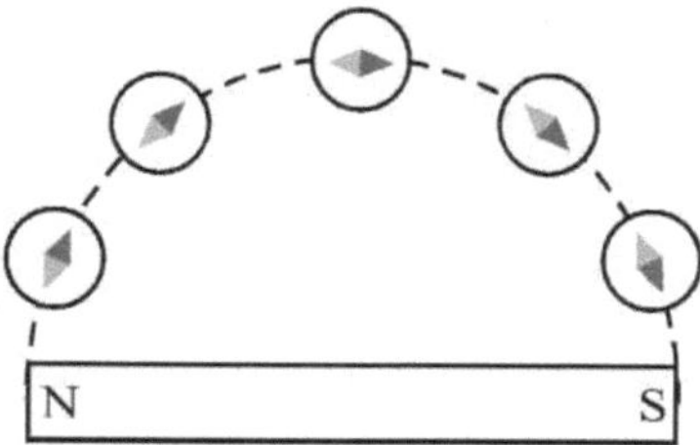

   (vi) Go on marking the north and south positions of the compass needle by shifting the compass till it reaches the other end of pole of the bar magnet.
   (vii) All the pencil dots on the paper are joined to get a smooth curve. This curve is known as magnetic field line.
   (viii) Repeat the process to plot other smooth curves.
   (ix) The magnetic field lines of the bar magnet are obtained as shown in figure (1).

Magnetic field lines of a pair of opposite poles of two magnets placed close to each other are shown in figure (2).

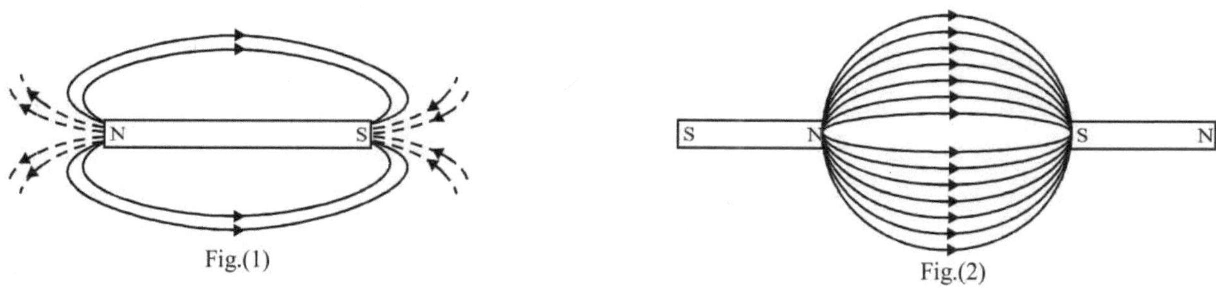

Fig.(1) Fig.(2)

Magnetic field lines of a pair of similar poles of two magnets placed close to each other are shown in figure.

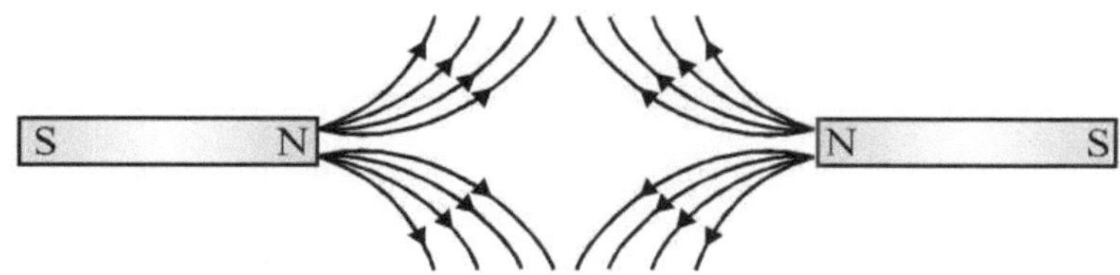

Properties of Magnetic Lines of Force :

1. **Magnetic field lines are closed continuous curves :**
Magnetic lines of force emerge from a magnet at N-pole and enter the magnet at S-pole. But magnetic field lines run from S-pole to N-pole within the magnet.

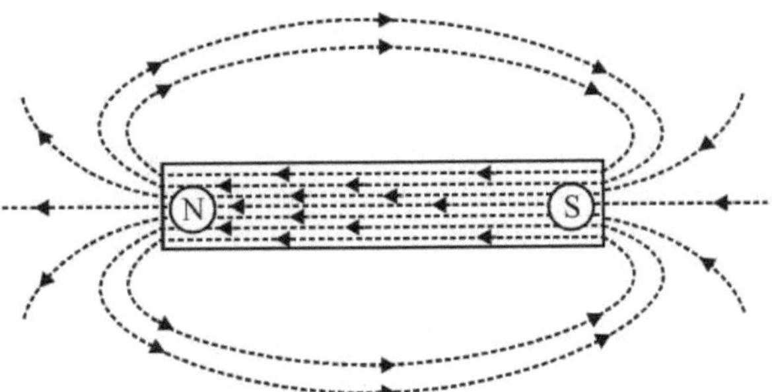

2. **The tangent at any point on the magnetic field lines gives the direction of the magnetic field at that point.**

3. **No two magnetic field lines can intersect each other.**
If two magnetic field lines intersect at a point (P) as shown in figure, then there will be two tangents at that point. It means, at the point of intersection, there will be two directions of the same magnetic field, which is not possible. Hence, no two magnetic field lines can intersect each other.

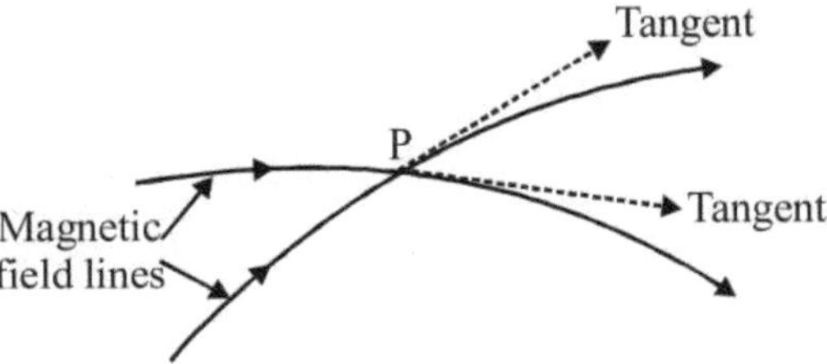

4. Magnetic field lines are crowded (i.e. close to each other) in a region of strong magnetic field. On the other hand, magnetic field lines are far from each other (or diverges) in a region of weak magnetic field.

5. These behave like a stretched bow and have a tendency to contract length wise, which shows attraction between two opposite poles as shown in figure given.

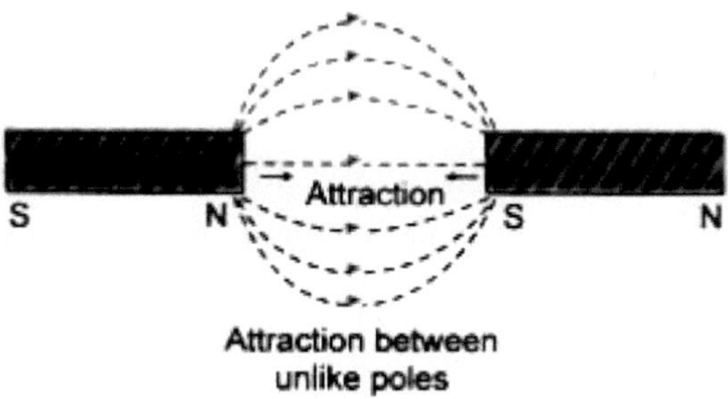

Attraction between unlike poles

6. Lines of force exert a lateral force of repulsion on each other which explains repulsion between two similar poles as shown in figure below. (No line of force exists in the region between two similar poles.

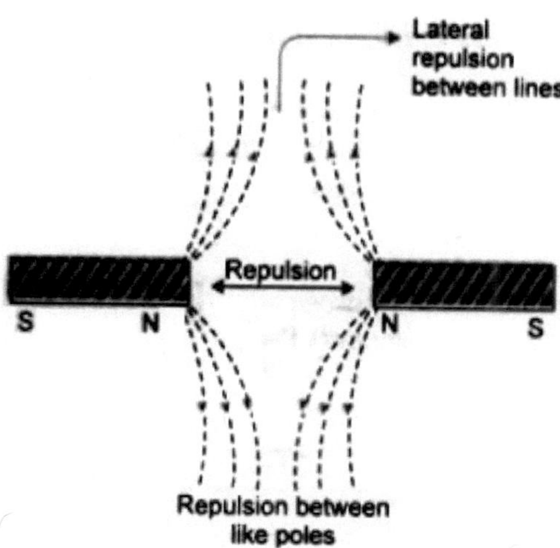

Types of Magnetic fields :

Uniform magnetic field : Magnetic field is said to be uniform if its magnitude is equal and direction is same at every point in the space.

Uniform magnetic field is represented by equidistant parallel straight field lines as shown in figure.

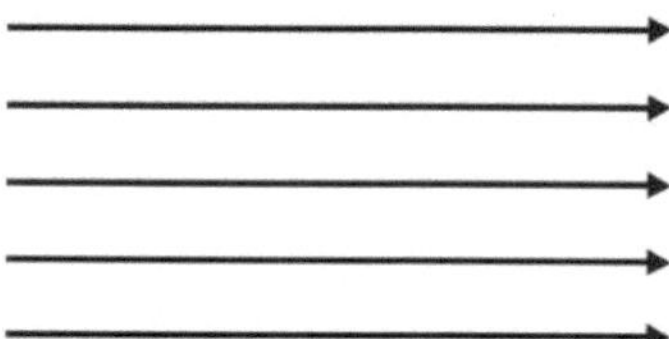

Non-Uniform magnetic field : Magnetic field is said to be non-uniform magnetic field if its magnitude is not equal and direction is not same at every point in the space.

Non-uniform magnetic field is represented as shown in figure.

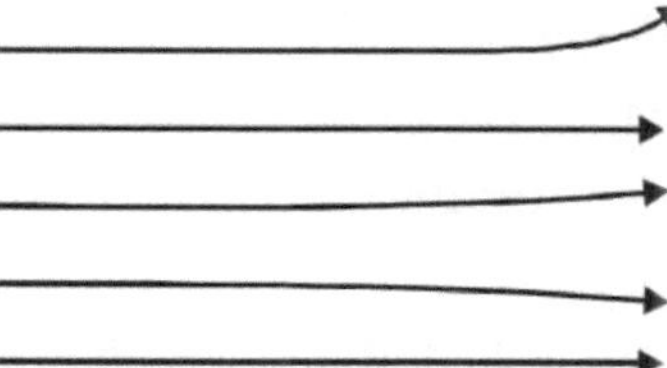

The SI unit of Strength of magnetic field is Tesla (T)

1 Tesla = 1 Newton ampere^{-1} metre^{-1} ($NA^{-1}m^{-1}$)

or = |Weber meter^{-2} | (wbm^{-2})

The cgs unit is gauss (G)

Illustration

What is neutral region in a magnetic field.

Solution

The region in the magnetic field where magnetic field lines do not exist is called neutral region.

Try yourself

3. What do you mean by magnetic lines of force?
4. At what angle magnetic lines of force lie w.r.t. a bar magnet.
5. What is the use of a magnetic compass?

2.4 AN ELECTRIC CURRENT PRODUCES A MAGNETIC FIELD

A magnet is not the only thing that produces a magnetic field. An electric current in a conductor also produces a magnetic field. This was first observed in 1820 by the Danish physicist Hans Christian Oersted (1777-1851). The magnetic effect of electric current can be very easily be demonstrated by bringing a magnetic compass near a current-carrying wire. The compass needle gets deflected, showing that a magnetic field is produced near the wire.

PRACTICAL LEARNING

Place a magnetic compass on a wooden or plastic block, away from all magnetic material.

When the compass needle comes to rest, fix a wire over the compass, parallel to the needle. Connect the wire to a battery through a switch, as shown in figure. Close the switch to pass a current through the wire. The compass needle will get deflected, and come to rest at right angles to its original position. If the direction of the current is from south to north, the north pole of the needle will come to rest pointing west. Now, hold the compass above the wire. The needle will get deflected in the opposite direction. The direction of deflection will also change if you reverse the direction of the current in the wire by interchanging the battery connections. If you switch off the current in the wire, the needle will go back to its original position.

Make sure that you pass a current through the wire only for short periods of time (say 5 seconds). Allowing current to pass through the wire for long will heat the wire considerably and also drain the battery rapidly.

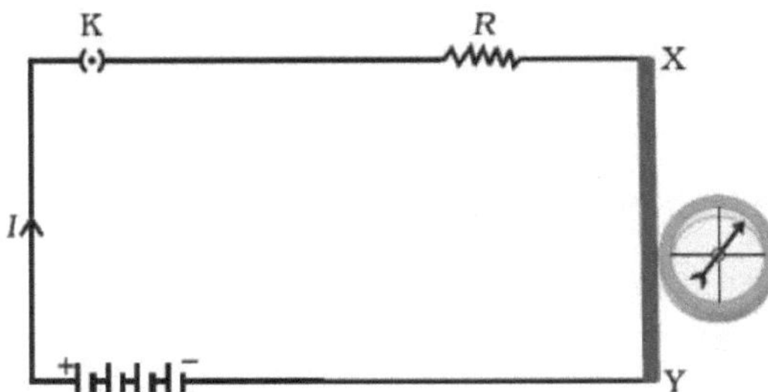

Figure: A current-carrying wire produces a magnetic field that deflects the needle of the compass.

2.5 MAGNETIC FIELD OF A CURRENT CARRYING CONDUCTOR

2.5.1 Oersted Experiment:

Oersted performed an experiment to show that a magnetic field is set up around a current carrying conductor. The experiment was performed as follows :

1. Electric current was allowed to pass through a metallic wire AB, placed parallel to the axis of a magnetic compass kept directly below the wire. The needle of the magnetic compass was found to deflect from its normal position as shown in figure (a).

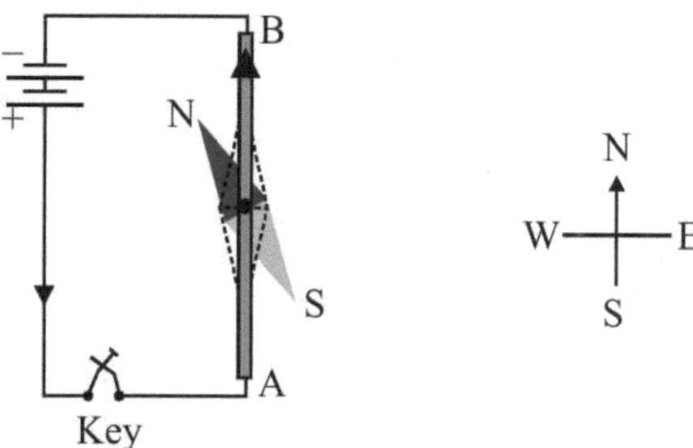

2. Electric current was again allowed to pass through the same wire AB but now in opposite direction. It was found that the needle of the magnetic compass again deflected from its normal position in opposite direction as shown in figure (b).

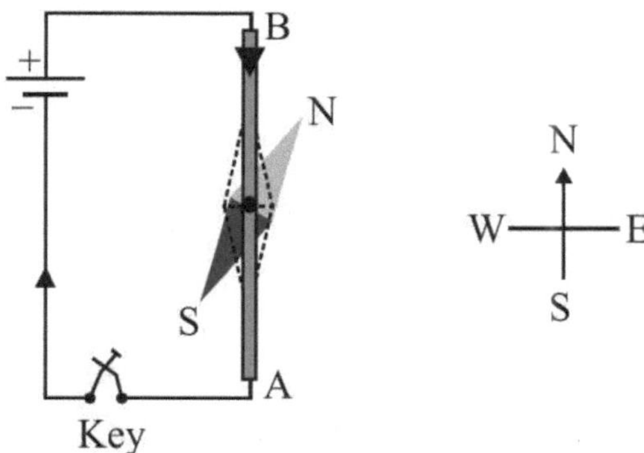

These observations led Oersted to conclude that there must be a magnetic field around the conductor (carrying electric current) which deflected the magnetic compass.

2.5.2 Direction of deflection of the needle of the magnetic compass :

Direction of deflection of the magnetic compass due to the electric current passing through the wire can be found by applying Ampere's swimming rule.

Consider a man swimming along the direction of current in the wire. If the electric current enters his feet and leaves his head, then the north pole of the needle of the magnetic compass will be deflected towards his left hand.

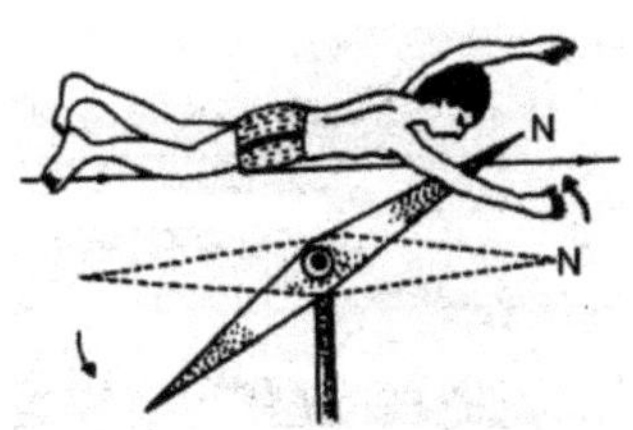

Ampere's swimming rule is also known as SNOW rule. It can be started as : If electric current flows from South to North direction in a wire kept Over a magnetic compass, then the north pole of the needle of a magnetic compass will be deflected towards West.

2.6 MAGNETIC FIELD DUE TO A CURRENT THROUGH A STRAIGHT CONDUCTOR :

When a straight conductor carries electric current (dc), a magnetic field is set up around the conductor. This magnetic field causes the deflection in the needle of the magnetic compass.

PRACTICAL LEARNING

Describe an activity to shown that magnetic field exists around a wire (or conductor) through which electric current is passing.

(i) Take the thick piece of wire consisting of turns of insulated copper wire and a card board.

(ii) Pass this thick wire through a hole in the card board placed horizontally as shown in figure.

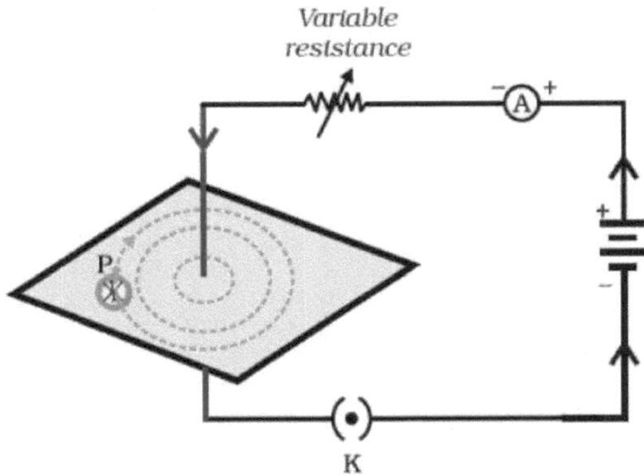

(iii) Now pass electric current (about 4 Amp) through the wire by pressing the key and sprinkle some iron filings on the card board around the wire.

(iv) Tap the card board gently.,

Observation :

We find that the iron filings are arranged in concentric circles around the wire as shown in above figure. If magnetic compass is placed near the current carrying wire and at different position, we get concentric circles around the wire as above figure. These concentric circles around the wire carrying current represent the magnetic field around the wire.

HIGHER ORDER THINKING OR SKILL BASED INFORMATION :

A sketch of the earth's magnetic field is shown in figure (a). If the key in arrangement shown in figure (b) is not closed i.e. no current in the wire flows, then the magnetic field lines over the car board will represent the magnetic field of the earth. These magnetic field lines will be straight lines parallel to each other.

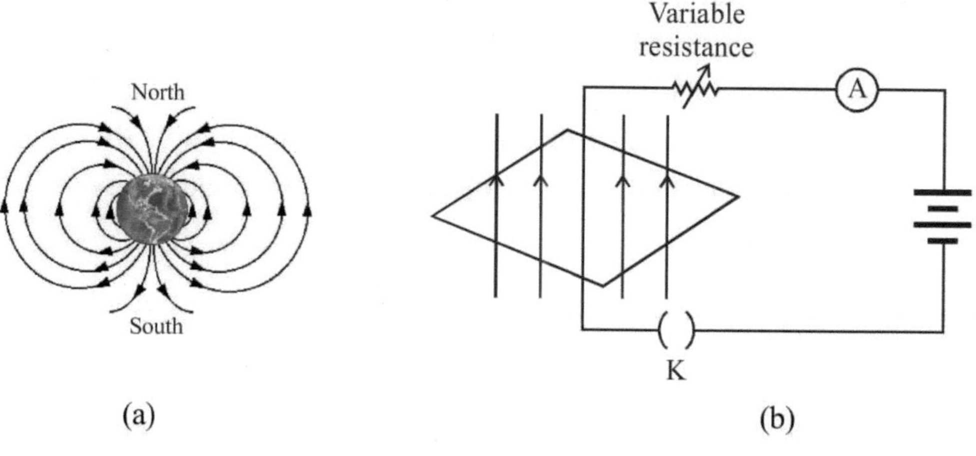

(a) (b)

Factors on which the intensity (or strength) of the magnetic field due to a current carrying conductor depends.

1. **The amount of current flowing through a conductor :** If current flowing through a conductor is increased with the help of a rheostat (figure 13(b)), then the deflection of the needle of the magnetic compass placed near the conductor (or wire) also increases. On the other hand, if current is flowing through the conductor is decreased, then the deflection of the needle of the magnetic compass placed near the conductor also decreases. This shows that the strength of the magnetic field due to a current carrying conductor is directly proportional to the amount of current flowing through it. That is,

$$B \propto I$$

2. **Distance (r) from the conductor :** If the magnetic compass is placed near the current carrying conductor, the deflection of the needle of the magnetic compass is large. On the other hand, if the magnetic compass is placed away from the current carrying conductor, then the deflection of the needle of the magnetic compass is small. This shows that the strength of the magnetic field due to the current carrying conductor decreases with the increase of the distance. Thus, the strength of the magnetic field due to current carrying conductor is inversely proportional to the distance from the conductor. That is,

$$B \propto \frac{1}{r}$$

The direction of the magnetic field around a straight conductor carrying current can be determined by Right Hand Thumb Rule.

RIGHT HAND THUMB RULE :

If a current carrying conductor is imagined to be held in the right hand such that the thumb points in the direction of the current, then the curled fingers of the hand indicate the direction of magnetic field (figure). If current in a conductor flow in the upward direction, then the direction of magnetic field around the conductor is in anticlockwise direction. On the other hand, if current in a conductor flows in the downward direction, then the direction of the magnetic field around the conductor is in clockwise direction.

Magnitude of magnetic field due to an infinitely long, current carrying conductor or wire at a distance r (in air/vacuum) from the conductor (figure) is given by

$$B = \left(\frac{\mu_0}{4\pi}\right)\frac{2I}{r} \Rightarrow \text{Biot-savart Law} \qquad .....(1)$$

[SI unit of current (I) is ampere (A), SI unit of distance r is metre (m) and SI unit of magnetic field (B) is tesla (T)].

$\mu_0 = 4\pi \times 10^{-7}$ tesla metre/ampere (TmA^{-1}) is the permeability of free space or vacuum.

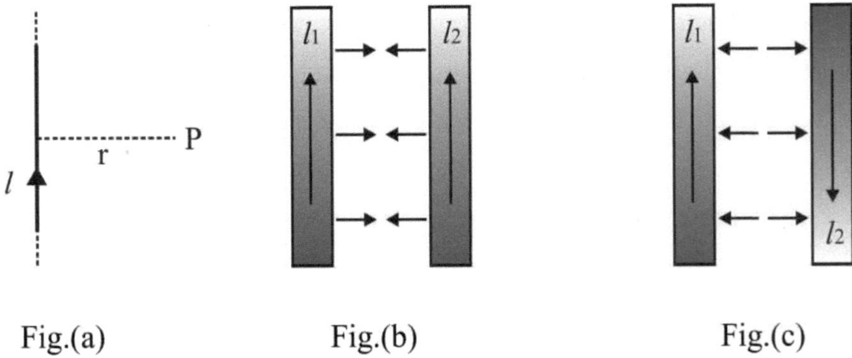

Fig.(a) Fig.(b) Fig.(c)

Application

Eqn. (1) is used to find the magnetic field due to electric power line or telephone line.

- Two parallel conductors carrying current in same direction attract each other (Figure-b). It was a French Physicist Andre Ampere who first of all demonstrated that two parallel wires carrying current in the same direction attract each other just as unlike poles of a bar magnet.
- Two parallel conductors carrying current in the opposite directions repel each other (Figure-c).

Magnetic field due to the beam of charged particles :

(i) Moving beam of positively charged particles like protons and alpha (α) particles constitute electric current in the direction of their movement. Hence, magnetic field is also set up around the beam of these charged particles as shown in figure.

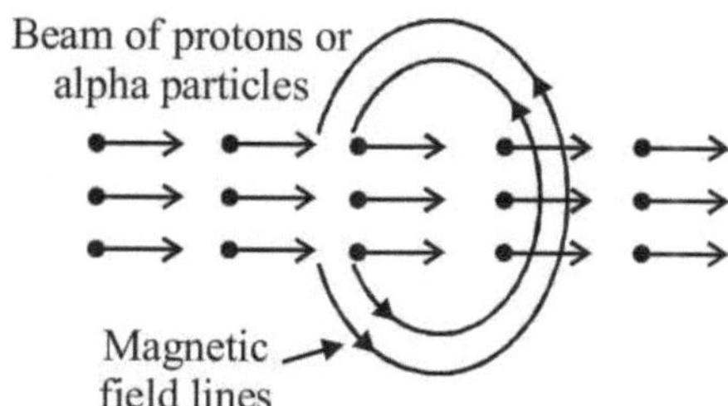

(ii) Moving beam of neutrons (i.e. neutral particles) does not constitute electric current. Hence, magnetic field is not set up around the beam of neutrons.

2.7 MAGNETIC FIELD DUE TO A CURRENT THROUGH A CIRCULAR WIRE OR LOOP :

The magnetic field around a straight current carrying conductor or wire can be increased by bending the wire into a circular loop. A circular wire is made up of large number of very-very small straight wires. Each small straight section of the current carrying wire contributes to the magnetic field lines and the direction of all these lines is in the same direction as shown in figure.

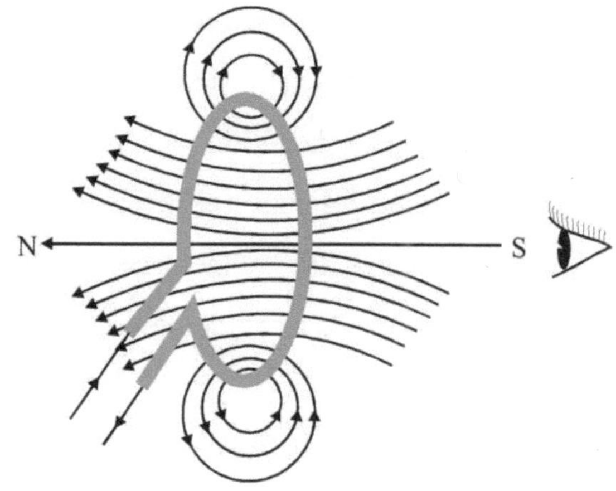

PRACTICAL LEARNING

Describe an activity to show that a magnetic field is produced by an electric current flowing through a circular coil of a wire.

(i) Take a thick copper wire in the form of a circular loop. Pass this circular wire through a cardboard supported over a table in the horizontal position (figure).

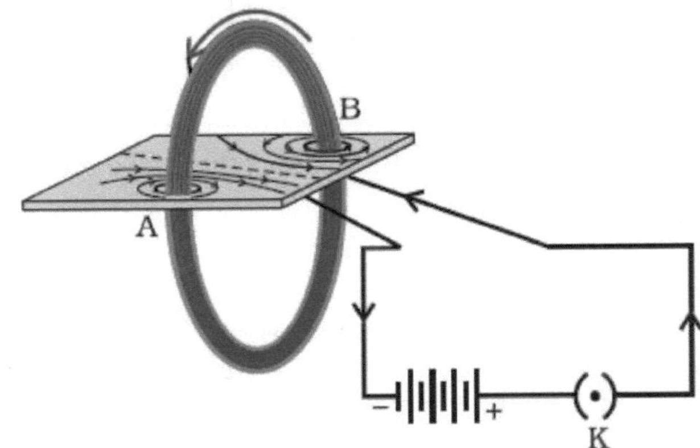

(ii) Now connect the ends of this wire with a battery through a key (K), rheostat and ammeter (A).

(iii) Allow the current to flow through the circular wire by closing the key K.

(iv) Now plot magnetic field lines around the wire with the help of a magnetic compass needle.

Observations : Magnetic field lines as shown by dotted circles are observed. This shows that a magnetic field is produced by an electric current flowing through a circular coil of a wire. The size of these circles increases as we move away from the wire. At the centre of the circular wire, the field lines become straight and perpendicular to the plane of the coil.

2.7.1 Factors on which the magnetic field produced at the centre of a current carrying circular wire depends

1. **The amount of current flowing through the wire :** If the amount of current flowing through the circular wire is increased, then the deflection of the needle of the magnetic compass placed inside the wire also increases. On the other hand, if the amount of current flowing through the wire is decreased, then the deflection of the needle of the magnetic compass also decreases. This shows that the strength of the magnetic field due to current carrying circular wire is directly proportional to the amount of current (dc) flowing through it.

   That is, $\mathbf{B \propto I}$

2. **The radius of the circular wire :** Take two circular wires of different radii through which the same amount of current is flowing. It is found that the deflection of the needle of the magnetic compass placed at the centre of the circular wire of smaller radius is more than that when placed at the centre of the circular wire of larger radius. This shows that the strength of the magnetic field at the centre of current carrying circular wire is inversely proportional to its radius (r).

   That is, $\mathbf{B \propto \frac{1}{r}}$

3. The number of turns (n) of the circular wire : If the number of turns (n) of the circular wire or loop are increased, then the magnetic field at the centre of the loop increases. This shows that the magnetic field at the centre of current carrying wire (or loop) is directly proportional to the number of turns of the wire (or loop).

   That is, $\mathbf{B} \propto \mathbf{n}$

2.7.2x Direction of Magnetic Field due to a current carrying circular wire or loop

Right Hand Thumb Rule is used to determine the direction of the magnetic field produced due to a current carrying circular wire.

Maxwell's Right-Hand Thumb Rule

The direction of the magnetic field due to a current in a straight conductor is given by Maxwell's right-hand thumb rule.

If a straight current-carrying wire is imagined to be held in the right hand, with the thumb stretched along the direction of the current, the direction of the magnetic field produced by the current is in the direction in which the fingers are curled (figure a).

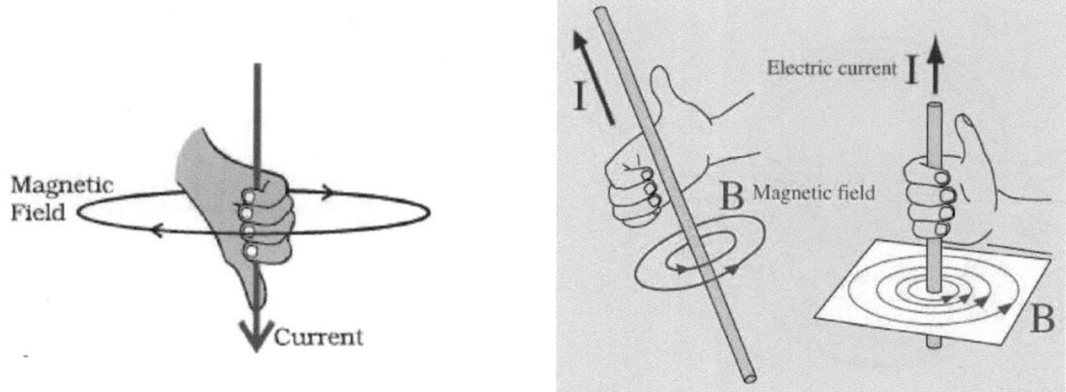

Figure: (a) Maxwell's right-hand thumb rule and (b) corkscrew rule are two ways of finding the direction of the magnetic field due to a current in a straight wire.

This rule is also called Maxwell's corkscrew rule. Suppose the tip of a rotating corkscrew (or a screw) advances in the direction of the current. Then the direction of rotation of its handle (or head) gives the direction of the current.

Magnitude of magnetic field's strength at the centre of a current carrying circular wire or loop is given by $B = \frac{\mu_0 I}{2r}$

Here, B is expressed in tesla (T), current (I) in ampere (A) and radius (r) in metre (m). $\mu_0 = 4\pi \times 10^{-7}\ TmA^{-1}$

Magnitude of magnetic field's strength at the centre of a current carrying circular wire or loop having n turns is given by $B_1 = \frac{\mu_0 nI}{2r}$

2.8 MAGNETIC FIELD DUE TO A CURRENT IN A SOLENOID :

A solenoid is a coil of many turns of an insulated copper wire closely wound in the shape of a tight spring.

OR

A solenoid is a long, helically wound coil of insulated copper wire. A solenoid is shown in figure (b).

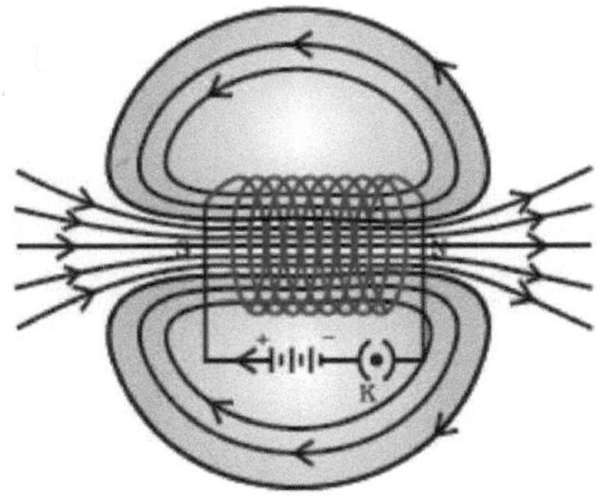

figure (a)

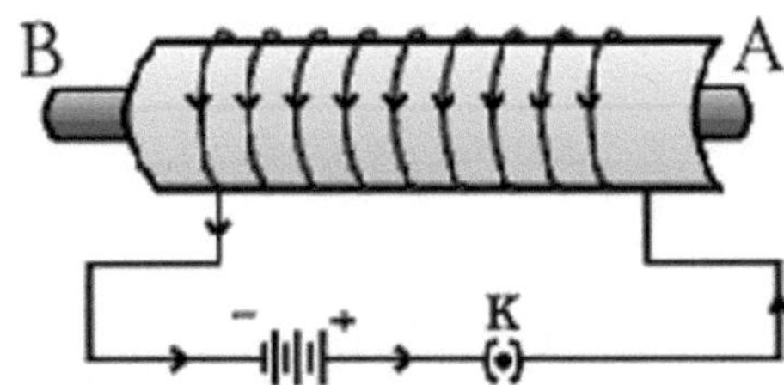

figure (b)

When an electric current flows through a solenoid, a magnetic field is set up around the solenoid which is similar to the magnetic field of a bar magnet. The magnetic field due to a solenoid carrying current is shown in figure (a).

One end of the solenoid acts as South pole and the other end acts as North pole. If the current flows in a clockwise direction when the coil is seen end-on, then that end of the solenoid acts as a South pole. On the other hand, if the current flows in anticlockwise direction when the coil is seen end-on, then that end of the solenoid acts as a North pole.

Thus, face or end B of the solenoid behaves as South pole and face or end A of the solenoid behaves as North pole in figure (b). In other words, a current carrying solenoid behaves as a bar magnet.

(i) Magnetic field inside a long solenoid is uniform (i.e. same at all points) and strong. This magnetic field is represented by straight magnetic field lines parallel and very close to each other.

(ii) Magnetic field inside a long solenoid decreases as we move towards the ends of the solenoid because magnetic field lines near the ends of the solenoid start spreading out.

(iii) Magnetic field outside the solenoid is non-uniform and weak.

(iv) Magnetic field lines inside the solenoid are from South pole to North pole and outside the solenoid, these lines of force are from North pole to South pole.

(v) The magnetic field of the solenoid resembles the magnetic field of the bar magnet as shown in figure.

(vi) The strong magnetic field produce inside a solenoid is used to magnetize the rod of a magnetic material like soft iron, when placed inside the solenoid.

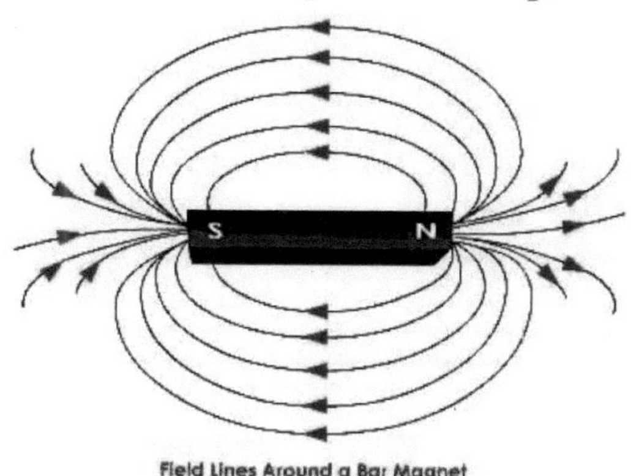

Field Lines Around a Bar Magnet

2.9 ELECTROMAGNETS

When a soft iron bar is placed inside a solenoid carrying current, it becomes a magnet as long as current flows through the solenoid. Such a magnet is known as electromagnet.

In fact, the magnetic field inside the solenoid magnetizes the soft iron bar placed in it, which acts as on electromagnet. (figure).

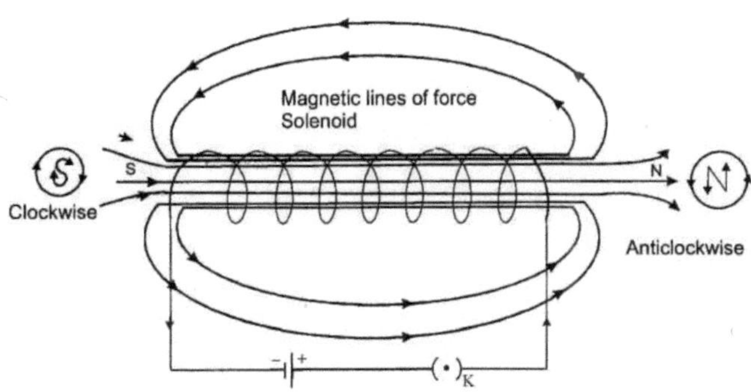

Uses of electromagnets

(i) They are used to lift heavy iron pieces. They are fitted on cranes for lifting heavy objects of scrap iron.

(ii) They are used in many devices like electric bell, electric horn, telephone receiver, electric relay, microphones, radio set, television, loudspeakers etc.

Difference between an Electromagnet and a Permanent Magnet (Bar Magnet)

	Electromagnet		Permanent Magnet (Bar Magnet)
1	It behaves as a magnet as long as electric current passes through the solenoid surrounding it. It is demagnetised when electric current stops passing through the solenoid. Thus, electromagnet is a temporary magnet.	1	It cannot be demagnetised easily.
2	Electromagnet gives a strong magnetic field and the strength of the magnetic field produced by the electromagnet can be increased or decreased by increasing or decreasing electric current through the solenoid.	2	Magnetic field of a permanent magnet is weak. The strength of magnetic field of the permanent magnet cannot be changed.
3	The polarity (i.e. North and South poles) of an electromagnet can be reversed by reversing the direction of electric current through the solenoid.	3	The polarity of a permanent magnet cannot be reversed.

(i) **Hard Steel, alnico (an alloy of aluminium, nickel, cobalt and iron) Nipermag (an alloy of aluminum, iron and titanium) are used to make permanent magnets.**

(ii) **Soft iron is used to make electromagnets.**

(iii) **A steel rod can be made a permanent magnet if it is placed inside a solenoid carrying direct current.**

(iv) **Permanent magnets are used in loudspeakers, galvanometers, voltmeters, ammeter, and speedometers.**

(v) **Permanent magnet can be demagnetised by heating it or throwing it again and again on the ground.**

2.10 FORCE ON A CURRENT CARRYING CONDUCTOR PLACED IN A MAGNETIC FIELD

When a current carrying conductor is placed in a magnetic field, the conductor experiences a force. This fact can be demonstrated with the help of the following activity.

PRACTICAL LEARNING

Describe an activity to show that a current carrying conductor placed perpendicular to the magnetic field experiences a force.

(i) Fix a horse shoe magnet on the top of the table.

(ii) Place a long and thin strip of aluminium on two wooden supports such that it passes between the North and South poles of the magnet.

(iii) Connect a battery across the ends of the aluminium strip through a key (K) as shown in figure.

(iv) Now close the key so that current (I) flows through the strip (figure)

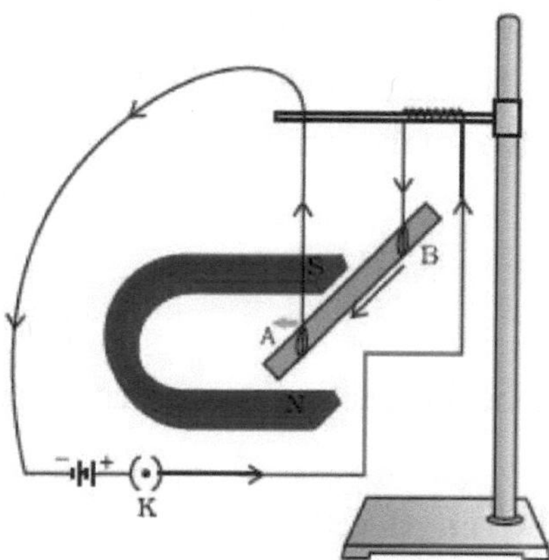

Observation : When current flows through the aluminium strip, it moves upward. If the direction of current is reversed, the aluminium strip moves downward.

Conclusion : A current carrying conductor (aluminium strip) placed in a magnetic field experiences a force in a direction perpendicular to the direction of the magnetic field. Due to this force, the current carrying conductor is displaced from its rest position.

Direction of force experienced by a current carrying conductor placed in a magnetic field is given by Fleming's left hand rule.

2.10.1 Fleming's left hand rule

Stretch the left hand such that the thumb, first finger and the central finger are mutually perpendicular to each other. If the First finger points in the direction of the magnetic Field and the Central finger points in the direction of Current, then the thumb will point in the direction Motion (or Force) as shown in figure.

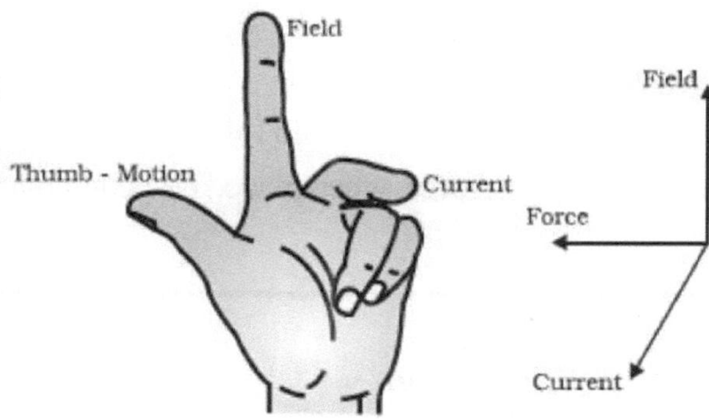

2.10.2 Factors on which the force acting on the current carrying conductor depend

The force acting on a current carrying conductor placed in the magnetic field depends upon :

(i) **The strength of the magnetic field :** If the conductor is placed in a strong magnetic field, it experiences a large force. That is, $F \propto B$ (strength of magnetic field)

(ii) **The strength of the electric current :** If large current flows through the conductor placed in the magnetic field, it experiences a large force. That is, $F \propto I$.

(iii) **The length of the conductor :** A long conductor experiences a greater force than the short conductor, when placed in the magnetic field. That is, $F \propto l$.

2.10.3 Magnitude of the force acting on a current carrying conductor placed in a magnetic field

We have seen that the force acting on a current carrying conductor placed perpendicular to the magnetic field depends upon (i) the strength of the magnetic field (B), (ii) the amount of current (I) flowing through the conductor and (iii) the length (l) of the conductor.

That is $F \propto BIl$

or $F = kBIl$ .....(1)

If k = 1, $F = BIl$ .....(2)

Eqn. (2) gives the magnitude of the force acting on a current carrying conductor placed perpendicular to the magnetic field.

Definition of Magnetic field strength (B)

From eqn. (2),

$$B = \frac{F}{Il} \qquad .....(3)$$

If $I = 1$ and $l = 1$, then $B = F$

Thus, magnetic field strength (B) is defined as the force acting per unit current per unit length of a conductor placed perpendicular to the direction of the magnetic field.

SI unit of magnetic field strength

SI unit of magnetic field strength is tesla. The symbol of tesla is T.

From eqn. (3),

$$\text{SI unit of magnetic field strength} = \frac{\text{SI unit of force}}{\text{SI unit of current} \times \text{SI unit of length}}$$

i.e. $$1 \text{ tesla} = \frac{1 \text{ newton(N)}}{1 \text{ ampere} \times 1\text{m}} = 1\text{NA}^{-1}\text{m}^{-1}$$

Thus, magnetic field strength is said to be 1 tesla if 1 metre long conductor carrying 1 ampere current experiences 1 newton force, when placed perpendicular to the direction of the magnetic field.

Illustration

Calculate the force acting on a wire of length 1m through which a current of 0.2 A flows and the wire is placed perpendicular to the direction of magnetic field of strength 0.4T.

Solution

Here, $l = 1\text{m}$; $I = 0.2$ A ; $B = 0.4$T

Using $F = BIl$,

we get $F = 0.4\text{ T} \times 0.2\text{ A} \times 1\text{m} = 0.4\text{ NA}^{-1}\text{m}^{-1} \times 0.2\text{ A} \times 1\text{m}$

$= 0.08$ N $(\because 1\text{T} = 1\text{NA}^{-1}\text{ m}^{-1})$

FORCE ACTING ON A MOVING CHARGE IN A MAGNETIC FIELD :

The current flowing in a conductor or a metallic wire is due to the moving free electrons. Each electron has an electric charge of magnitude 1.6×10^{-19} C. The force acting on a current carrying conductor placed perpendicular to a magnetic field is equal to the force acting on a net charge moving in the conductor. The net charge is equal to the sum of the charges on the electrons moving in the conductor to form an electric current.

We know, force acting on a current carrying conductor placed perpendicular to the magnetic field is given by

$$F = BIl \qquad ....(1)$$

But $I = \frac{Q}{t}$, where Q is the net charge moving through the conductor.

$\therefore$ Eqn. (1) becomes

$$F = B\left(\frac{Q}{t}\right)l = BQ\left(\frac{l}{t}\right)$$

Now $\frac{l}{t}$ = v, velocity of charge (or electron)

$$\therefore \quad F = BQv \qquad ....(2)$$

Eqn. (2) is the expression for the force acting on a charge Q moving with velocity v perpendicular to the magnetic field B. This force makes the charged particle to move in a circular path with a constant speed. However, the velocity and hence momentum of the charged particle change continuously due to the change in the direction of its motion.

NOTE : If a charged particle having charge Q moves with a velocity $\vec{v}$ at angle θ with the magnetic field $\vec{B}$, then force acting on the charge is given by

$$F = QvB \sin \theta$$

The charge Q will experience no force in a magnetic field if it is at rest (i.e. v = 0) or (ii) if it moves parallel or anti-parallel (i.e. θ = 0° or 180°) to the direction of magnetic field. Direction of force experienced by a moving charge in a magnetic field is determined by Right Hand Rule.

Illustration :

A particle having charge 1.6×10^{-19} C travelling at a speed 3.0×10^{6} ms^{-1} passes perpendicular to a uniform magnetic field of 0.04 T. Calculate the force acting on the particle.

Solution

Here, $Q = 1.6 \times 10^{-19}$ C; $v = 3.0 \times 10^{6}$ ms^{-1} ; B = 0.04 T

Using, F = BQv, we get

$$F = 0.04\ T \times 1.6 \times 10^{-19}\ C \times 3.0 \times 10^{6}\ ms^{-1}$$
$$= 0.04\ NA^{-1}\ m^{-1} \times 1.6 \times 10^{-19}\ C \times 3.0 \times 10^{6}\ ms^{-1} = 19.2 \times 10^{-15}\ N$$

(i) If charge Q is at rest (i.e. Q is static charge) in the magnetic field, then no force acts on this charge.

(ii) When a charge Q moves in the direction of magnetic field, no force acts on the charge. Thus, charge continues to move in the same direction and with same speed.

- **The fact that charged particles are deflected by magnetic field is used no focus electrons onto the inner surface of a TV tube and provide picture.**
- **When a stream of high energy charged particles (i.e., solar wind) enters the earth's atmosphere, these particles experience a deflecting force due to the earth's magnetic field. In fact, these charged particles are trapped near the earths magnetic equator. The regions, where these charged particles from the sun are trapped are called Van Allen radiation belts. They are named so after American scientist James Van Allen suggested their existence from the data collected by the U.S. satellite Explorer I in 1958.**
- **Importance of Earth's magnetic Field :Earth's magnetic field has saved us from the ill effect of the high energy charged particles coming out of the sun in the form of solar wind. The earth's magnetic field deflects these particles away from the surface of the earth. Thus, the intensity of these high energy charged particles striking the surface of the earth decreases considerably.**

2.11 ELECTRIC MOTOR

Electric motor converts electrical energy into mechanical energy.

Principle : Electric Motor is based on the fact that a current carrying conductor placed perpendicular to the magnetic field experiences a force.

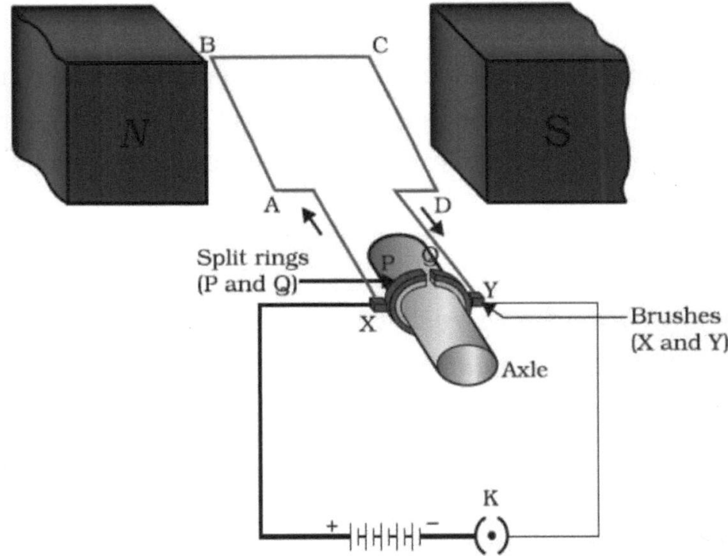

Construction :

(i) **Armature coil :** It consists of large number of turns of insulated copper wire wound soft core in the form of a rectangular coil. Rectangular coil ABCD shown in figure is an armature coil.

(ii) **Strong field magnet :** Armature coil is placed between two pole pieces (N and S poles) of a strong magnet. This magnet provides a strong magnetic field.

(iii) **Split-ring type Commutator :** It consists of two halves (P and Q) of a metallic ring. The two ends of the armature coil are connected to these two halves of the ring. Commutator reverses the direction of current in the armature coil.

(iv) **Battery :** A battery is connected across the carbon brushes. This battery supplies the current to the armature coil.

Working and Theory of Electric Motor :

1. When current flows through the coil as shown in figure, arms AB and CD experience magnetic force. According to Fleming's left hand rule, arm AB of the coil, experiences a force in the downward direction. Similarly, arm CD of the coil experiences a force in the upward direction. Both these force are equal but opposite in direction.
   Two equal and opposite force acting at different position of the armature constitute a couple. This couple rotates the coil in clockwise direction until the coil is in the vertical position figure. At this position, the contacts of commutator and brushes break. So the supply of current to the coil is cut off. Hence, no force acts on the arms of the coil. But the coil does not come to rest. It goes on rotating due to the inertia of motion of the coil until commutator again comes in contact with the brushes B_1 and B_2.
2. When the commutator comes in contact with brushes (X and Y) after rotation, the direction of the current in arms AB and CD is reversed as shown in figure.
   The force acting on arm AB is in the downward direction and the force acting on the arm CD is in the upward direction. These two equal and opposite forces again constitute a couple. This couple rotates the coil again in the clockwise direction.
   Thus, the coil of d.c. motor continues to rotate in the same direction. Hence, electrical energy is converted into mechanical energy (i.e. kinetic energy of rotation).

Uses of D.C. Motor

1. It is used in electric cars, rolling mills, electric cranes and electric lifts.
2. It is used in drilling machines, electric fans, hair dryers, record players tape recorder and blowers.
3. It is used in centrifugal machines like mixers and blenders, refrigerator and washing machines.

2.12 ELECTROMAGNETIC INDUCTION

It was Michael Faraday, who performed a simple experiment to show that an electric current can be produced in a closed circuit without the use of an electrochemical cell or battery but by moving a bar magnet towards or away from the closed circuit.

Faraday's Experiments

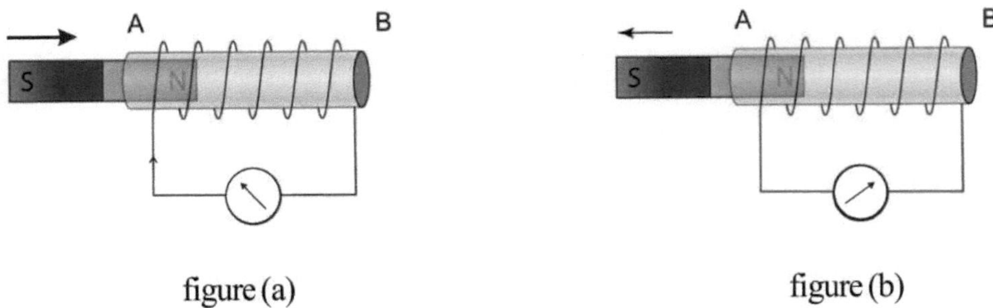

figure (a) figure (b)

***Experiment-1* :**

Faraday connected a coil of wire with a sensitive galvanometer as shown in figure-a. He observed that

(i) When a bar magnet with its North pole facing the coil was moved towards the coil [figure(a)], the galvanometer showed a deflection. Deflection in the galvanometer was also observed when the bar magnet with its South pole facing the coil moved towards the coil.

(ii) When the bar magnet was moved away from the coil as shown in figure (b), galvanometer again showed the deflection but now in opposite direction.

(iii) When the bar magnet was stationary near the coil, no deflection in the galvanometer was observed.

Conclusion :

When a bar magnet moves towards or away from the closed coil, galvanometer shows a deflection. The deflection in the galvanometer indicates that current is flowing through the coil.

Explanation :

(i) When a magnet is moved towards the coil, more and more magnetic field lines pass through the coil as shown in figure (b). Thus, magnetic field around the coil increases. The increase in magnetic field induces potential difference (or voltage) across the ends of the coil. As the coil connected to the galvanometer forms a closed circuit, so induced potential difference makes the current to flow through the circuit. The presence of this current in the circuit is shown by the deflection of the galvanometer.

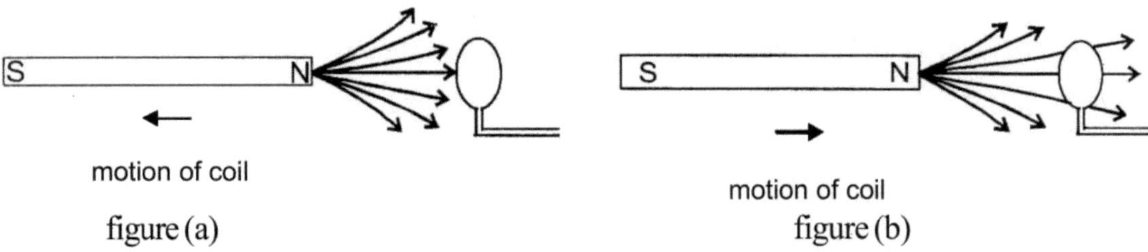

figure (a) figure (b)

(ii) When a magnet is moved away from the coil, the magnetic field around the coil decreases. The decrease in magnetic field induces potential difference across the ends of the coil. This presence of the current in the circuit is shown by the deflection of the galvanometer. The current in the circuit is known as induced current.

(iii) When the magnet is stationary, the magnetic field around the coil is constant. Therefore, no potential difference is set up across the coil. Hence, no current flows through the circuit.

Experiment-2 :

Take an iron rod. Now wrap a coil of an insulated copper wire near left end of the iron rod. Connect this coil (called Primary coil) with a battery through a one way key (K). Wrap another coil of an insulated copper wire near right end of the iron. Connect this coil (called Secondary coil) with a galvanometer as shown in figure.

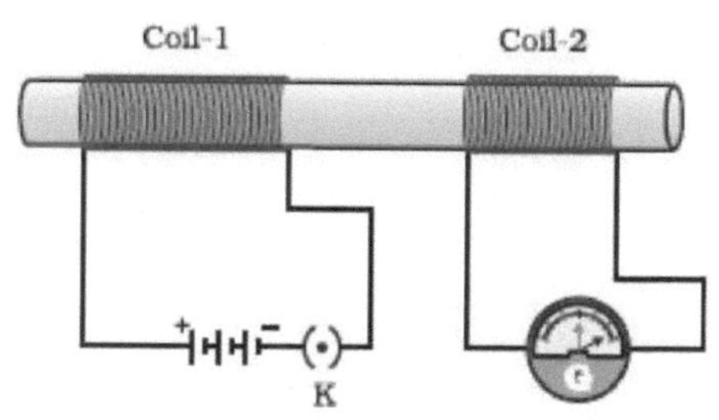

Observation : When key K is closed, current begins to flow in the left coil and the galvanometer connected with right coil shows momentary deflection. After short period of time, deflection of galvanometer becomes zero.

Explanation : When current begins to grow in the left coil, a changing magnetic field is set up around the coil. This changing magnetic field is also associated with the right coil. The changing magnetic field produced an induced potential difference in the right coil. This induced potential difference sets up induced electric current in the secondary coil. This induced electric current is shown by the deflection in the galvanometer. This is known as electromagnetic induction. The deflection of galvanometer becomes zero when current in the left coil becomes constant. This is because, constant current sets up magnetic field which does not change.

Faraday's Experiments : Wind an insulated copper wire on a wooden cylinder so as to form a solenoid coil. Connect the two ends of the coil to the centre of galvanometer. A magnet is placed along the axis of the coil.

(i) When the magnet is stationary, there is no deflection in the galvanometer. The pointer reads zero as shown in figure (A).

(ii) When the north pole of the magnet is brought near the coil, the current flows in the coil in direction shown in the figure (B) and the galvanometer shows the deflection towards the right.

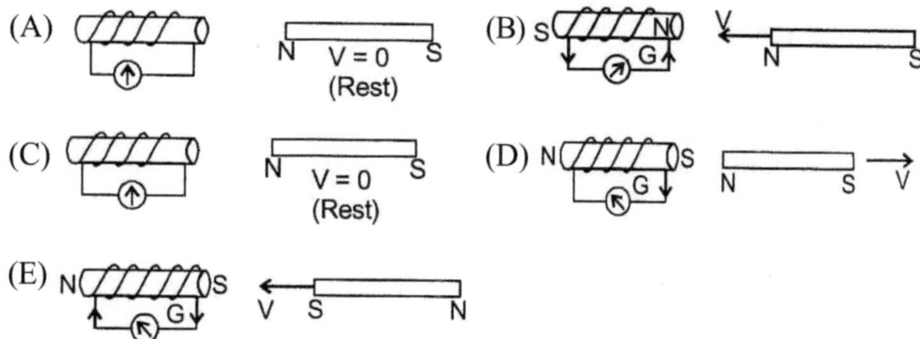

(iii) If we stop the motion of the magnet, the pointer of the galvanometer comes to the zero position as shown in figure (C). Thus the current in the coil flows as long as the magnet is moving. If the magnet is taken away from the coil, the current again flows in the coil but in the direction opposite to that shown in figure (D) and therefore the pointer of the galvanometer deflects towards the left side.

(iv) If south pole of the magnet is brought towards the coil, the current in the coil flow in the direction opposite to that shown in figure (E) and so the pointer of the galvanometer deflects towards the left.

(v) Similar deflection is observed in the galvanometer if the magnet is kept stationary and the coil is moved.

From this experiment Faraday concluded that :

(i) The galvanometer shows a deflection (i.e. current flow in the coil) only when there is relative motion between the coil and the magnet.

(ii) The direction of deflection is reversed if the direction of motion is reversed.

(iii) The value of the current in the coil (i.e. deflection of the pointer) is increased by :

(A) The rapid motion of the magnet or the coil.

(B) The use of a strong magnet.

(C) Increasing the area and number of turns in the coil.

2.13 DEFINITION OF ELECTROMAGNETIC INDUCTION :

The phenomenon of producing induced current in a closed circuit or coil due to the change in magnetic field in the circuit or a closed coil is known as electromagnetic induction.

2.13.1 Factors on which induced current depends : The value of induced current depends upon :

(i) The number of turns in the coil. If coil has large number of turns, then large induced current is produced in the closed coil.

(ii) The strength of the magnet. A strong magnet moved towards or away from the closed coil produced a large induced current.

(iii) The speed with which the magnet moves towards the coil. If the magnet moves very quickly, then large induced current is produced in the closed coil.

2.13.2 Direction of Induced current : The direction of induced current can be obtained by :

Fleming's right hand rule : Stretch the thumb, middle finger and the forefinger of your right hand mutually perpendicular to each other as shown in figure. If the forefinger indicated the direction of the magnetic field and the thumb indicated the direction of motion of the conductor, the middle finger will indicate the direction of induced current

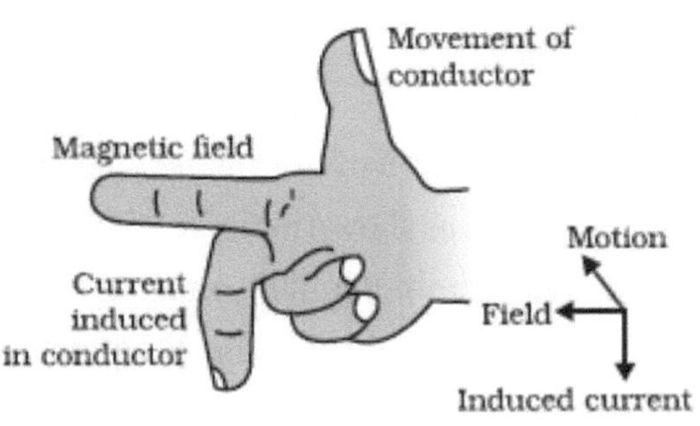

2.13.3 Direct and alternating current :

Direct current : An electric current whose magnitude is either constant or variable but the direction of flow in a conductor remains the same is called direct current. It is denoted by D.C.

D.C. can be represented as shown in figure.

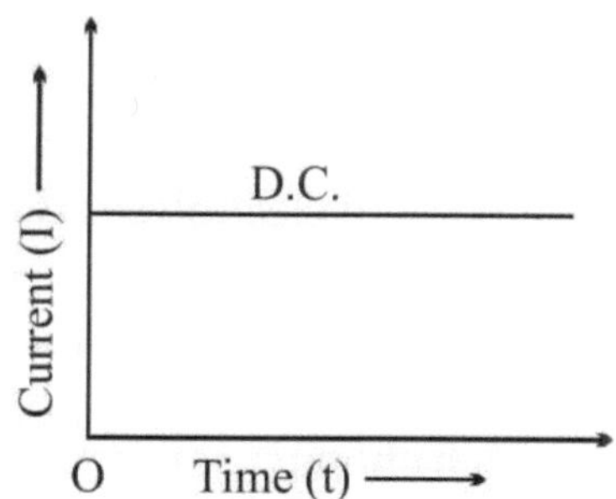

Note : (i) Sources of direct current (D.C.) are a voltaic cell, a dry cell, a battery, a solar cell, D.C. generator etc.

(ii) Frequency of D.C. is zero.

Alternating Current : An electric current whose magnitude changes with time and direction reverse periodically is called alternating current. It is denoted by A.C.

Alternating current is expressed as

$$I = I_0 \sin \omega t$$

or $I = I_0 \sin \frac{2\pi}{T} t$ $\quad$ $(\because \omega = \frac{2\pi}{T}$, T = Time period)

or $I = I_0 \sin 2\pi ft$ $\quad$ ... (1)

In equation (1), I_0 = maximum or peak value of A.C.

I = value of A.C. at any time t

The variation of a.c. with time is shown in figure

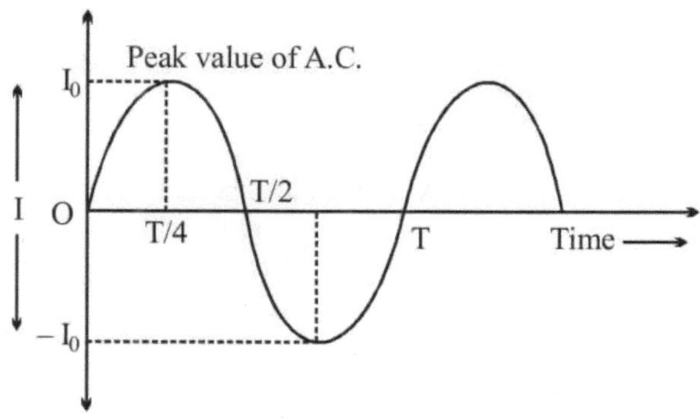

Where $f = \frac{1}{T}$ is called frequency of A.C.

The frequency of household supply of A.C. in India is 50 Hz. This means, A.C. completes 50 cycles in one second. Thus, A.C. changes direction after every $\frac{1}{100}$ second. In other words, A.C. used in India changes direction 100 times in one second.

Frequency of A.C. means how many cycles it completes in one second.

Advantages of A.C. over D.C.

1. The cost of generation of A.C. is less than the cost of generation of D.C.
2. A.C. can be easily converted into D.C.
3. A.C. can be controlled without much loss of electric power than D.C.
4. A.C. can be transmitted to distant places without much loss of electric power than D.C.

Disadvantages of A.C. over D.C.

1. A.C. is more dangerous than D.C.
2. A.C. cannot be used in the process of electrolysis. But D.C. is used for this process.

***Transformer* is a device which changes small A.C. potential difference to a larger A.C. potential difference. Transformer consists of two coils of wire wound around a core of soft iron. One coil is known as primary coil and the other is known as secondary coil as shown in figure.**

Transformer is used to transmit a.c. to distant places through conductors (called transmission lines) without much loss of electric energy or power.

2.14 ELECTRIC GENERATOR

An electric device used to convert mechanical energy (kinetic energy) into electric energy (electricity) is called an electric generator.

Principle : Electric generator works on the principle of electromagnetic induction. When the coil of electric generator rotates in a magnetic field, induced current flows in the circuit connected with the coil.

Types of electric generator : (i) AC generator **and** (ii) DC generator

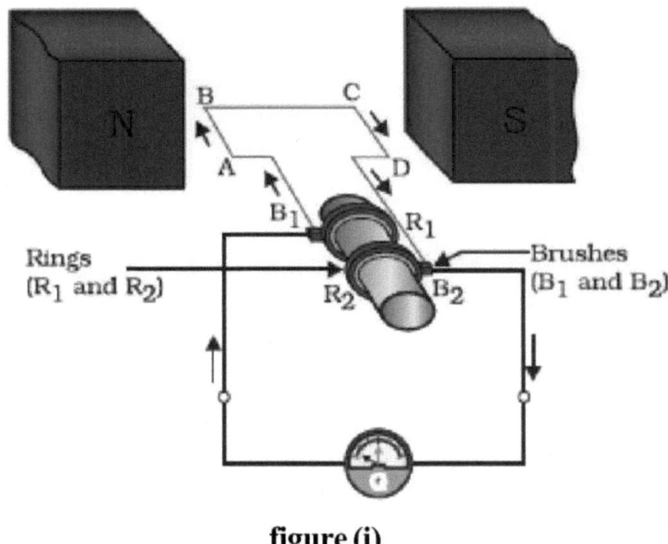

figure (i)

AC Generator :

AC generator converts mechanical energy into electrical energy in the form of alternating current of AC.

Construction : The main components of AC generator are :

(i) **Armature :** Armature coil (ABCD) consists of large number of turns of insulated copper wire wound over a soft iron core.

(ii) **Strong field magnet :** A strong permanent magnet or an electromagnet whose pole (N and S) are cylindrical in shape is a field magnet. The armature coil rotates between the pole pieces of the field magnet. The uniform magnetic field provided by the field magnet is perpendicular to the axis of rotation of the coil.

(iii) **Slip Rings :** The two ends of the armature coil are connected to two brass slip rings R_1 and R_2. These rings rotate alongwith the armature coil.

(iv) **Brushes :** Two carbon brushes (B_1 and B_2), are pressed against the slip rings. The brushes are fixed while slip rings rotate along with the armature. These brushes are connected to the external circuit across which the output is obtained.

Working : When the armature coil ABCD rotates in the magnetic field provided by the strong field magnet, it cuts the magnetic lines of force. Thus, the changing magnetic field produced induced current in the coil. The direction of the induced current in the coil is determined by the Fleming's right hand rule. The current flows out through the brush B_1 in one direction in the first half of the revolution and through the brush B_2 in the next revolution in the reverse direction. This process is repeated. Therefore, induced current produced is of alternating nature. Such a current is called alternating current.

DC generator or Dynamo

DC generator converts mechanical energy into electrical energy in the form of direct current or DC.

Construction : The main components of DC generator are :

(i) **Armature coil :** It consists of large number of turns of insulated copper wire wound soft core in the form of a rectangular coil. Rectangular coil ABCD shown in figure is an armature coil.

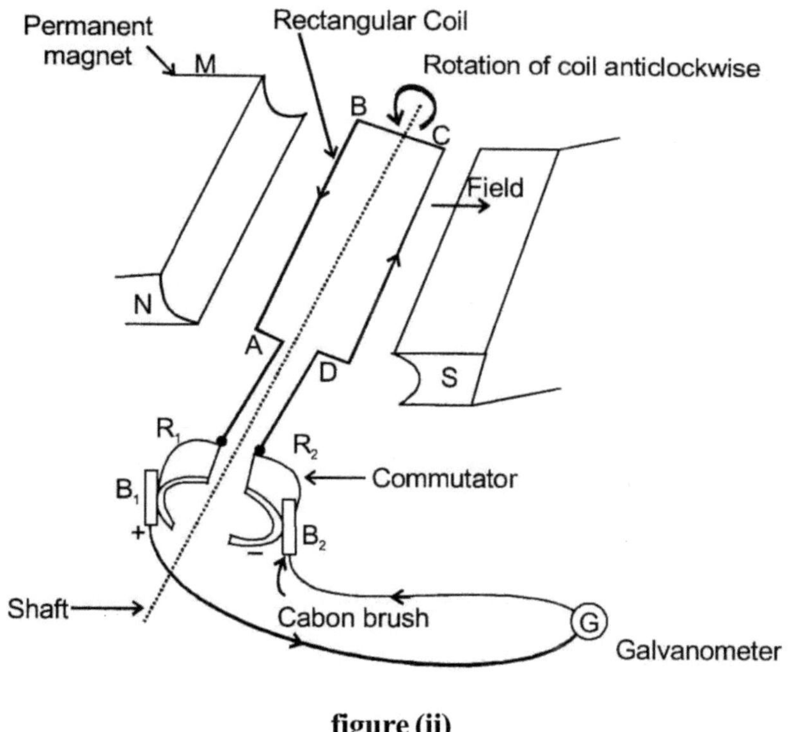

figure (ii)

(ii) **Strong field magnet :** Armature coil is placed between two pole pieces (N and S poles) of a strong magnet. This magnet provides a strong magnetic field.

(iii) **Split-ring Type Commutator :** It consists of two halves (R_1 and R_2) of a metallic ring. The two ends of the armature coil are connected to these two halves of the ring.

(iv) **Brushes :** Two carbon brushes B_1 and B_2 press against the commutator.

(v) **Galvanometer :** The output is shown by the galvanometer connected across the carbon brushes.

Working of D.C. generator : When the coil of D.C. generator rotates in the magnetic field, induced potential difference is produced in the coil. This induced potential difference gives rise to the flow of current through the bulb and hence the bulb glows.
In d.c. generator, the flow of current in the circuit is in the same direction as long as the coil rotates in the magnetic field. This is because one brush is always in contact with the arm of the armature moving up and the other brush is in contact with the arm of the armature moving downward in the magnetic field.

Note : A.C. generator can be converted into D.C. generator by replacing slip rings (used in A.C. generator) by a split ring type commutator.

2.15 DOMESTIC ELECTRIC CIRCUITS :

Electricity Board of a State is responsible for the electric power supply to the houses and factories. The electric power is supplied to the houses or factories through underground cable or overhead wires on poles. Overhead wires or cables are three in number. They are known as phase wire (or live wire), neutral wire and earth wire. These wire coming from power sub-station are connected to an electric meter installed in a house or a factory. The potential difference between the live wire and neutral wire is 220V. An electric fuse is placed in the path of the phase wire before it is connected to the electric meter (known as KWh metre). This fuse is known as pole fuse and has a definite current rating. The current rating of pole fuse depends upon the load sanctioned by the Electricity Board to a particular house or a factory. The load sanctioned is calculated on the basis of the number of appliances (like bulbs, tubes, heaters, geysers, fans etc.) to be used in a house. If the owner of the house draws more current than the sanctioned one, then the pole fuse melts and the power supply is cut off.

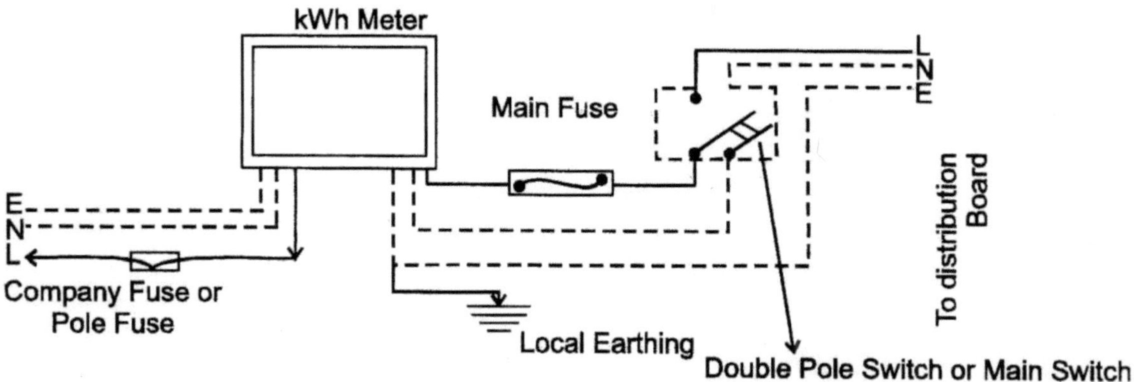

The output power from electric meter is taken to the main switch. Another fuse known as main fuse is placed in the path of the live or phase wire. Main switch consists of a double pole iron clad switch. This switch can cut off the power supply from the domestic electric circuit with the help of a lever. The body of main switch is earthed by connecting it with a metallic wire buried deep into the earth.

The output electric power from the main switch is distributed to the domestic electric circuit. The arrangement of power supply from the electric power sub-station to the main switch of a house or a factory is shown in figure.

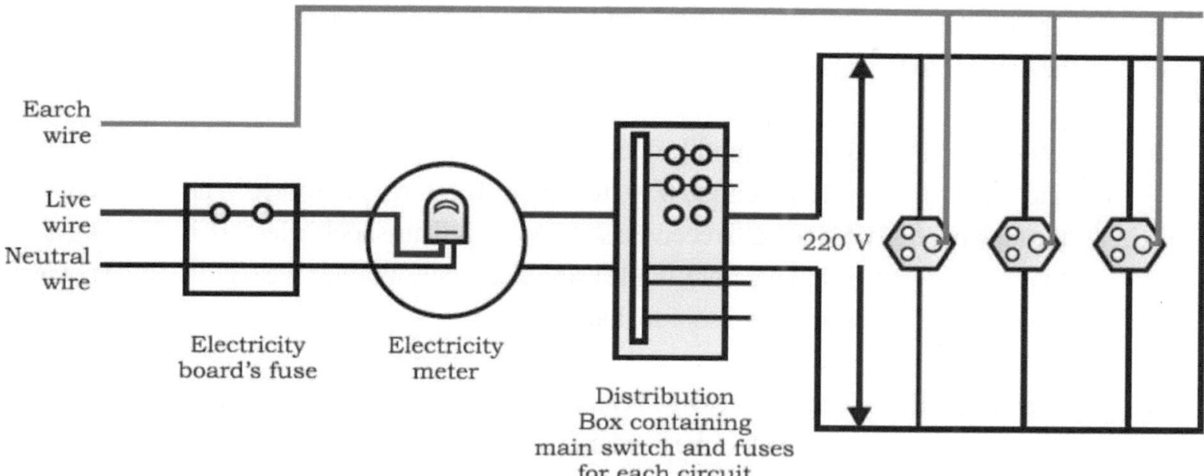

Alternating current flowing through a wire is dangerous if the wire is touched with bare hands. Moreover, when current flowing through the wire exceeds a certain limit, it can burn the electric circuit. So, we have to take safety measures while using electricity. These safety measures are given below :

2.16 ELECTRIC FUSE :

1. An electric fuse is a safety device that is used to save the electrical appliances like electric bulbs, electric tubes. T.V. etc. from burning when large current flows in the circuit. Electric fuse is a wire made of copper or aluminium or tin-lead alloy. The melting point of the material of which the electric fuse wire is made should be low. Commonly used, electric fuses are shown in figure.

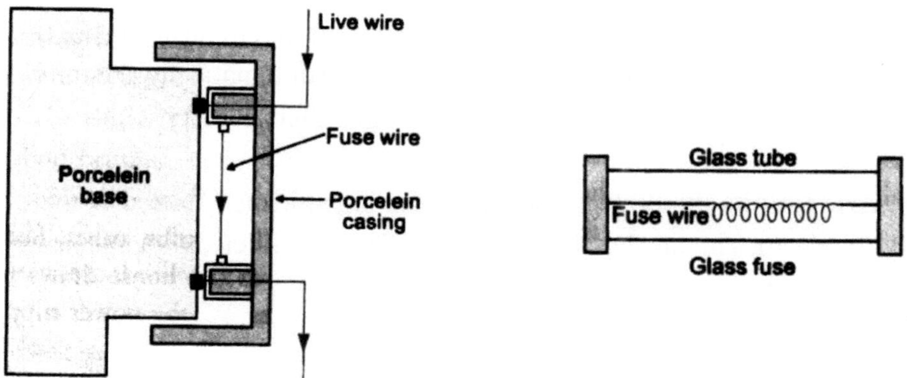

Suppose a fuse is not connected in the path of a live wire of the circuit. In such case, the circuit may be over heated if the current in the circuit exceeds the safe limit. There is a chance of short circuiting of the circuit which causes the fire. So to avoid short circuiting of the circuit, a fuse must be put in the path of the circuit.

Fuse wires are usually rated as 5A or 15A. A circuit in which bulb or a tube is to be connected, the fuse is rated as 5A. It means, this circuit can draw maximum 5A current. If current in this circuit becomes greater than 5A, the fuse wire melts and the circuit is switched off automatically. Hence the circuit can be saved from burning.

Similarly, a circuit in which a heating appliance like an electric heater or a geyser is to be connected, the fuse rated as 15A is used.

2. The insulation on the wire should be of high strength so that it may not melt easily when wires are heated due to large current flowing through them.

3. Wires carrying electricity should not be touched bare footed. The live wire is at higher potential and the earth is at zero potential. If we touch the live wire bare footed, a large current will pass through our body. So we will receive a severe shock. This shock affects our nervous system and may cause even death. Therefore, while using electricity, we must wear gloves made of insulated material and shoes of rubber sole so that current may not flow through our body.

4. **Earthing :** Electric appliances like heater, toaster, refrigerator etc. are frequently touched by us with bare hands. If by chance, the insulation on live wire melts, then the live wire may touch the metallic case of the appliance. In that case, current passes through the metal casing of the appliance. If we touch this casing with bare hands, we will receive a severe shock. To avoid such an accident, metal casings of all electric appliances must be earthed. One end of copper wire is connected with metal casing of the electric appliance. The other end of the copper wire is connected to the copper plate which is buried deep inside the earth. This system of connecting the metal casing of an electric appliance with a copper plate buried deep inside the earth is known as earthing.
How is earthing of an electric appliance is useful ?
When the live wire touches the metal casing of an electric appliance, the electric current flows from the casing of the appliance to the earth through the copper wire. As the earth offers very low or almost no resistance to the flow of current, so large current passes through the copper wire instead of human body. This large current heats the circuit and hence the fuse in the circuit melts. As a result of this, the circuit is switched off automatically and the electric appliance is saved from burning. Moreover, the human body suffers no electric shock.

5. **Electric circuits should be switched off during lighting :** Whenever there is lightning in the sky, the electric circuits should be switched off to save the electric appliances connected in these circuits from burning.

2.17 SHORT-CIRCUITING AND OVERLOADING :

Short-Circuiting takes place when the live wire and the neutral wire come in direct contact (or touch each other). It can happen accidently or if the insulation on these wire melts. When short circuiting occurs, the resistance of the circuit becomes very small and hence huge amount of current flows through it. Large amount of current in the circuit produces large amount of heat which raises the temperature of the circuit to very high value. As a result of this, the circuit catches fire.

Overloading means flow of large amount of current in the circuit beyond the permissible value of current. It occurs when many electrical appliances of high power rating like geyser, heater, refrigerator, motor etc. are connected in a single socket or in a single circuit. High current flowing in the circuit due to overloading causes fire.

LET US RECAPITULATE

- Hans Christian oersted discovered a relationship between electricity and magnetism.
- A current carrying wire behaves as a magnet.
- When a current passes through a wire, a magnetic field is set up around the wire. This effect of current is called magnetic effect of current.
- Like magnetic poles repel each other and unlike magnetic poles attract each other.
- ***Magnetic field*** is space or region around a current carrying wire or a magnet within which its influence is felt by another magnet.
- ***Magnetic field line :*** The path along which a free unit north pole moves in a magnetic field is called magnetic field line. The tangent at any point on a magnetic field line gives the direction of the magnetic field at that point.
- Two magnetic field lines can't intersect or cross each other.
- Magnetic field lines are crowded in a region of strong magnetic field.
- Magnetic field lines are far apart in a region of weak magnetic field.
- When current passes through a straight wire or conductor, a magnetic field is set up around the wire or conductor.
- Magnetic field around a current carrying wire or conductor is represented by concentric circles centred at the wire or the conductor.
- The direction of magnetic field around the current carrying conductor is determined by Right Hand Thumb Rule.
- Magnetic field around a current carrying wire increases with the increase in the current passing through the wire.
- Magnetic field around a current carrying wire or conductor is represented by concentric circles centred at the wire or the conductor.
- The direction of magnetic field around the current carrying conductor is determined by Right Hand Thumb Rule.
- Magnetic field around a current carrying wire increases with the increase in the current passing through the wire.
- Magnetic field around a current carrying wire decreases as we go away from the wire.
- Magnetic field due to a very long wire like a power transmission line carrying current I and at a distance r from the wire is given by

$$B = \left(\frac{\mu_0}{4\pi}\right)\frac{2I}{r}\ ;\ \text{where, } \mu_0 = 4\pi \times 10^{-7}\ TmA^{-1}$$

- Two parallel wires or conductors carrying current in the same directs attract each other.
- Two parallel wires or conductors carrying current in the opposite directions repel each other.
- The magnetic field around a straight current carrying conductor or wire can be increased by bending it into a circular loop.
- The strength of magnetic field produced at the centre of a circular loop of a wire is
  (i) directly proportional to the amount of current passing through the loop of the wire.
  (ii) directly proportional to the number of turns of the circular loop of the wire.
  (iii) inversely proportional to the radius of the circular loop of the wire.
- Magnetic field produced by a current carrying circular wire or loop decreases on both sides along the axis of the circular wire.
- A solenoid is a coil of many turns of an insulated copper wire closely wound in the shape of a tight spring.
- Magnetic field inside a current carrying solenoid is uniform magnetic field.

- A solenoid carrying current behaves like a bar magnet.
- A soft iron rod placed in a current carrying solenoid is known as electromagnet.
- A current carrying conductor placed perpendicular to the magnetic field experience a force.
- The force acting on a current carrying conductor placed perpendicular to the magnetic field B is given by
$$F = BIl$$
- Direction of force experienced by a current carrying conductor placed in a magnetic field is determined by Fleming's Left Hand Rule.
- No Force acts on a current carrying conductor when placed parallel to the magnetic field.
- SI unit of magnetic field is tesla (T).
- Force acts on a charge moving perpendicular to the magnetic field. This force is called Lorentz force.
- Force acting on a charge Q moving with velocity v perpendicular to the magnetic field B is given by
$$F = BQV$$
- No force acts on a charge moving parallel to the magnetic field B.
- Direction of force experienced by a moving charge in a magnetic field is determined by Right Hand Rule.
- Electric motor is a device which converts electrical energy into mechanical energy.
- Principle of electric motor : Electric motor works on the principle that a current carrying conductor placed perpendicular to a magnetic field experiences a force.
- The phenomenon of producing induced current in a closed circuit due to the change in magnetic field in the circuit is known as electromagnetic induction.
- More induced current flows through a closed coil if a bar magnet is brought towards or away from the coil with large speed.
- No induced current flows through a closed coil if magnetic field linked with it does not change.
- Direction of induced current in a conductor is determined by Fleming's Right hand rule.
- Direct current is an electric current whose magnitude is either constant or variable but the direction of flow in a conductor remains the same.
- Frequency of direct current is zero.
- Alternating current is an electric current whose magnitude changes with time and direction reverse periodically.
- In India, frequency of A.C. is 50 Hz.
- A.C. is more dangerous than D.C.
- Electric generator is a device used to convert mechanical energy into electrical energy.
- Electric generator works on the principle of electromagnetic induction.
- To supply electric power from one place to another place, three wires known as phase wire (or live wire), neutral wire and earth wire are used.
- The potential difference between the live wire and neutral wire in a household supply of electric power is 220 V.
- Current rating of a fuse is the maximum amount of electric current that can be passed through the fuse wire without melting it.
- Current rating of a fuse wire in a circuit having bulbs and tubes is 5A.
- Current rating of a fuse wire in a circuit having heating appliances is 15A.
- Electric fuse is a safety device used to save the electrical appliances from burning when large current flows in the circuit.
- Electric fuse is made of a material of low melting point.
- Material used for making a fuse wire is made of copper / aluminium / tin-lead alloy.
- Short Circuiting : When live wire and neutral wire come in direct contact, the resistance of the circuit becomes very small. Hence huge current flows through the circuit. This huge current produces large amount of heat in the circuit and the circuit catches fire. This is known as short circuiting.

CONCEPT APPLICATION LEVEL - I [NCERT Questions]

Q.1 Which of the following correctly describes the magnetic field near a long straight wire ?
(a) the field consists of straight lines perpendicular to the wire
(b) the field consists of straight lines parallel to the wire.
(c) the field consists of radial lines originating from the wire.
(d) the field consists of concentric circles centered on the wire.

Ans. (d) the field consists of concentric circles centered on the wire.

Q.2 The phenomena of electromagnetic induction is
(a) the process of charging a body
(b) the process of generating magnetic field due to current passing through a coil
(c) producing induced current in a coil due to relative motion between a magnet and the coil
(d) the process of rotating a coil of an electric motor.

Ans. (c) producing induced current in a coil due to relative motion between a magnet and the coil

Q.3 The device used for producing electric current is called a
(a) generator (b) galvanometer (c) ammeter (d) motor

Ans. (a) generator

Q.4 The essential difference between an AC generator and a DC generator is that
(a) AC generator has an electromagnet while a DC generator has permanent magnet
(b) DC generator will generate a higher voltage
(c) AC generator will generate a higher voltage
(d) AC generator has slip rings while the DC generator has a commutator.

Ans. (d) AC generator has slip rings while the DC generator has a commutator.

Q.5 At the time of short circuit, the current in the circuit.
(a) reduces substantially (b) does not change
(c) increases heavily (d) vary continuously

Ans. **(c) increases heavily**

Q.6 State whether the following statements are true or false :
(a) an electric motor converts mechanical energy into electrical energy
(b) an electric generator works on the principle of electromagnetic induction
(c) the field at the centre of a long circular coil carrying current will be parallel straight lines.
(d) a wire with a green insulation is usually the live wire.

Ans. (a) False. It converts electrical energy into mechanical energy.
(b) True
(c) True
(d) False, Live wire has red insulation cover.

Q.7 List three sources of magnetic fields.

Ans. (i) a permanent magnet (ii) a current carrying conductor
(iii) a current carrying solenoid

Q.8 How does a solenoid behave like a magnet ? Can you determine the north and south poles of a current carrying solenoid with the help of a bar magnet. Explain.

Ans. When electric current flows through a solenoid, magnetic field is set up around the solenoid. The pattern of the magnetic field is same as that of the magnetic field of a bar magnet. One end of the solenoid behaves as north pole and the another end behaves as south pole.

To determine the north and south poles of a current carrying solenoid with the help of a bar magnet, suspend it with a strong thread. Now bring the north pole of a bar magnet towards one end of the solenoid. If the solenoid attracts towards the magnet, then that face of the solenoid is south pole. If the solenoid moves away from the bar magnet, then that face of the solenoid is the north pole.

Q.9 When is the force experienced by a current carrying conductor placed in magnetic field is the largest ?

Ans. When current carrying conductor is placed perpendicular to the magnetic field.

Q.10 Think you are sitting in a chamber with your back to one wall. An electron beam moving horizontally from back wall towards the front wall, is deflected by a strong magnetic field to your right side. What is the direction of magnetic field ?

Ans. Movement from electron beam from back wall to the front wall is equivalent to the flow of electric current from front wall to the back wall. The deflection of the beam means, the force is acting towards our right side. According to Fleming's Left Hand Rule, the direction of magnetic field is vertically downward. That is, the magnetic field is perpendicular to the plane of the paper and directed inward. Such magnetic field is shown by

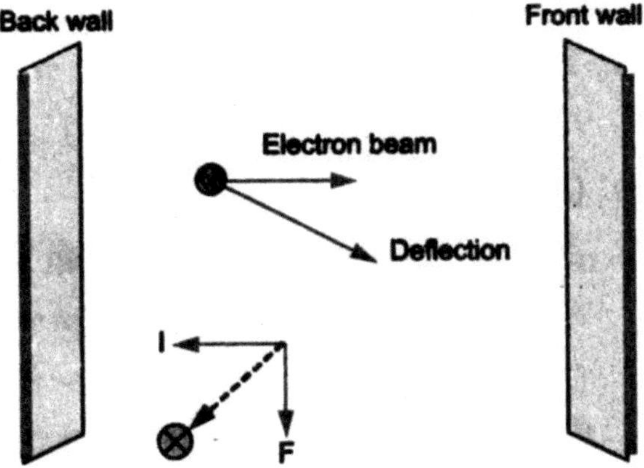

Q.11 Draw a labelled diagram of an electric motor. Explain its principle and working. What is the function of a split ring in an electric motor ?

Ans. Refer text

Q.12 Name some devices in which electric motors are used.

Ans. Electric cars, rolling mills, electric fans, hair dryers, mixers, blenders etc.

Q.13 A coil of insulated copper wire is connected to a galvanometer. What will happen if a bar magnet is (i) pushed into the coil. (ii) withdrawn from inside the coil (iii) held stationary inside the coil ?

Ans.

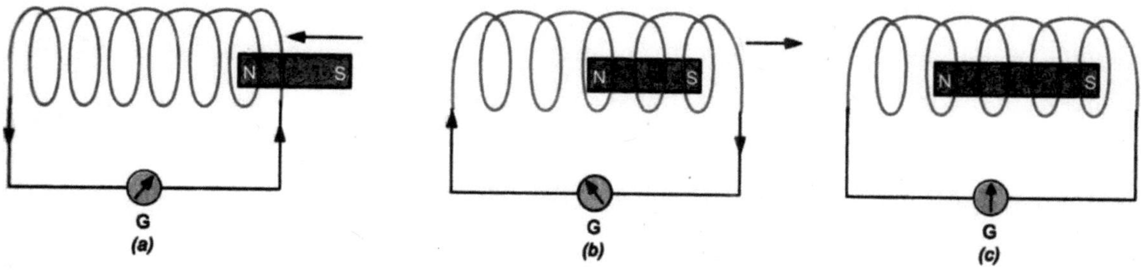

(i) When a bar magnet is pushed into the coil, induced current flows through the coil due to the phenomenon of electromagnetic induction. This induced current is indicated by the deflection of the needle of the galvanometer as shown in figure(a).

(ii) When bar magnet is withdrawn from inside the coil, again induced current flows through the coil due to the phenomenon of electromagnetic induction. In this case, the direction of induced current is opposite to the direction of the current in case (i) as shown in figure (b).

(iii) When the bar magnet is held stationary inside the coil, there is no change in magnetic field around the coil. Hence, no induced current flows through the coil. Therefore, galvanometer shows no deflection as shown in figure(c).

Q.14 Two circular coils A and B are placed close to each other. If the current in the coil A is changed, will some current be induced in the coil B ? Give reason.

Ans. When current in coil A is changed, a changing magnetic field is set up around it. This changing magnetic field also links with coil B and hence some current will be induced in coil B due to electromagnetic induction.

Q.15 State the rule to determine the direction of a (i) magnetic field produced around a straight conductor carrying current, (ii) force experienced by a current-carrying straight conductor placed in a magnetic field which is perpendicular to it, and (iii) current induced in a coil due to its rotation in a magnetic field.

Ans. (i) Right hand thumb rule (ii) Fleming's left hand rule (iii) Fleming's right hand rule

Q.16 Explain the underlying principle and working of an electric generator by drawing a labelled diagram. What is the function of brushes ?

Ans. Refer text.

Q.17 When does an electric short circuit occur ?

Ans. When live wire and neutral wire touch each other (i.e. come in direct contact)

Q.18 What is the function of an earth wire ? Why is it necessary to earth metallic casings of electric appliances ?

Ans. Earth wire acts as a safety measure. When the live wire touches the metallic casing of an electric appliance, the electric current flows from the casing of the appliance to the earth through the copper wire. As the earth offers very low or almost no resistance to the flow of current, so large current passes through the copper wire instead of human body. This large current heats the circuit and hence the fuse in the circuit melts. As a result of this, the circuit is switched off automatically and hence the electric appliance is saved from burning and the human body suffers no electric shock.

CONCEPT APPLICATION LEVEL - II

SECTION–A

Q.1 Why does a compass needle get deflected when brought near a bar magnet ?

Ans. Compass needle is a small magnet which experiences a force in the magnetic field of a bar magnet. Due to this force, it gets deflected.

Q.2 Draw magnetic field lines around a bar magnet.

Ans.

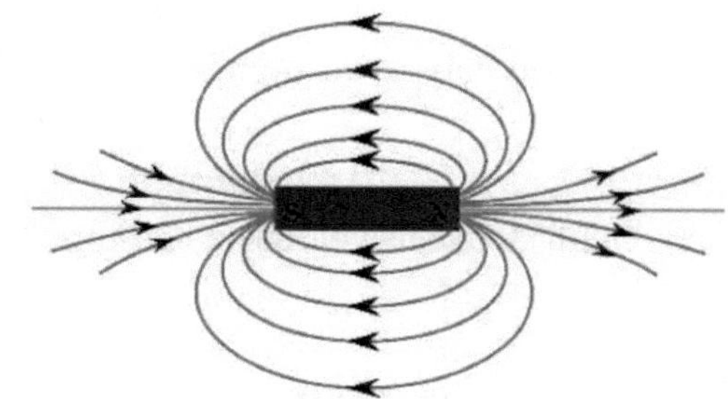

Q.3 List the properties of magnetic lines of force.

Ans.
(i) Magnetic lines of force are closed continuous curves.
(ii) The tangent at any point on the magnetic line of force gives the direction of the magnetic field at that point.
(iii) Two magnetic lines of force can not cross each other.

Q.4 Why do not two magnetic lines of force intersect each other ?

Ans. The tangent at any point on a magnetic field line gives the direction of magnetic field at that point. If two magnetic field lines cross each other, then at the point of intersection, there will be two tangents. Hence, there will be two directions of the magnetic field at the point of intersection. This is not possible. Hence, no two magnetic field lines can cross each other.

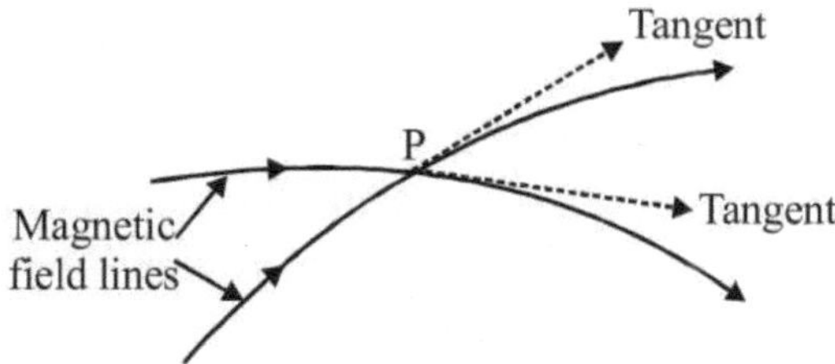

Q.5 Consider a circular loop of wire lying in the plane of the table. Let the current passing through the loop clockwise. Apply the right hand rule to find out the direction of magnetic field inside and outside the loop.

Ans. Magnetic field inside the loop is perpendicular to the plane of table and in the downward direction. However, outside the loop, magnetic field is perpendicular to the plane of the table and in the upward direction.

Q.6 The magnetic field in a given region is uniform. Draw a diagram to represent it.

Ans. →→→→→ (five parallel equally spaced arrows)

Q.7 Choose the correct option :
The magnetic field inside a long straight solenoid carrying current is :
(a) zero (b) decreases as we move towards its ends
(c) increases as we move towards its ends (d) is the same at all points.

Ans. (d) is the same at all points.

Q.8 Which of the property a proton can change when it moves freely in a magnetic field ? (There may be more than one correct answer).
(a) mass (b) speed (c) velocity (d) momentum

Ans. A force acts on a proton when it moves freely in a magnetic field. Hence its velocity and momentum can change.

Q.9 In activity (Force on a current-carrying conductor in a magnetic field), how do we think the displacement of rod AB will be affected if (i) current in rod AB is increased (ii) a stronger horse shoe magnet is inserted (iii) length of the rod AB is increased.

Ans. Force acting on a current carrying conductor of length l placed perpendicular to magnetic field B is given by : $F = BIl$

(i) When I increase, F also increases. Hence the displacement of the rod increase.

(ii) When a stronger horse shoe magnet is inserted, magnetic field at B increases. So force also increases. Hence displacement increases.

(iii) When l increases, force increases and hence displacement increase.

Q.10 A positively charged particle (alpha particle) projected towards west is deflected towards north by a magnetic field. The direction of magnetic field is
(a) towards south (b) towards east (c) downward (d) upward

Ans. (d) upward

Q.11 State Fleming's left hand rule.

Ans. Stretch the left hand such that the thumb, first finger and the central finger are mutually perpendicular to each other. If the First finger points in the direction of the magnetic Field and the Central finger points in the direction of Current, then the thumb will point in the direction Motion (or Force) as shown in figure.
Stretch the left hand such that the thumb, first finger and the central finger are mutually perpendicular to each other. If the First finger points in the direction of the magnetic Field and the Central finger points in the direction of Current, then the thumb will point in the direction Motion (or Force) as shown in figure.

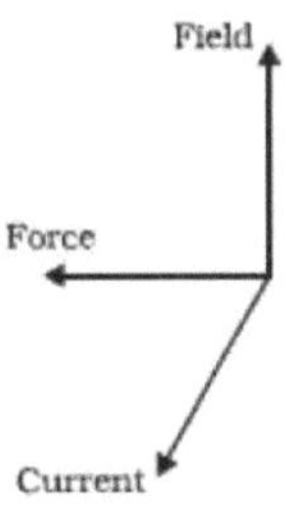

Q.12 What is the principle of electric motor ?

Ans. Electric motor works on the principle that a current carrying conductor placed perpendicular to a magnetic field experiences a force.

Q.13 What is the role of the split ring in an electric motor ?

Ans. The split-ring in an electric motor reverses the direction of current in the armature coil of the motor. Therefore, the direction of the force acting on the two arms of the coil is also reversed. As a result of this, the coil of d.c. motor continues to rotate in the same direction.

Q.14 Explain different ways to induce current in a coil.

Ans. (i) By moving a bar magnetic towards or away from the coil.

(ii) By placing a coil near another coil connected across a battery.

Q.15 State the principle of electric generator.

Ans. It is based on the principle of electromagnetic induction. That is, the changing magnetic field induces current in the coil.

Q.16 Name some sources of direct current.

Ans. A dry cell, a battery, a solar cell, d.c. generator etc. are some sources of direct current/

Q.17 Which source produces alternating current ?

Ans. AC generator (which converts mechanical energy into alternating current or electricity) and an oscillator (device which converts D.C. into A.C.) are the sources which produce alternating current.

Q.18 Choose the correct option :

A rectangular coil of copper wires is rotated in a magnetic field. The direction of the induced current changes once in each

(a) two revolutions (b) one revolution (c) half revolution (d) one-fourth revolution

Ans. (c) half revolution

Q.19 Name two safety measures commonly used in electric circuit and appliances.

Ans. (i) Electric fuse and (ii) earthing

Q.20 An electric oven of 2 kw power rating is operated in a domestic electric circuit (220V) that has a current rating of 5A. What result do you except ? Explain.

Ans. P = 2kW = 2000 W and V = 220 V

$$\therefore \quad I = \frac{P}{V} = \frac{2000}{220} = 9.09 \text{ A}$$

This shows that current flowing through the oven is more than the current rating (5A). Hence, the fuse in the circuit melts and oven is saved from damage.

Q.21 What precautions should be taken to avoid the overloading of domestic electric circuit ?

OR

Write any two precaution to be taken to avoid overloading of a domestic electric circuit.

Ans. (i) We should not connect many appliances in the same socket.

(ii) Electrical appliances of high power rating should not be switched on simultaneously.

SECTION–B

Q.1 State the factors on which the strength of magnetic field at a point due to a current carrying conductor depends.

Ans. (i) Strength of electric current flowing in the conductor.

(ii) The distance of the point from the conductor.

Q.2 On what factors does the magnetic field produced by a current carrying solenoid depend?

Ans. (i) The strength of the current flowing through the solenoid.

(ii) The number of turns of the wire of the solenoid.

(iii) The nature of the material inside the solenoid i.e., permeability of the material inside the solenoid.

Q.3 Mention at least five uses of an electric motor. What is the differences between electric motor and electric generator?

or

Name four appliances wherein an electric motor (a rotating device that converts electrical energy into mechanical energy is used as an important component. In what respect electric motors are different from generator?

Ans. It is used in mixers, blenders, refrigerators, washing machines, hair dryers. Electric motor converts electrical energy into mechanical energy and electric generator converts mechanical energy into electric energy.

Q.4 What is the function of brushes in an electric generator?

Ans. The brushes in a electric generator supply the induced current from the coil to the external circuit.

Q.5 Describe an activity to show that magnetic field in generated around straight current carrying wire.

Ans. Refer text.

Q.6 Describe an activity to show that magnetic field is produced by an electric current flowing through a circular coil of a wire.

Ans. Refer text.

Q.7 A horizontal power line carries current in east to west direction. What is the direction of the magnetic field due to the current in the power line at a point above and at a point below the power line?

Ans. According to right-hand thumb rule: (i) the direction of magnetic field at a point above the power line is from south to north, (ii) the direction of magnetic field at a point below the power line is from north to south.

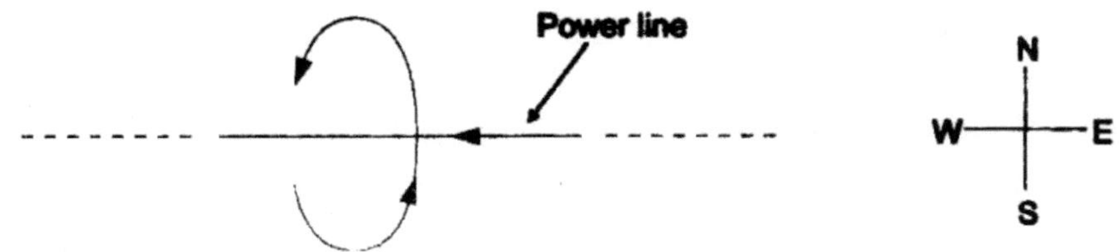

Q.8 The magnetic field produced by a current carrying circular coil having n turns is equal to n times the magnetic field produced by a current carrying circular coil having a single turn. Explain, why?

Ans. As the direction of the current flowing in each turn of the coil is same, so the direction of the magnetic field produced by each turn is also the same. The magnetic field produced by each turn will therefore get added up to give the magnetic field produced by a coil of n turns. Hence, magnetic field produced by a coil of n turns = n times the magnetic field produced by a coil having a single turn.

Q.9 Current is flowing anticlockwise in a circular coil lying in the plane of a table. Using Right Hand Thumb Rule, state the direction of the magnetic field inside and outside the coil.

Ans. Magnetic field inside the coil is perpendicular to the plane of the table and in upward direction. However, the magnetic field outside the coil is perpendicular to the plane of the table and in downward direction as shown in figure.

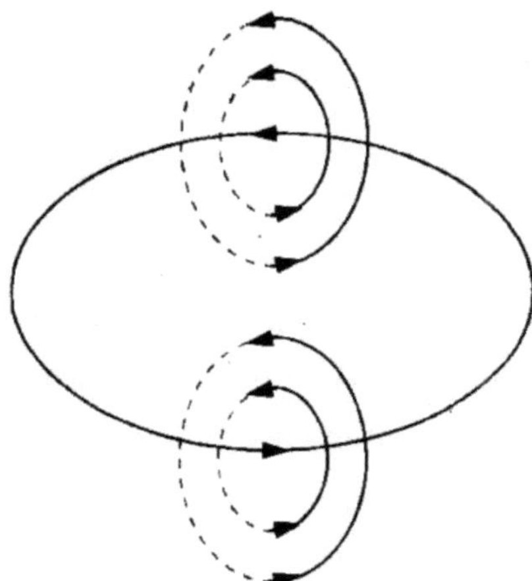

Q.10 Why does a current carrying conductor kept in a magnetic field experience force?

Ans. A current carrying conductor contains moving negatively charged particles (i.e., electrons). Each electron experiences a force (= Bev). The total force experienced by electrons is equal to the force experienced by the conductor.

Q.11 A proton enters a magnetic field at right angle to it as shown in figure. What is the direction of the force acting on the electron?

Ans. According to Fleming's left hand rule, the force acting on a current carrying conductor placed at right angles to a magnetic field is perpendicular to the directions of current (i.e. flow of positive charges) and the magnetic field.

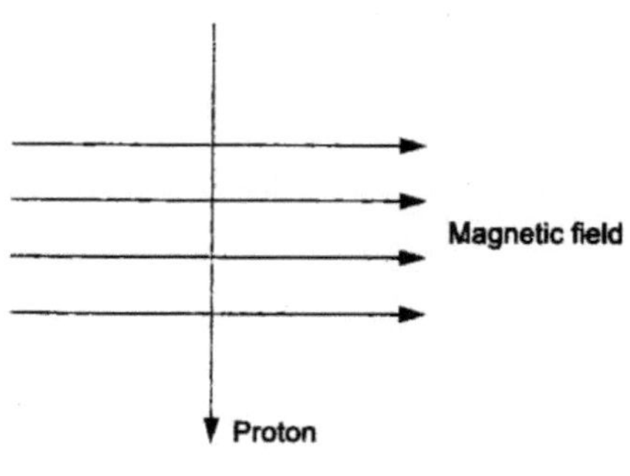

The arrow showing the direction of proton represents the direction of current in a conductor, therefore, the force acting on the conductor is perpendicular to the plane of the paper and in upward direction.

Q.12 Explain the meaning of the word "electromagnetic" and "induction" in the term electromagnetic induction.

Ans. "Electromagnetic" means production of induced current in a closed coil due to the change in magnetic field. "Induction" means the induced current is produced without the actual contact of the closed coil and the moving magnet.

Q.13 Current-time graphs from two different sources are shown in the following diagrams.

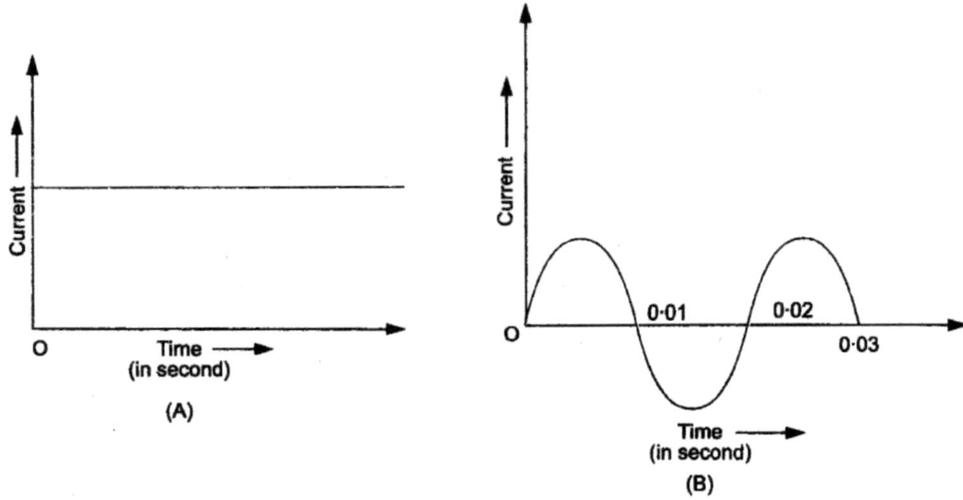

Now answer the following questions.

(i) Name the type of current shown by graph A and graph B.

(ii) Name any one source of the current shown by graph A and graph B

(iii) What is the frequency of current in case B?

(iv) Write two difference between the current shown by graphs A and B.

Ans. (i) Graph A represent direct current (DC). Graph B represents alternating current (AC).

(ii) A dry cell is the source of current shown by graph A. An AC generator is the source of current shown by the graph B.

(iii) From graph B, time period, T = 0.02s, Therefore, frequency of current, $f = \frac{1}{T} = \frac{1}{1/50\,s} = 50$ Hz.

(iv) **Direct current**

(i) The magnitude of direct current is constant and flows in one direction only.

(ii) Direct current cannot be used for large scale supply of electricity for household purpose.

(iii) The frequency of direct current is zero.

Alternating current

(i) The magnitude and direction of alternating current reverses periodically.

(ii) Alternating current is used to run electrical appliances like electric bulb, electric heater, electric iron, refrigerator etc.

(iii) Frequency of alternating current in India is 50 Hz.

Q.14 What is the basic difference between AC generator and DC generator?

Ans. (i) In AC generator, slip-ring are used while in DC generator split ring type commutator is used.

(ii) AC generator converts mechanical energy into electrical energy in the form of alternating current. DC generator converts mechanical energy into electrical energy in the form of direct current.

Q.15 A magnetic compass is placed near current carrying wire. What will you observe

(i) When current in the wire is increased.

(ii) When the magnetic compass is displaced away from the wire?

OR

A magnetic compass shows a deflection near a current carrying wire. How will the deflection of the compass get affected if current in the wire is increased? Support your answer with reason.

Ans. (i) We observer that the deflection of the needle of the magnetic compass increases. This is because the magnetic field strength due to a current carrying wire increases, when current in the wire is increased.

(ii) We observe that the deflection of the needle of the magnetic compass decreases. This is because the magnetic field strength due to a current carrying wire decreases with the increase of the distance from the wire.

Q.16 Two copper wires A and B are wrapped on a hollow card board as shown in figure. Wire A is connected across a battery through one way key. The wire B close to wire A is connected across a galvanometer. What do you observe when key is closed.

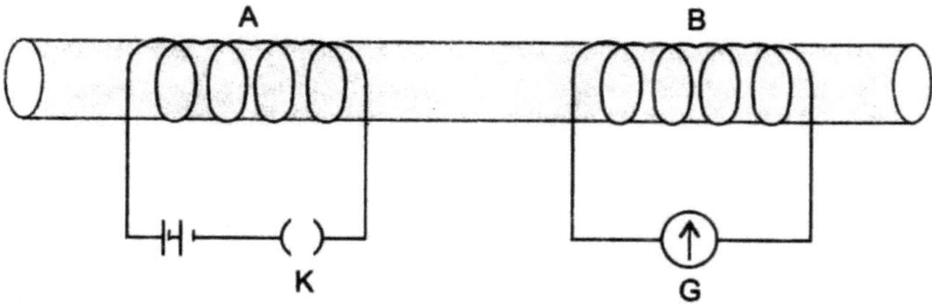

Ans. We observe that galvanometer shows a deflection for a short moment. This is because, when current flows through wire A, a changing magnetic field is set up around the wire A. Due to electromagnetic induction, induced current flows through the wire B. Hence galvanometer shows deflection.

Q.17 On what factors does the value of induced current produced in a circuit depend? Name and state the rule used for determination of direction of induced current. State one application of this phenomenon in every day life.

Ans. Refer Text.

Fleming's Right Hand Rule is used for determining the direction induced current.

For the statement of Fleming's Right Hand Rule, Refer Text.

Electric generator to produce large electric current works on the principle of electromagnetic induction.

SECTION–C [PREVIOUS YEARS QUESTIONS (1 MARK)]

Q.1 Mention the shape of the magnetic field lines around a current-carrying straight conductor. **[SAI-2015]**

Ans. In the form of concentric rings around the straight conductor

Q.2 What happens to the magnetic field lines due to a current-carrying conductor when the current is reversed ? **[SAI-2010, 2011, 2012]**

Ans. The direction of magnetic field lines gets reversed on reversing the direction of the current.

Q.3 State the observation made by Oersted on the basis of his experiment with current-carrying conductors. **[SAI-2013]**

Ans. Every current-carrying conductor has a magnetic field around it.

Q.4 What type of core is used to make electromagnet? **[SAI-2013]**

Ans. Soft iron.

Q.5 Mention the voltage and frequency of current that we receive at our house? **[SAI-2014]**

Ans. 220 V, 50 Hz

SECTION–D [PREVIOUS YEARS QUESTIONS (2 MARKS)]

Q.1 List two factors on which strength of induced current depends. **[SAI-2010]**

Ans. The strength of the induced current depends directly upon the following factors:
(i) Strength of the magnetic field. (ii) Number of turns in the coil.

Q.2 What is the nature of magnetic field produced by a current-carrying circular coil? Explain with the help of an experiment. **[SAI-2013,2014]**

Ans. Bend a copper wire in a circular shape. Pass the coil through a cardboard. Connect the free ends of the coil to a battery and a key. Sprinkle some iron filings on the cardboard. Put on the key. You will find that the iron filings arrange themselves in the form of concentric circles. The magnetic lines of force near each segment of wire are circular and form concentric circles whereas the lines of force near the centre of the coil are almost straight lines. Note that at the centre of the coil, the magnetic field is uniform and 'perpendicular to the plane of the coil.

Q.3 Describe an activity to show that the magnetic field produced by given electric current in the wire decreases as the distance from the wire increases. **[SAI-2013]**

Ans. (i) A circuit is made using battery (12 V), a plug key, an ammeter (0-5 A) and a long thick copper as shown below.

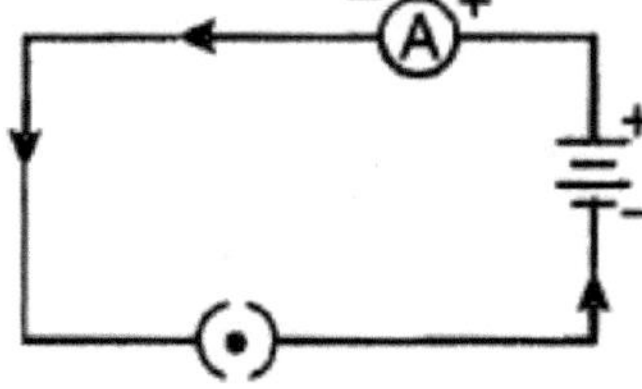

(ii) Then the key is switched on and a compass is brought near and moved away from the copper wire keeping the current through the wire same. The observation is noted down.

(iii) It is observed that the deflection of the compass needle increases as it is brought near the wire and decreases when it is moved away.

Q.4 State two ways by which the strength of an electromagnet can be increased. **[SAI-2013]**

Ans. The strength of an electromagnet can be increased by :

(i) Increasing the number of turns in the solenoid.

(ii) Increasing the strength of current flowing through the solenoid.

Q.5 (a) Name the type of electric current generated by the most of the power stations in our country.

(b) Why is it preferred over the other type ?

(c) State the frequency of the power supply generated in India. **[SAI-2014]**

Ans. (a) Alternating current (ac).

(b) Alternating current (ac) is preferred because in comparison to direct current (de), it can be transmitted over long distance effectively.

(c) 50 Hz.

Q.6 Explain why a fuse should be joined with the live wire and not with the neutral wire in a domestic circuit. **[SAI-2012]**

Ans. In a domestic circuit, the phase wire is always at a much higher potential than the neutral wire. Moreover, the neutral wire is connected to the earth at the sub-station. Thus, during short-circuit the fuse will break the connection with the neutral wire and not the live wire.

SECTION–D [PREVIOUS YEARS QUESTIONS (3 MARKS)]

Q.1 Define magnetic field. Describe an activity to draw magnetic field lines around a bar magnet from one pole to another pole. **[SAI-2015]**

Ans. It is the region around a magnet where the magnetic force of the magnet can be felt. Take a small compass and a bar magnet. Place the magnet on a sheet of white paper fixed on a drawing board, using some adhesive material. Mark the boundary of the magnet. Place the compass near the north pole of the magnet. We find that the south pole of the needle points towards the north pole of the magnet. The north pole of the compass is directed away from the north pole of the magnet. Mark the position of two ends of the needle; Now, move the needle to a new position such that its south pole occupies the position previously occupied by its north pole. In this way, proceed step by step till you reach the south pole of the magnet as shown in Fig.

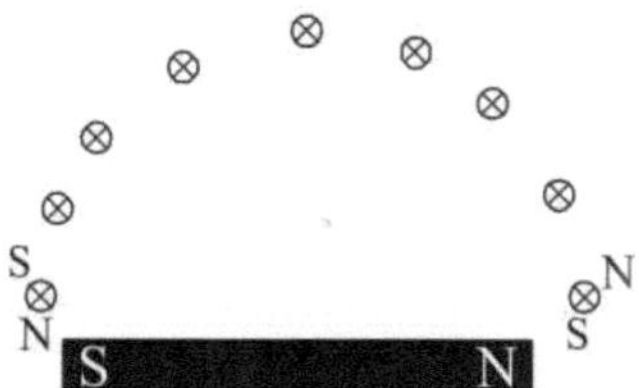

Q.2 Explain an activity to show that a current carrying conductor experiences a force placed in a magnetic field. **[SAI-2010, 2011, 2012]**

Ans. **Activity :** A small aluminium rod is suspended horizontally from a stand using 'connecting wires. A strong horseshoe' magnet is placed in such a way that the rod lies in the two poles with the magnetic field directed upwards. For this, the north pole magnet is kept vertically below and south pole vertically above the aluminium rod.

The aluminium rod is connected in series with a battery, a key and a rheostat. A current is passed through the aluminium rod from one end to other (B to A). The rod is displaced towards left. When the direction of current flowing through the rod is reversed, the displacement of rod is towards right.

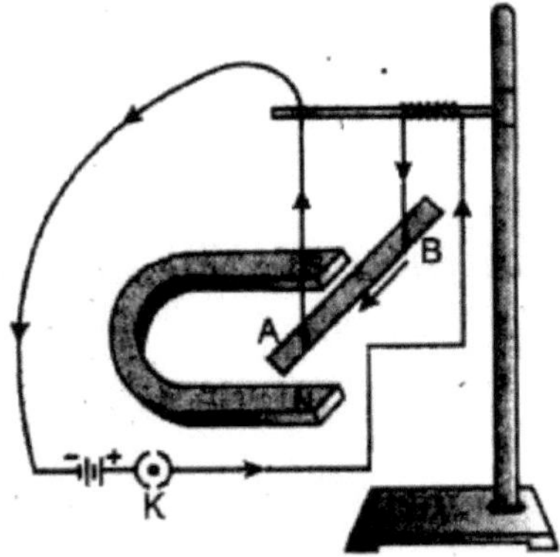

Q.3 What is short-circuiting ? State one factor that can lead to it. Name a device in the household that acts as a safety measure for it. State the principle of its working. **[SAI-2012,2013]**

Ans. It is a situation in which live and neutral wires come in direct contact, abruptly increasing the current in the circuit. **Factors :** (i) Damaged insulation of wire. (ii) Fault in appliance.
Safety device: Electric fuse/MCB. Electric fuse is an application of Joule's heating effect.

Q.4 Name the three types of wires used in household circuits. Out of these three which wire is used as a safety measure especially for those appliances that have metallic body? State the colour of insulation used for this wire. How it ensures the safety of the user ? **[SAI-2012, 2013]**

Ans. (i) Live wire, (ii) Neutral wire, (iii) Earth wire.
Earth wire, colour of insulation is green. The metallic body connected to the earth wire keeps its potential to that of the earth and if there is any leakage, the user does not get any kind of electric shock.

Q.5 A uniform magnetic field is directed vertically upwards. In which direction in this field should an α -particle (which are positively charged particles) be projected so that it is deflected south ward? Name and state the rule you have used to find the direction in this case. **[SAI-2015]**

Ans. An α-particle carries positive charge, applying Flemings left hand rule we find that the direction of motion of positively charged alpha particle is from west to east. -

Q.6 Can a freely suspended current carrying solenoid stay in any direction? Justify your answer. What will happen when the direction of current in the solenoid is reversed? Explain. **[SAI-2015]**

Ans. A current-carrying solenoid behaves like a magnet.
$\therefore$ When suspended freely it will stay in
north -south direction.
On reversing current its polarity will be .
reversed and so it will turn at 180°.

Q.7 Find the minimum rating of fuse that can be safely used on a line on which two 1.1 kW, electric geysers are to run simultaneously. The supply voltage is 220 V. **[SAI-2015]**

Ans. $I = \frac{nP}{V} = \frac{2 \times 1.1 \times 1000}{220} = \frac{2200}{220} = 10A$

Q.8 The following diagram shows two straight wires carrying current. Copy the diagram and draw the pattern of lines of force around them and mark their directions. **[SAI-2013]**

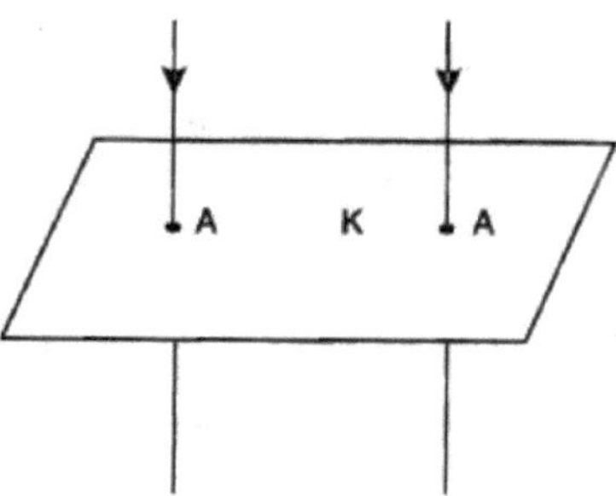

Ans. The pattern of lines is a as shown in the figure below

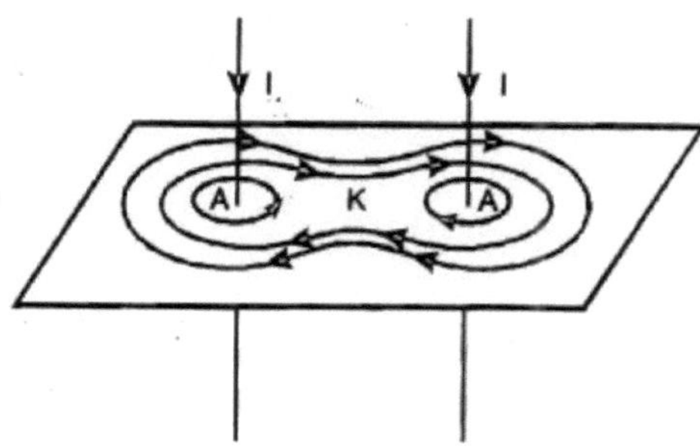

Q.9 (a) In a pattern of magnetic field lines due to a bar magnet, how can the regions of relative strength be identified ?

(b) Compare the strength of field near the poles and middle of a bar magnet. **[SAI-2013]**

Ans. (a) The relative strength of the magnetic field is shown by the degree of closeness of the field lines

(b) The strength of field near the poles is highest and in the middle of a bar magnet it is lowest.

SECTION–D [PREVIOUS YEARS QUESTIONS (5 MARKS)]

Q.1 Draw the lines of force (indicating field direction) of the magnetic field Through an around (a) single loop wire carrying electric current, and (b) a solenoid carrying electric current. **[SAI-2013]**

Ans. (a) The magnetic field lines are as shown :

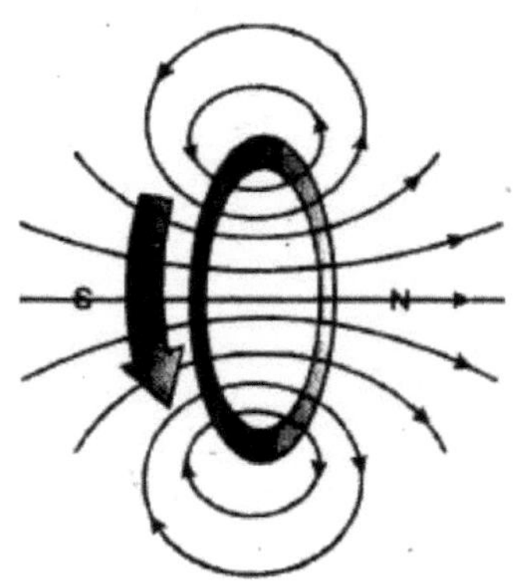

(b) The magnetic field lines are as shown :

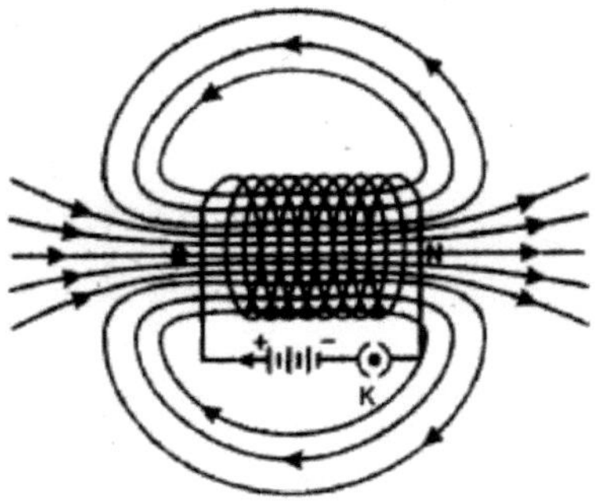

Q.9 What is an electromagnet ? What decides its polarity ? How it differs from a permanent magnet ? List the three factors and explain how strength of an electromagnet depends on these. **[SAI-2013]**

Ans. When a soft iron is placed inside a solenoid and current is passed through it then the soft iron gets magnetised. The magnet so formed is called an electromagnet.

Its polarity is decided by the direction of current flowing through the solenoid.

Permanent magnets have constant magnetic field around them whereas magnetic field of electromagnet is temporary.

Strength of an electromagnet depends on :

(i) The number of turns in the solenoid.

(ii) Strength of current flowing through the solenoid

(iii) Position of soft iron core within the solenoid.

Q.12 (a) Write three differences between ac and dc.

(b) State the frequency of ac supply in India and mention the potential difference between neutral and live wire in domestic circuit.

(c) How many times does ac change its direction in one second ? **[SAI-2013]**

Ans. (a) The difference between ac and dc are shown in the table below :

ac	dc
(i) It can be transmitted over long distance effectively	(i) It cannot be transmitted over long distance effectively.
(ii) It changes its direction at regular interval of time	(ii) It does not change direction
(iii) It is represented by : 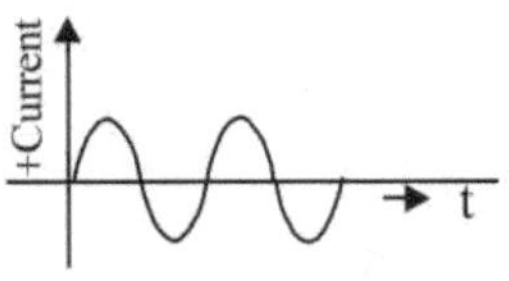	(iii) It is represented by : 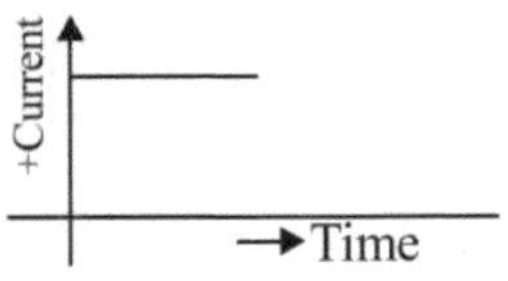

(b) 50 Hz, 220 V

(c) 100 times

CONCEPT APPLICATION LEVEL - III

SECTION-A

- **Multiple choice question with one correct answers**

Q.1 A vertical wire is carrying current in the upward direction. Then the direction of magnetic field in the west direction will be

(A) towards south (B) towards east (C) towards west (D) towards north

Q.2 A charge of 1.6×10^{-19} C enters in the magnetic field of 3 tesla normally with a velocity of 10^6 m/s. The force on the charge will be

(A) 4.8×10^{-12} N (B) 4.8×10^{-13} N (C) 4.8×10^{-14} N (D) 2×10^{-19} N

Q.3 The magnetic field due to an infinitely long wire carrying a current of 2A at a distance of 10 m from it is

(A) 2×10^{-8} T (B) 4×10^{-8} T (C) $4\pi \times 10^{-8}$ T (D) 2×10^{-6} T

Q.4 The device used for producing electric current is called a

(A) generator (B) galvanometer (C) ammeter (D) motor

Q.5 A circular loop is suspended in air as shown in figure. When the loop is seen from above, current flows anti clock wise and when seen from below, current flows clock wise. This loop behaves as a magnet. The N-pole of this magnetic is on.

(A) the upper face

(B) lower face

(C) the lower face if current is large

(D) None of these

Q.6 A student connects a coil of wire with a sensitive galvanometer as shown in figure. He will observe the deflection in the galvanometer if bar magnetic is

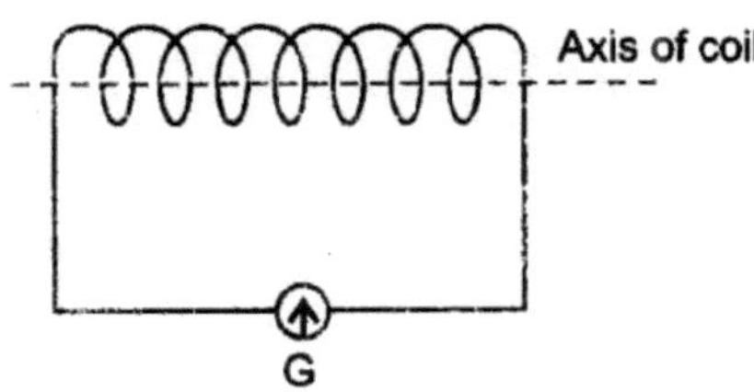

(A) placed near and parallel to the axis of the coil.

(B) placed near one of the faces of the coil and perpendicular to the axis of the coil.

(C) placed inside the coil.

(D) moved towards or away from the coil parallel to the axis of the coil.

Q.7 Which of the following statements is incorrect regarding magnetic filed lines.
(A) The direction of magnetic field at a point is taken to be the direction in which the north pole of a magnetic compass needle points.
(B) Magnetic field lines are closed curves
(C) If magnetic field lines are parallel and equidistant, they represent zero field strength
(D) Relative strength of magnetic field is shown by the degree of closeness of the field lines.

Q.8 Magnetic field lines determine
(A) the shape of the magnetic field
(B) only the direction of the magnetic field
(C) only the relative strength of the magnetic field
(D) both the direction and the relative strength of the magnetic field

Q.9 The magnetic field near a long straight wire is described by
(A) straight field lines parallel to the wire (B) straight field lines perpendicular to the wire
(C) concentric circle centred on the wire (D) radial field lines starting from the wire

Q.10 The phenomenon of electromagnetic induction is
(A) the process of charging a sphere
(B) the process of producing magnetic field in a coil
(C) the process of producing induced current in a coil whenever there is a relative motion between the coil and the magnet.
(D) the process of producing cooling effect

Q.11 Electric generator converts
(A) electrical energy into mechanical energy (B) mechanical energy into heat energy
(C) electrical energy into chemical energy (D) mechanical energy into electrical energy

Q.12 Electric motor converts
(A) mechanical energy into electric energy (B) mechanical energy into heat energy
(C) electrical energy into heat energy (D) electric energy into mechanical energy

Q.13 Potential difference between a live wire and the neutral wire in India is
(A) 200 volt (B) 150 volt (C) 210 volt (D) 220 V

Q.14 Magnetic field inside a intemetaly long solenoid carrying current is
(A) same at all points (B) minimum in the middle
(C) more at the ends than at the centre (D) found to increase from one end to the other

Q.15 Commercial electric motors do not use
(A) an electromagnetic to rotate armature (B) a soft
(C) aluminium, nickel, and iron (D) aluminium, nickel, cobalt and iron

Q.16 The frequency of direct current is
(A) zero (B) 50 Hz (C) 60 Hz (D) 100 Hz

Q.17 The frequency of household supply of a.c in India is
(A) zero (B) 50 Hz (C) 60 Hz (D) 100 Hz

Q.18 Who invented generator?
(A) Oersted (B) Coulomb (C) Rutherford (D) Michael Faraday

Q.19 The most important safety device or method used for protecting electrical appliances from short circuiting or overloading is
(A) earthing (B) use of stabilizers (C) use of electric meter (D) use of fuse

Q.20 To convert AC generator to DC generator
(A) slip rings and brushes must be used (B) split ring type commutator must be used
(C) rectangular wire loop is to be used (D) stronger magnetic field is to used

Q.21 Figure shows the magnetic field lines between the two faces A and B of two bar magnets.

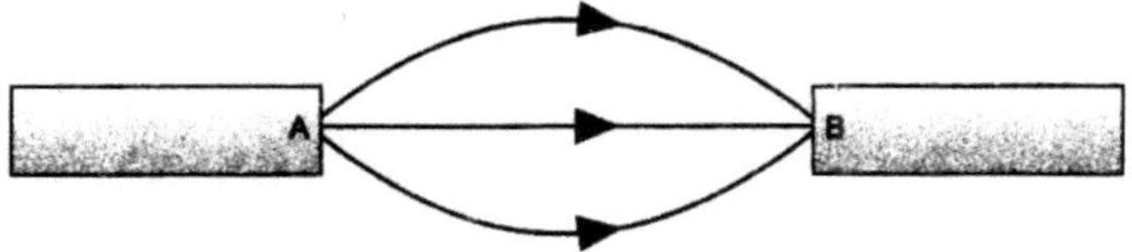

(A) Both faces A and B of two bar magnets are North poles
(B) Both faces A and B of two bar magnets are South poles
(C) Face A is South pole, while face B is North pole
(D) Face A is North pole, while face B is South pole

Q.22 Same amount of current flows in the same direction along the two parallel conductors separated by a small distance.
(A) both conductors attract each other
(B) both conductors repel each other
(C) conductors neither attract each other nor repel each other
(D) both conductors rotates about their axis

Q.23 When an electric current flows through a long solenoid, magnetic field is set up in and around the solenoid.
(A) magnetic field inside the solenoid is non-uniform and weak
(B) magnetic field outside the solenoid is uniform and strong
(C) magnetic field inside the solenoid increases as we move towards the ends of the solenoid
(D) magnetic field of solenoid resembles the magnetic field of the bar magnet

Q.24 Magnetic field produced at the centre of a current carrying circular wire is
(A) directly proportional to the square of the radius of the circular wire
(B) directly proportional to the radius of the circular wire
(C) inversely proportional to the square of the radius of the circular wire
(D) inversely proportional to the radius of the circular wire.

Q.25 The basic difference between an AC generator and a DC generator is that
(A) AC generator has slip ring while the DC generator has a split ring type commutator
(B) DC generator will generate a higher voltage
(C) AC generator will generate a higher voltage
(D) AC generator has an electromagnet while a DC generator has permanent magnet.

Q.26 Two parallel conductor carrying current in the opposite directions.
(A) repel each others
(B) attract each other
(C) sometimes attract and sometimes repel each other
(D) none of these

Q.27 Force acting on a stationary charge Q in the magnetic field B is
(A) BQv (B) BQ/v (C) Bv/Q (D) zero

Q.28 A current carrying conductor placed perpendicular to the magnetic field experience a force. The displacement of this conductor in the magnetic field can be increased by
(A) decreasing the magnetic field (B) decreasing the current in the conductor
(C) increasing the magnetic field (D) decreasing the length of the conductor

Q.29 A conductor of length 50 cm, carrying current of 0.1 A, when placed perpendicular to direction of magnetic field 0.2 T experience force.
(A) 1.0 N (B) 0.1 N (C) 0.01 N (D) 0.001 N

Q.30 A conductor of length ℓ, carrying current of 0.2 A, when placed perpendicular to direction of magnetic field 0.4 T experience of force of 0.08 N. The length ℓ of the conductor is
(A) 10 cm (B) 40 cm (C) 50 cm (D) 100 cm

Q.31 A charge particle having charge 3.2×10^{-19} C is travelling with a speed of 1.0×10^{6} ms^{-1}. When it passes perpendicular to the magnetic field 0.4 T, the force experienced by it is
(A) 12.8×10^{-13} N (B) 1.28×10^{-13} N (C) 19.2×10^{-15} N (D) 1.92×10^{-15} N

Q.32 A charged particle having charge 1.6×10^{-19} C travels with a speed of 3.2×10^{6} ms^{-1} in a direction parallel to the direction of magnetic field 0.04 T. The force experienced by the particle is
(A) 2.0×10^{-14} N (B) 0.2×10^{-14} N (C) zero (D) 4.0×10^{-14} N

Q.33 When North pole of magnetic approaches a circular coil, then the current in the coil as seen from the magnet side is
(A) clockwise (B) anticlockwise (C) parallel (D) antiparallel

Q.34 A vertical wire carries a current upward. The magnetic field at north of the wire will be directed
(A) upward (B) eastward (C) westward (D) northward

Q.35 The magnetic flux is expressed in
(A) dyne (B) Oersted (C) Gauss (D) Weber

SECTION-B

- **Multiple choice question with one or more than one correct answers**

Q.1 The magnetic field lines have which of the following properties

(A) They are closed curves (B) Field lines don't intersect

(C) The are discontinuous (D) None of the above

Q.2 Magnetic field due to a current carrying solenoid on its axis is

(A) constant (B) variable (C) $B = \mu_0 nI$ (D) At ends $B = \frac{\mu_0 nI}{2}$

Q.3 Lenz's law explains the following

(A) direction of induced emf (B) direction of induced current

(C) conservation of energy (D) direction of induced magnetic field

SECTION-C

- **Assertion & Reason**

Instructions: In the following questions as Assertion (A) is given followed by a Reason (R). Mark your responses from the following options.

(A) Both Assertion and Reason are true and Reason is the correct explanation of 'Assertion'

(B) Both Assertion and Reason are true and Reason is not the correct explanation of 'Assertion'

(C) Assertion is true but Reason is false

(D) Assertion is false but Reason is true

Q.1 **Assertion:** A magnetic field is produced around a current carrying conductor.

Reason: This was experimentally proved by Oersted.

Q.2 **Assertion:** A charged particle (+vely charged) when enters normally to the magnetic field follows an elliptical path

Reason: The magnetic force on the charged particle provides the necessary centripetal force

SECTION-D

- **Match the following (one to one)**

Column-I and **column-II** contains **four** entries each. Entries of column-I are to be matched with some entries of column-II. Only One entries of column-I may have the matching with the same entries of column-II and one entry of column-II Only one matching with entries of column-I

Q.1

	Column I		Column II
(A)	$B=\frac{\mu_o}{4\pi}\frac{2I}{r}$	(P)	Force on a charged particle q moving with a velocity v in a magnetic field
(B)	$F = Bqv\sin\theta$	(Q)	Fleming's left-hand rule
(C)	Force on a current carrying conductor in a magnetic field	(R)	$r=\frac{mv}{qB}$
(D)	Radius of the circular path of a charged particle in a magnetic field	(S)	Magnetic field due to an infinitely long wire.

- **Match the following (one to many)**

Column-I and **column-II** contains **four** entries each. Entries of column-I are to be matched with some entries of column-II. One or more than one entries of column-I may have the matching with the same entries of column-II and one entry of column-II may have one or more than one matching with entries of column-I

Q.2

	Column-I *(Devices)*		Column-II *(Components used in given devices)*
(A)	Electric motor	(P)	Current carrying conductors
(B)	Electromagnet	(Q)	Magnets
(C)	AC Generator	(R)	Commutator
(D)	Loud speakers	(S)	Brushes

ANSWER KEY

Knowledge Based Questions:

1.	C	2.	C	3.	C	4.	B	5.	A	6.	B	7.	A
8.	B	9.	C	10.	A								

CONCEPT APPLICATION LEVEL - III

SECTION-A

Q.1	A	Q.2	B	Q.3	B	Q.4	A	Q.5	A	Q.6	D	Q.7	C
Q.8	D	Q.9	C	Q.10	C	Q.11	D	Q.12	D	Q.13	D	Q.14	A
Q.15	D	Q.16	A	Q.17	B	Q.18	D	Q.19	D	Q.20	B	Q.21	D
Q.22	B	Q.23	D	Q.24	D	Q.25	A	Q.26	B	Q.27	A	Q.28	C
Q.29	C	Q.30	D	Q.31	B	Q.32	C	Q.33	B	Q.34	C	Q.35	D
Q.36	D												

SECTION-B

Q.1 AB Q.2 ACD Q.3 ABC

SECTION-C

Q.1 A Q.2 D

SECTION-D

Q.1 (A)-(S), (B)-(P),(C)-(Q),(D)-(R) Q.2 (A)-(PQRS), (B)-(P), (C)-(QS), (D)-(PQ)

3 SOURCES OF ENERGY

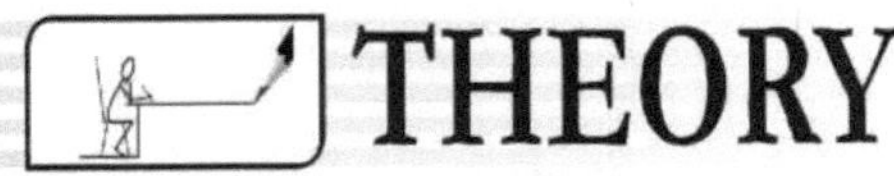

THEORY

3.1 INTRODUCTION

Energy is an essential requirement of our life. No activity in our daily life can be performed without the use of energy. Energy in one or the other form has been used by a man since long time. For example, energy is required to undertake the activities like cooking food, heating water, heating rooms, glowing bulbs and tubes in our homes. Energy is also needed to operate radios, televisions, computers washing machines, refrigerators, ovens, scooters, buses, trucks, aeroplanes, ships, motorboats, rockets etc. Energy is needed to operate machines in factories to produce goods.

Thus , we can say that energy is required in every field. Usually, energy in the form of fuel and electricity is used to carry out all the activities mentioned above. Energy can be derived from various sources. However, the sun is the ultimate source of all forms of energy.

Knowledge Based Questions:

1. Which of the following is renewable source of energy?
   (A) Coal (B) Natural gas (C) Sun light (D) Uranium
2. The source of energy in a hydro power station is:
   (A) Coal (B) Water (C) Sunlight (D) Diesel
3. The radiations that are responsible for the heating effect of solar radiations are:
   (A) Visible radiations (B) X-rays
   (C) Ultra-violet radiations (D) Infra-red-radiations
4. A renewable source of energy is
   (A) exhaustible (B) non-replenishable (C) limited (D) inexhaustible
5. Which one of the following is not used as a cooking fuel:
   (A) Compressed natural gas (B) Biogas
   (C) Liquified petroleum gas (D) Coal
6. Biogas is made mainly of_____________ gas.
   (A) CH_4 (B) CO_2 (C) H_2SO_4 (D) N_2
7. Which of the following is a product of a biogas plant.
   (A) Fertiliser (B) Nutritious food (C) Cleaning detergent (D) Poisonous gas
8. Which of the following is not an example of a biomass energy source:
   (A) Wood (B) Gobar gas (C) Nuclear energy (D) Coal
9. Most of the sources of energy use by us represent stored solar energy. Which of the following is not ultimately derived from the Sun's energy:
   (A) geothermal energy (B) wind energy (C) nuclear energy (D) biomass
10. Which of the following materials is used to make a photovoltaic solar cell:
    (A) Silicon (B) Carbon (C) Lead (D) Aluminium

3.2 DIFFERENT SOURCES OF ENERGY

Anything which supplies useful energy to us is carry out the various activities like cooking, heating, lighting, running buses, cars, trains, scooters, motorcycles, aeroplanes, ships, operating many devices like TV, radio, tape recorder, computer etc. is known as a source of energy.

There are many sources of energy like plants, wind , water , coal, petroleum, natural gas, gobar gas or bio-gas etc. However, all these sources of energy derive energy from the sun.

It is estimated that the sun is about 5 billion years old and continue to shine for another 5 billion year. So this source of energy will be available to us for a very - very long period of time. **The Sun is the ultimate source of all forms of energy available on the earth.**

Sources of Energy :

(i) Plants, wind, water, coal, petroleum, natural gas, gobar gas or bio-gas.

(ii) Solar Energy + Air $\rightarrow$ Wind Energy

(iii) Photosynthesis is the process of making food by leaves of plants using sunlight.

This can be illustrated as follows:

Solar energy heats up the surface of the earth and the air around it. The hot air rises up and the cool air from the surroundings rushes to occupy its space. This makes the air to move. Moving air is known as wind and possesses kinetic energy. Thus, solar energy + Air $\rightarrow$ Wind energy.

Green leaves of plants make their food using sunlight (i.e. Sun's energy) by the process of photosynthesis. The energy stored in the food is known as chemical energy. The food eaten by a man or an animal provides him the muscular energy. This muscular energy is used to do work. In other words, muscular energy is converted into mechanical energy.

Thus, **Solar energy + Green leaves + Food (chemical energy) $\rightarrow$ Muscular energy $\rightarrow$ Mechanical energy (work).**

The Solar energy evaporates the water in oceans, rivers, lakes and ponds. The evaporated water is converted into clouds (having both kinetic energy and potential energy). These clouds after cooling give rain. The rain water flows through rivers and has kinetic energy. This water is stored in dams and hence possess potential energy. When this water is allowed to fall from some height, potential energy of water is converted into its kinetic energy. The kinetic energy of flowing water rotates the turbine of a generator. The generator in turn produces the hydro electricity or hydro electric power. Thus hydro electric energy is also derived from the solar energy.

Solar energy + H_2O $\rightarrow$ Clouds (K.E. + P.E.) $\rightarrow$ Rain (flowing water K.E.) $\rightarrow$ Hydro electricity (electrical energy).

Even the energy of fossil fuels like coal, petroleum and natural gas also available by the solar energy. Long years ago, plants and animals which had derived the energy from the sun in the form of food after their death were buried under the earth. Due to high temperature and pressure, the bio-mass of dead animals and plants was converted into the fossil fuels like coal, petroleum and natural gas. These fuels store chemical energy which is converted into heat energy when the fuel burns. This heat energy can be converted into mechanical energy with the help of heat engines. Moreover, the heat energy produced by burning the fuel is also used to produce electricity. Thus, we conclude that all forms of energy are derived from a single source the Sun.

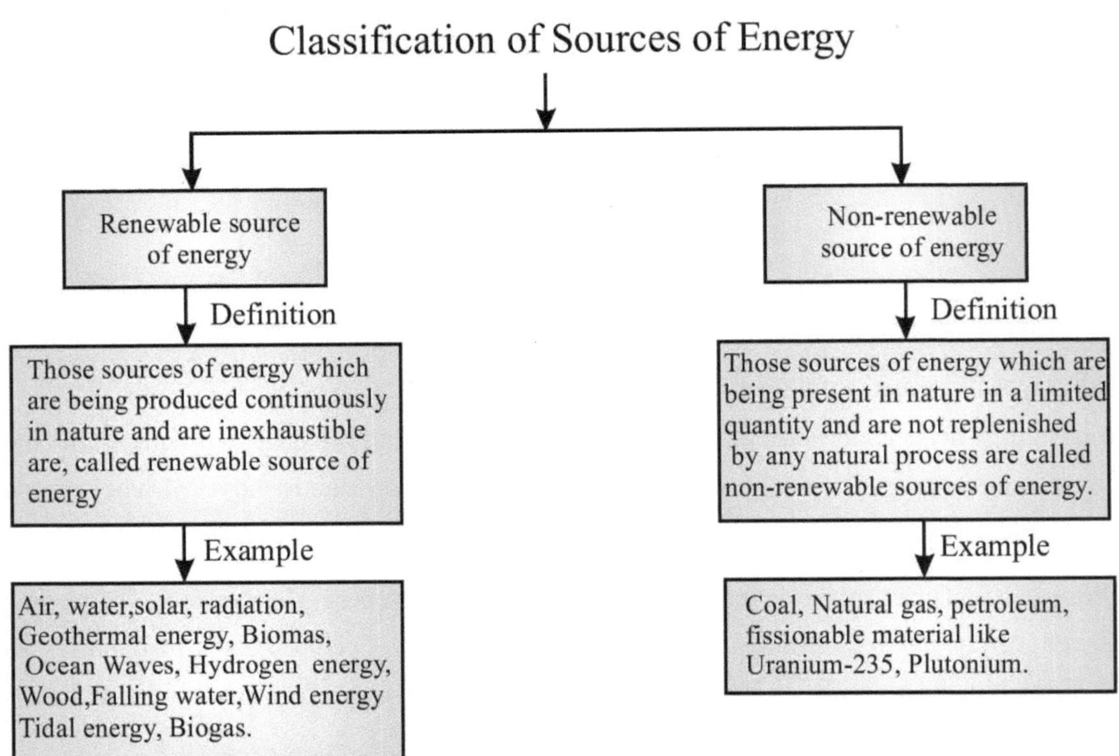

3.3 WHAT ARE CHARECTERISTICS OF A GOOD SOURCE OF ENERGY ?

A good source of energy should have the following characteristics.

(i) It should supply enough amount of useful energy.

(ii) It should be easily stored.

(iii) It should be easily transported.

(iv) It should occupy less space for storage.

(v) It should supply useful energy in a controlled manner.

(vi) It should be easily available or accessible.

(vii) It should be cheap i.e., it should be economical.

(viii) It should cause minimum environmental pollution.

Calorific value of a fuel is defined as the amount of heat energy released in joule or kilojoule by the complete burning of 1 gram fuel.

UNITS OF CALORIFIC VALUE :

(i) Calorific value of a fuel is expressed as joule /gram (Jg^{-1}) or kilojoule/g($kJ\ g^{-1}$).

(ii) Calorific value of gaseous fuel is expressed as kilocalorie/metre^3($kcal\ m^{-3}$).

Calorific values of different fuels are given below in the table.

Table: Calorific values of some fuels

Nature of fuel	Name of fuel	Calorific value (kJg^{-1})
Solid Fuels	Animal dung cake	8
	Wood	17
	Charcoal	33
	Coal	35
	Anthracite	37
Liquid fuels	Alcohol	30
	Diesel	45
	Kerosene oil	48
	Petrol	50
Gaseous fuels	Biogas	35-40
	LPG	55
	Hydrogen	150

$$\text{Calorific value of fuel} = \frac{\text{heat produced by burning fuel}}{\text{mass of fuel}}$$

$$= \frac{Q}{m} = \frac{m_1c_1t + m_2c_2t}{m} = \frac{(m_1c_1 + m_2c_2)t}{m} \quad (\because \Delta H = mc\Delta T)$$

3.4 CONVENTIONAL (NON-RENEWABLE) SOURCES OF ENERGY :

The sources of energy which are exhaustible (i.e., which can be finished) and have been formed in nature long years ago are known as conventional sources of energy or non- renewable sources of energy. Fossil fuels are the examples of conventional sources of energy.

3.5 FOSSIL FUELS

The combustible substances formed from the dead animals and plants which were buried deep under the surface of the earth over millions of years are called fossil energy sources or fossil fuels. At present, a major part of our energy requirement is being supplied by fossil fuels.

Examples of fossil fuels : Coal, petroleum and natural gas.

3.5.1 COAL

Coal is a fossil fuel and the major source of energy. It is a black material which is a mixture of carbon and compounds of carbon containing oxygen, nitrogen and sulphur.

Uses of coal

(i) Coal is used for cooking food and heating water.

(ii) Coal is used in thermal power plants to produce electricity

(iii) Coal is used by black smiths to melt iron and other metals

(iv) Coal is used in brick kilns and other industries.

The total estimated resources of coal in India are placed now around 148790 million tonnes, but the mineable reserves may amount to about 60000 million tones. The total lignite reserves, found mostly at Neyveli in South Arcot district of Tamil Nadu, are contains 3300 million tones of which 1900 million tones are in the proved category. Annual production of coal including lignite was around 437 million tonnes (2006-07) According to the present and future demand projections, the coal reserves in India would be just sufficient for about 130 years.)

The carbon contents calorific values and main application of these fuels are given in the table below:

S.N.	Fuel	Percentage Carbon	Calorific value k cal/kg	Main applications
1	Wood	50	4000 to 4500	Domestic fuel
2	Peat	57	4125 to 5400	Used when there is deficieny of high rank coals.
3	Lignite	67	6500 to 7100	Used for steam generation in thermal power plants and for the production of producer gas
4	Bituminous	83	8000 to 8500	Used for steam generation in thermal plants and for domestic heating. It is also used for making coal gas and metallurgical coke.
5	Anthracite	93	8650 to 8700	Used in metallurgical purposes where no smokes and high calorific heat is desired.It is also used in household purposes and steam rising.

DESTRUCTIVE DISTILLATION OF COAL

The process of strong heating of coal in closed retorts in the absence of air is called destructive distillation of coal.

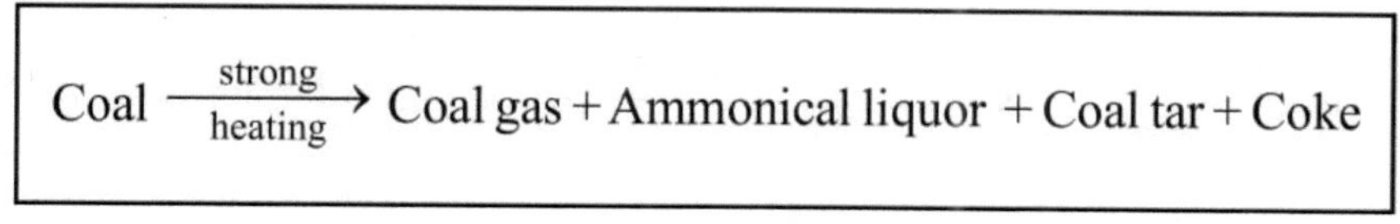

$$\text{Coal} \xrightarrow[\text{heating}]{\text{strong}} \text{Coal gas} + \text{Ammonical liquor} + \text{Coal tar} + \text{Coke}$$

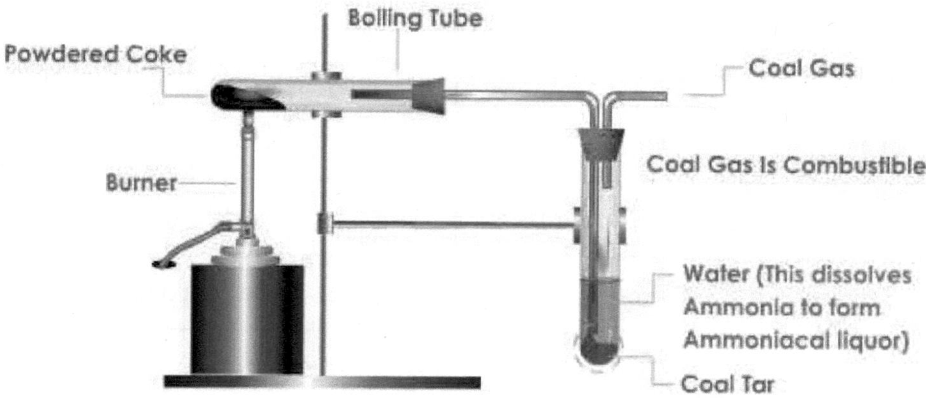

3.5.2 PETROLEUM

Petroleum is derived from two words **petra** (in greek) = **rock** and **oleum** = **oil**. Thus, petroleum means **rock oil**.

The average composition of petroleum is as follows.

1. $C \rightarrow 80$ to 87% 2. $H \rightarrow 11.1$ to 15% 3. $N \rightarrow 0.1$ to 3.5%
4. $O_2 \rightarrow 0.1$ to 0.9% 5. $S \rightarrow 0.4$ to 0.9%

3.5.2.1 NATURE AND COMPOSITION OF PETROLEUM

Petroleum in general is a mixture of natural hydrocarbons (compounds consisting of carbon and hydrogen) in the form of gas, liquid or solid found in rocks. In common use, the liquid form of hydrocarbons is called petroleum. It is a greyish-black viscous liquid .

3.5.2.2 REFINING OF PETROLEUM

Petroleum which exists in the rocks of the earth is in a crude state. This crude oil is a mixture of gaseous, liquid and solid hydrocarbons. Some of the hydrocarbons are the most volatile (i.e flying off like vapours) and some are the least volatile. Thus, various hydrocarbons present in the petroleum are to be separated and purified.

The process of separating and purifying the various hydrocarbons, the constituents of petroleum by fractional distillation taking into account their different boiling points is called refining of petroleum. The product of petroleum are petroleum gas, petrol, kerosene oil, diesel oil, lubricating oil, paraffin wax and bitumen (Asphalt). Out of these products, lubricating oil, paraffin wax and bitumen or asphalt are not combustible.

Sr. No.	Product or fraction	Composition or number of carbon atoms	Boiling range	Uses (°C)
1	Petroleum gas	$C_1 - C_4$	Below 10°	Gaseous fuel, LPG.
2	Petrol	$C_5 - C_{12}$	40° to 220°	Motor and Aviation fuel.
3	Kerosene oil	$C_{12} - C_{16}$	150°to 300°	Fuel for tractors and kerosene stove, jet engine
4	Diesel oil	$C_{15} - C_{18}$	300°to 400°	Fuel for diesel engine and ships
5	Lubricating oil	$C_{16} - C_{40}$	Above 400°	Lubricants for machinery
6	Paraffin wax	C_{20} onward	Non - volatile solid	Candles, ointments
7	Bitumen	$C_{12} - C_{16}$	Residue	Road making

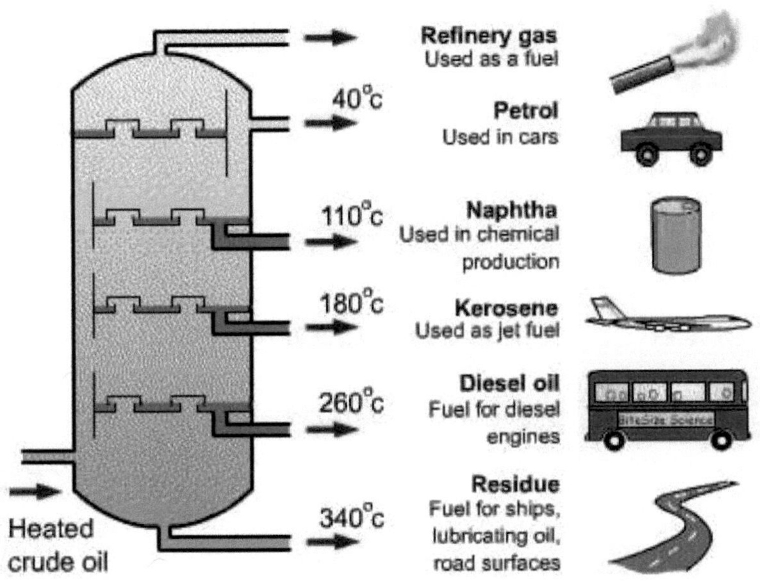

3.5.2.3 PETROLEUM GAS

Petroleum gas is a mixture of three hydrocarbons i.e. butane of petroleum gas (C_4H_{10}), propane (C_3H_8) and ethane (C_2H_6) .However, the main constituent is butane. All these constituents of petroleum gas are in gaseous state at room temperature. They burn easily and hence act as a source of heat energy. Out of these gases, butane can be easily liquefied under pressure. Petroleum gas which is liquefied under pressure is known as liquefied petroleum gas (L.P.G.)

3.5.2.4 LIQUEFIED PETROLEUM GAS (L.P.G.)

Liquefied Petroleum gas (L.P.G.) consists mainly of butane with small amount of propane and ethane under pressure. This gas is filled in metal cylinders and used as a domestic fuel. Liquefied Petroleum gas (L.P.G.) is highly inflammable. Any leakage of this gas can be dangerous. So to detect the leakage of LPG, some traces of sulphur compound (ethyl mercapton = C_2H_5SH) giving a peculiar detectable smell is added in it.

(i) **Petroleum Refineries in India :** Digboi (Assam), Barauni (Bihar), Haldia (West-Bengal), Mathura (U.P.), Koyali (Gujarat), Trombay, Cochin, Chennai (Madras) and Visakhapatnam.

(ii) The main constituent of LPG is butane.

(iii) Main constituent of CNG is methane.

3.5.3 NATURAL GAS

Natural gas is another source of heat energy. It is a fossil fuel. It is also called 'Marsh gas'.

Composition: It mainly consists of methane (about 97%) and small quantities of ethane and propane.

Constituents	Methane CH_4	Ethane C_2H_6	Propane C_3H_8	Butane C_4H_{10}	Pentane, H_2, CO, CO_2 and higher hydrocarbons
Percentage	88.50%	5.50%	3.70%	1.80%	0.50%

3.5.3.1 COMPRESSED NATURAL GAS (CNG)

When natural gas in liquid form is subjected to high pressure, we get compressed natural gas (CNG).

3.5.3.2 USE OF NATURAL GAS AND CNG

(i) Natural gas and compressed Natural gas are used as fuel for scooters, buses and trucks.

(ii) Natural gas is used for cooking food and heating water

(iii) Natural gas is used to produce electricity.

(iv) Natural gas is used for manufacturing fertilizers.

3.5.4 DISADVANTAGES OF FOSSIL FUELS

Burning of fossil fuels has the followings disadvantages.

(i) Burning of fossil fuels give rise to smoke, which pollutes our environment. The air pollution is harmful to human health, animals and plants.

(ii) Burning of fossil fuels give rise to harmful gases like carbon-dioxide, carbon-monoxide, sulphur dioxide and nitrogen dioxide.

(iii) Gases produced due to the burning of fossil fuel give rise to acid rain after reacting with water vapours in air. For example, when carbon dioxide, sulphur dioxide and nitrogen dioxide combine with water vapours in the atmosphere, acids are formed as follows:

Carbon dioxide + Water $\rightarrow$ Carbonic acid

Sulphur dioxide + Water $\rightarrow$ Sulphuric acid

Nitrogen dioxide + Water $\rightarrow$ Nitric acid

These acids come down to the earth in form of rain. The rain containing acids is known as acid rain. Acid rain decreases the fertility of the soil, destroys forest, makes adverse effect on the buildings and human beings and pollute water resources.

(iv) Burning of fossil fuels do not produce much heat.

(v) Burning of fossil fuels leads to global warming.

WHY ARE WE LOOKING AT ALTERNATE SOURCES OF ENERGY ?

Inspite of number of disadvantages of fossil fuels, we mainly depend upon these fuels for our energy requirements. The growing demand for the energy to run industries and vehicles had accelerated the rate of extraction of the fossil fuels. However, the deposits of fossil fuels are limited in quantity and the formation of these fuel takes a very long period of time. Therefore, these sources of fuels can be completely finished or exhausted in future. Hence, every effort is being made to use and extract the fossil fuels effectively to conserve these sources of energy. Besides this, we look at alternate sources of energy like the sun, the wind the ocean etc. to reduce the pressure on the use of fossil fuels or conventional sources of energy. New techniques have been discovered to produce electricity by burning fossil fuels. Thermal power plant produces electricity by burning the fossil fuels like coal and oil.

3.6 THERMAL POWER PLANT

A thermal power plant produces electricity by burning the fossil fuels (i.e., coal or oil). A schematic diagram of a thermal power plant is shown in figure .

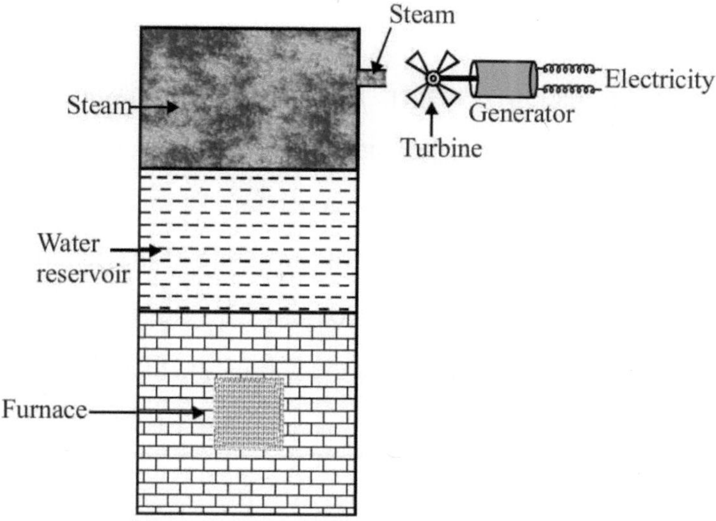

(i) **A power plant in which the heat required to make steam to drive turbines (to make electricity) is obtained by burning fuels (coal, oil, or gas) is called thermal power plant.**

(ii) **Note :**

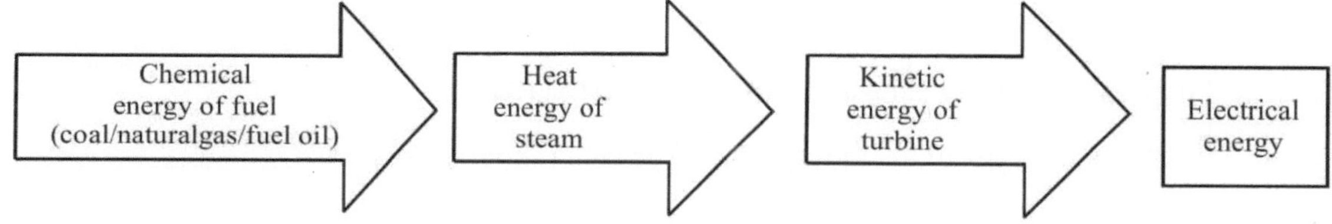

3.6.1 WORKING OF A THERMAL POWER PLANT

Coal or oil is burnt in a furnace to produce heat energy. This heat energy is used to boil water in a reservoir. The steam produced in the water reservoir is allowed to fall on a turbine under high pressure. The steam falling on the turbine rotates it with high speed. A generator or dynamo connected with the turbine through an axle rotates with high speed and produces electricity. In fact, the mechanical energy (kinetic energy of rotation) of the turbine is converted into electrical energy. The electricity so produced is transmitted to distant places through transmission wires. Thermal power plants are usually set up near coal fields or oil fields. This is because the fuel like coal or oil used in a thermal power plant is easily available and there is no problem in transporting the fuel.

Disadvantage : The burning of coal or oil in a thermal power plant causes environmental pollution and global warming.

3.7 HYDRO POWER OR HYDRO ELECTRIC POWER PLANT

Flowing water is the major source of energy. The electricity produced by the flowing water is known as hydro-electric power . A plant used to produce hydro-electric power is known as hydro-electric power plant.

A dam or water reservoir is made over a river . The energy of stored water in the dam is potential energy. The water in a dam is allowed to fall on the water wheel or turbine. As a result of this the turbine rotates whose axle is connected with the armature of the generator . The armature of the generator rotates within two poles of a strong magnet. The rotation of the armature of the generator between two poles of a strong magnet gives rise to electric current or electricity. This electricity is transmitted to the sub- station through a transformer for further distribution to the houses and factories.

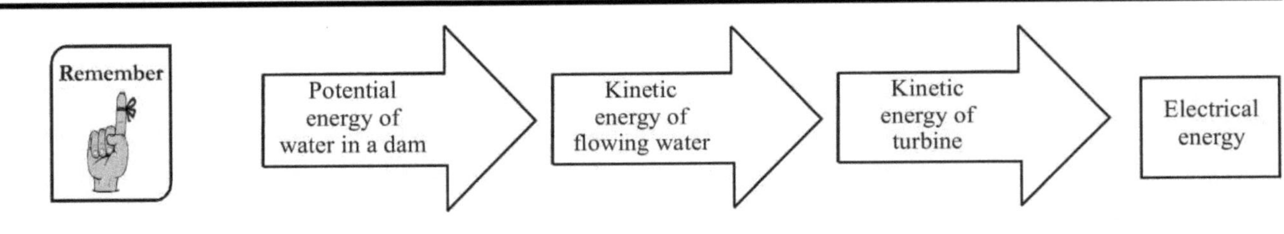

3.7.1 PRINCIPLE OF GENERATION OF HYDROELECTRICITY

Potential energy of water stored in a dam is converted into kinetic energy of the falling water. The water falls on the turbine, so kinetic energy of the flowing water is converted into the kinetic energy of the armature of the generator connected to the turbine. Then kinetic energy is converted into the electrical energy known as hydroelectricity.

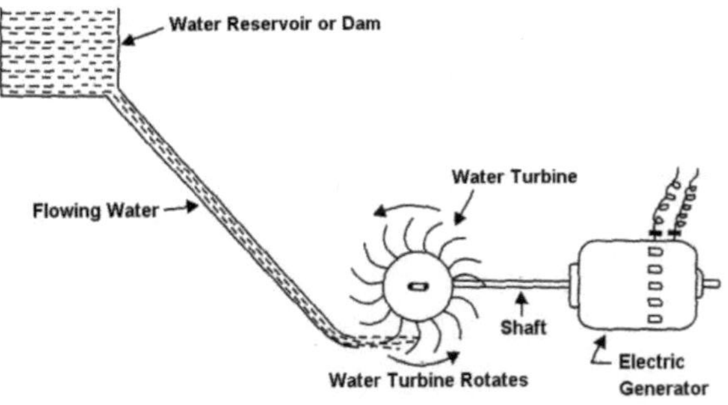

3.7.2 ADVANTAGES OF HYDROELECTRIC POWER

(i) Hydroelectric Power is pollution free.

(ii) Hydroelectric Power is dependable source of energy.

(iii) Lot of water is available in rivers, so the hydroelectric power is available free of cost. Money is spent only to construct dams and power stations.

3.7.3 DISADVANTAGES OF HYDROELECTRIC POWER

(i) Hydroelectric power is generated only near the rivers having water throughout the year. This electric power has to be carried to the substations for distribution to the houses and factories situated far off from the sites of hydro electric power stations. This is done through the transmission wires, so lot of money is to be spent on this process.

(ii) A large area of fertile land is submerged at the site of the dam constructed for tapping energy from the flowing water.

(iii) A large number of people residing near the site of a dam are dislocated. So, a lot of problems are to be faced in rehabilitating this population. That is why, there is a lot of opposition by the people around the site of dam for the construction of dam.

(iv) A large number of plants and wild life in the area of the dam is submerged in water. So, a large variety of flora (plants) and fauna (animals) is destroyed.

(v) Hydroelectric dams cannot be constructed everywhere, They are constructed mostly in hilly areas.

3.7.4 ADVANTAGES OF CONSTRUCTING DAMS OVER RIVERS

Dams are helpful to :

(i) control floods over rivers.

(ii) generate hydro electricity.

(iii) irrigate agriculture land.

(iv) develop water sports for recreation

(v) develop fishing zones.

Ultimate source of water energy/ hydro energy :

Water from oceans and lakes evaporates due to sunlight and goes into the atmosphere. These water returns back to the earth as rain water. Rain water or melted snow takes the form of river or dam water. The kinetic energy of this flowing water is used to produce electricity. Hence ultimate source of water energy is solar energy.

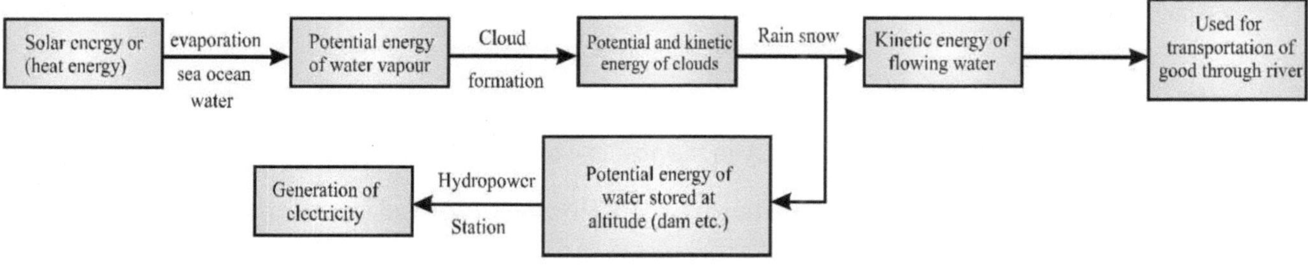

3.8 IMPROVEMENTS IN THE TECHNOLOGY FOR USING CONVENTIONAL SOURCES OF ENERGY

3.8.1 BIOMASS

Green leaves of plants manufacture their food using sunlight by a process called photosynthesis . In fact photosynthesis process converts solar energy into chemical energy. This chemical energy is stored in different parts of a plant in the form of biomass. Wood is a biomass which contains carbon and other combustible materials (i.e., cellulose and lignin). Any material containing carbon can be burnt in air to produce carbon-dioxide (CO_2) and energy in the form of heat energy i.e., it can be used as a fuel. Therefore, wood is used as the most conventional source of energy for household purposes and in industries.

(i) **The material contained in the bodies of plants and animals is called Biomass.**

(ii) **Biomass is a renewable sources of energy if more and more plants are grown periodically.**

3.8.2 USE OF WOOD AS A FUEL

Wood can be used for generating heat energy in the following ways :

(A) DIRECT METHOD

Firewood is burnt in traditional chulhas to generate heat for cooking food, heating water and warming rooms. Due to direct burning of wood, lot of smoke is produced which poses various problems like polluting the environment and hence causes serious health hazards. Moreover, complete combustion of wood does not take place, when wood is burnt directly and only small amount of heat is generated by burning huge quantity of wood. Thus, we conclude that direct method of burning wood is not suitable for generating good amount of heat energy.

(B) INDIRECT METHOD

When wood is heated indirectly in the absence of air, it is converted into charcoal. The process is known as destructive distillation of wood. However, charcoal is very expensive than the wood because 1 kg of wood produces only 250 g (0.25 kg) charcoal.

Charcoal is better source of heat energy than the wood itself. This is because :

(i) when charcoal burns it does not produce smoke. On the other hand when wood burns a lot of smoke is produced. Thus , burning of charcoal does not pollute the air, we inhale but burning of wood pollutes the air.

(ii) the heat energy produced by a given mass of charcoal is much higher than the heat energy produced by the equal mass of wood.

(iii) charcoal occupies less space, so no problem of storage.

(iv) charcoal is easily transported from one place to another.

(v) charcoal burns easily as compared to the wood.

$$\text{Wood} \xrightarrow[\text{in absence of air}]{\text{heat strongly}} \text{Charcoal + Volatile matter + Moisture}$$

DISADVANTAGES OF USING CHARCOAL AS A DOMESTIC FUEL

Although charcoal is clean and better source of heat energy but it is expensive fuel. Moreover, a lot of wood is needed to produce even a small amount of charcoal. So, huge amount of wood is required to produce charcoal for commercial purpose. It means, more and more trees are to be cut down for this purpose. It leads to deforestation which causes serious problems like soil erosion, floods, imbalance of eco-system etc. To avoid all these problems , it is not suggestive to use charcoal as a domestic fuel.

3.8.3 BIOGAS

Biogas is a mixture of various gases formed when the animal dung mixed with water is allowed to ferment (i.e. decompose) in the absence of air (or oxygen). Biogas is also called "gobar gas" as it is mostly obtained from the animals wastes. The animals and plants wastes contain large quantity of carbon compounds like carbohydrates, fats, proteins etc. The bacteria or anaerobic micro-organisms present in animal dung decompose these compounds into simple compounds like methane (CH_4) in the presence of water .

CONSTITUENTS OF BIOGAS

Biogas is a mixture of various gases such as methane (CH_4), carbon - dioxide (CO_2), hydrogen (H_2) and hydrogen sulphide (H_2S). The chief constituent of biogas is methane gas which is about 75% by volume. Methane is a very good fuel and acts as a source of heat energy because its heating capacity is high.

RAW MATERIALS USED FOR THE PREPARATION OF BIOGAS

The following materials are used for preparing biogas :

(i) Animal wastes like cow- dung, dung of buffaloes, horses etc. and poultry waste.

(ii) Human excreta.

(iii) Industrial and domestic wastes like fruits and vegetable wastes, willow dust, pulp etc.

BIOGAS PLANTS

The arrangement of producing biogas from animals dung, human excreta, industrial and domestic wastes is known as biogas plant. Based on mechanism, biogas plant can be of two types :

(A) FIXED-DOME TYPE BIOGAS PLANT

Construction : Fixed-dome type biogas plant is shown in figure. It consists of a well like underground tank made of bricks and cement. This tank is called digester and has inlet and outlet valves. The roof of the tank is dome shaped. A gas outlet pipe at the top of the dome is fitted. The dome of the digester acts as a storage tank of biogas.

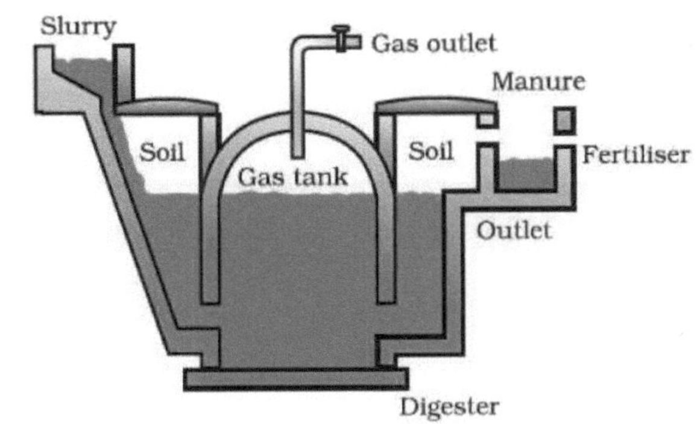

There is a mixing tank made above the ground level which is connected to the inlet valve of the digester through a slopping inlet chamber below the ground level. On the side of the digester, a rectangular tank called outlet chamber is constructed with bricks and cement. This outlet chamber is connected to the overflow tank which collects the used slurry.

Working : Animals - dung is mixed with water to make slurry in the mixing tank. This slurry enters the digester through the inlet chamber. The digester is filled partially with slurry so that enough space is left above it in the dome for the collection of biogas. The slurry in the digester is left for about two months for fermentation. Anaerobic micro organisms are responsible for this action As a result of fermentation, biogas is collected in the dome, it exerts a large pressure on the slurry and forced it to go into the overflow tank through the outlet chamber. The biogas is taken out from the dome through a pipe and used for cooking food or heating water whenever required.

Once the biogas plant starts functioning, more and more slurry may be fed into the digester to get the continuous supply of biogas. The used slurry collected in the overflow tank is rich in nitrogen and phosphorous which are essential for the growth of crops and plants. Hence this used slurry can be used as manure.

(B) FLOATING GAS HOLDER TYPE BIOGAS PLANT

Construction. It consists of a well shaped tank inside the ground called digester. Digester is divided into two chambers with a partition wall (T). A drum shaped gas holder made of steel in the inverted position over the mouth of the digester acts as a storage tank for biogas. This tank moves up and down over the slurry in the digester tank and hence this gas plant is called floating gas holder type. The motion of the drum is controlled by a pipe.

Mixing tank is connected to the digester with the help of the inlet pipe. The overflow tank used to collect the used slurry is also connected by a pipe. The biogas collected in the floating tank is taken out with a pipe having a valve.

Working : Animals - dung and water in equal proportion are mixed in the mixing tank. The slurry so prepared is fed to the digester through the inlet pipe. It is left for a month and so in the digester. The fermentation of the slurry takes place in the digester and biogas produced is collected in the floating steel tank.

When enough amount of biogas is collected in the tank, it moves up. The pressure of gas over the slurry begins to increase when the steel tank stops rising beyond a certain limit. The large pressure of biogas pushes the slurry into the overflow tank through the outlet pipe. The gas collected in the tank is taken out through a pipe for cooking food and heating water.

The slurry collected in the overflow tank is used as manure as it contains nutrients like nitrogen and phosphorous which are essential for the growth of crops and plants.

More slurry is added into the digester tank to get the continuous supply of biogas for daily use.

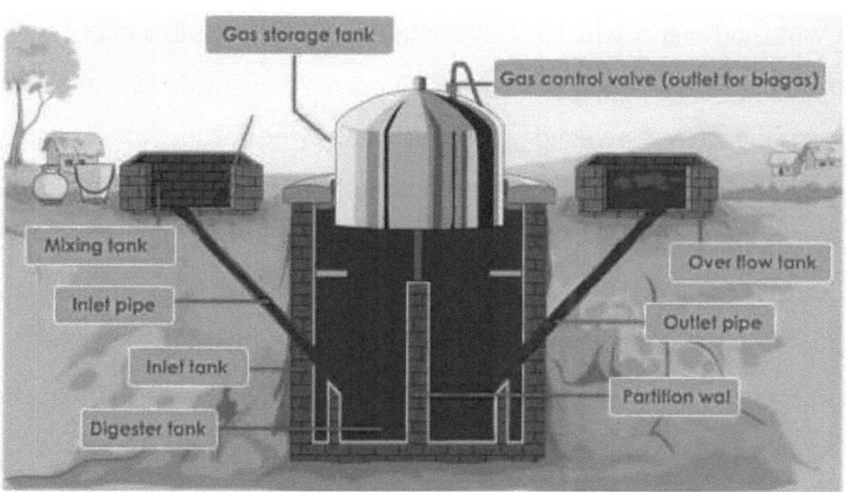

ADVANTAGES OF USING BIOGAS

Biogas is used for cooking food and heating water. It is a good source of energy because

(i) biogas does not produce smoke during burning and hence there is no air pollution.

(ii) it is a cheaper source of energy

3.8.4 HYDROGEN FUEL

Hydrogen has been recognized as a potential source of heat energy. When hydrogen is produced from renewable sources such as hydro (i.e., water), solar and wind energy, it becomes a renewable source of heat energy (i.e., fuel).

USES OF HYDROGEN AS A FUEL

(i) A mixture of hydrogen and carbon monoxide is burnt as a fuel for cooking food and heating water.

(ii) Hydrogen is used as a fuel to run vehicles.

(iii) Liquid hydrogen is used as a fuel in space ships or space crafts as it occupies less space.

ADVANTAGES OF USING HYDROGEN AS A FUEL

(i) Burning of hydrogen produces very large amount of heat energy.

(ii) Burning of hydrogen creates less air pollution.

DISADVANTAGES OF HYDROGEN AS A SOURCE OF ENERGY

(i) When hydrogen burns with oxygen, the reaction is explosive in nature. So using hydrogen as a source of energy is full of risk. As a result, hydrogen is not used as a domestic fuel.

(ii) Hydrogen cannot be stored and managed easily by a common man.

(iii) Hydrogen cannot be transported easily as it may explode during transportation.

(iv) Hydrogen is an expensive fuel.

3.9 WIND ENERGY

The blowing wind had energy which is called wind energy. Wind is associated with kinetic energies. Cause of wind to blow : Solar energy is responsible for the blowing of the wind. The intensity of sun rays is much more stronger near the equator of the earth than in the polar regions due to which the air near the surface of the earth in equatorial regions becomes quite hot. The hot air, being lighter, rises upward. The coolest air from the polar regions of the earth starts flowing towards the equatorial regions of the earth to fill the space vacated by the hot rising air. This flow of air from one place to another constitutes wind. The following three factors are responsible for blowing of wind.

1. The uneven heating of equatorial region and polar region of earth by sun rays.
2. Rotation of earth.
3. Local conditions.

3.9.1 USES OF WIND ENERGY

1. It is used to propel sail boats in lakes, rivers and seas.
2. It is used to operate water pumps to draw underground water.
3. It is used to drive windmills. They are used in water-lighting pumps and flour mills.
4. It is used to produce electricity.
5. The airplane makes use of wind energy, gliders depend totally on the wind energy.
6. Children and men used wind energy to move kites in space.

3.9.2 WIND MILL

A windmill is a machine, which works with the energy of blowing air or wind. It consists of large blades to catch the wind. When the wind strikes against these blades, they start rotating. The motion can then be passed on the other connected parts and is used to do useful work. A windmill consists of a system of big blades (or vanes) capable of rotating about a horizontal axis. The system of vanes is mounted on the top of a high tower. Its working is based on the transformation of kinetic energy of wind into the rotational energy of the blade.

The system of blades is connected to one end of the rod called shaft. The other end of the shaft is connected to a pump rod in case of water pump. This end is bent in form of inverted V and is connected to the free end of the pump rod of the water pump. When the wind blows, it rotates the blades of the windmill. The shaft turning about its axis rotates the crank. The rotation of the crank moves the piston rod of the water pump up and down and draws water from the well.

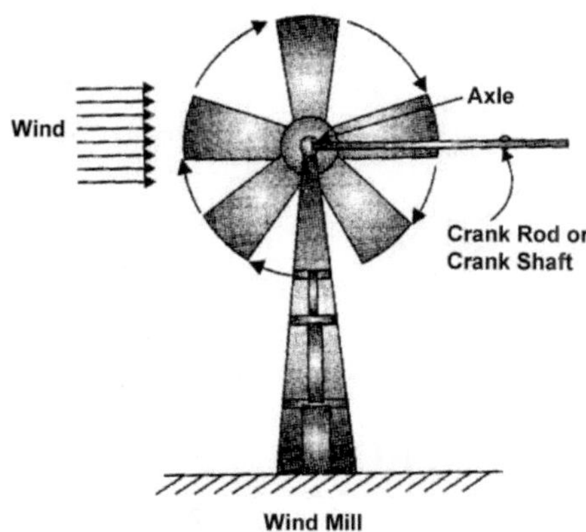

Wind Mill

3.9.3 APPLICATION OF WIND MILL

(A) Windmill to operate flourmill :

It is similar to one used to grind grains by suitable arrangements of toothed wheel & shafts. The other end of the shaft is connected to a toothed wheel. Grinding arrangement of flour mill has a fixed mill stone A and another heavy mill stone B. B is capable of rotating by a shaft rod (W2) having a toothed wheel (W2). The wheel (W1) is coupled with the wheel (W2) such that the rotation of wheel (W1) about a horizontal axis rotates the wheel (W2) about a vertical axis. The wheel (W1) rotates as the shaft (W1) connected to blades rotates due to rotation of blades of windmill. Thus the kinetic energy of wind by virtue of this motion rotates the windmill which in turn operates a flourmill and is able to grind grains.

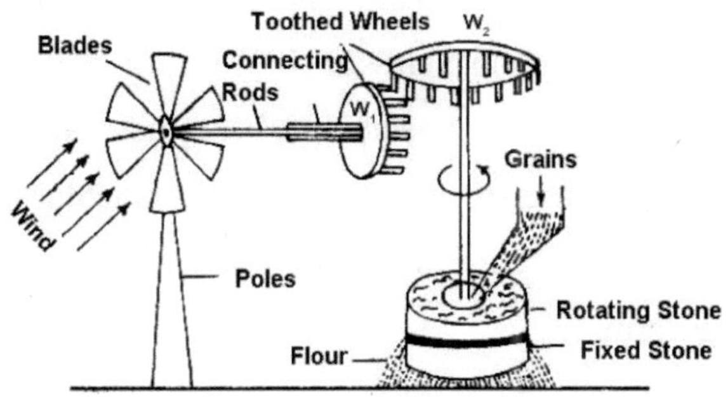

(B) Wind generator :

A modern generator, which is used to generate electricity by using wind energy is wind generator. When the fast moving wind strikes the blades of wind turbine, then the wind turbine startsrotating continuously. The coil of a small electric generator is attached to the shaft of wind turbine. So when the wind starts rotating and generates electricity. The electricity generated by a single wind turbine is quite small. So, in order to generate a large amount of electricity, a large amount of wind turbines are erected over a big area of land. Such a set-up of having a large number of wind turbines working at a place to generate electrical energy on a large scale is called a wind energy farm.

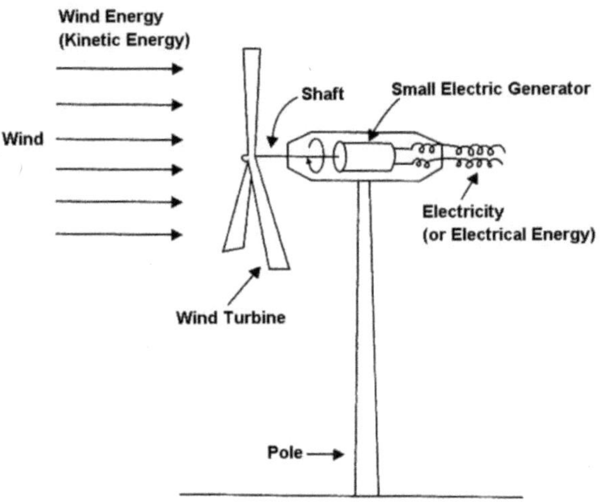

3.9.4 ADVANTAGES OF WIND ENERGY

(i) Wind energy produces no smoke and no harmful gases. So this form of energy is pollution free or environment-friendly.

(ii) Wind energy is free of cost and hence devices operated by wind energy are economical.

(iii) This source of energy is a renewable source of energy and is available for all times to come under favourable conditions.

3.9.5 LIMITATIONS OF WIND ENERGY

(i) We cannot depend upon wind energy as it is available only when air is in motion. The appliances or machines operating with wind energy stop working as soon as wind stops. The minimum speed of wind to operate generator to produce electricity is about 15 km/h. As soon as the speed of the wind becomes less then 15 km/h, the generator stops working

(ii) There are certain regions where wind is not available, so the use of wind energy is limited to certain places where wind is in plenty and blows most of the time.

(iii) Wind energy is not sufficient to operate very heavy machines.

(iv) Wind energy cannot be used to operate all types of machines.

(v) Wind mills are usually broken during storms and hence lot of money is spent for the maintenance of a wind energy farm.

Knowledge Enhancer

Wind energy is a renewable sourceof energy that colculates the total power in the wind. This energy is used to generate electricity or mechanical power. Here turbines are used which moves in wind power & converts the kineitc energy into mechanical power. This mechanical power is converted into electricity and acts as usefull power.

The wind energy formula is –

$$P = \frac{1}{2}\rho AV^3$$

Where P is power

ρ is air density

A is swept area of blades given

$$A = \pi r^2$$

Where r is radius of the blades, V is velocity of the wind.

Illustration 1

Caculate the power in the wind if the wind speed 15 m/s and blade length is 60 m.

Solution :

Given wind speed v = 15 m/s

blade length $l = 60$ m

Air density $\rho = 1.23$ kg/m^3

The area is given by, $A = \pi l^2$

$$A = \pi \times 60^2$$

$$A = 11309.7 \text{ m}^2$$

The wind power formula is given by

$$P = \frac{1}{2}\rho AV^3$$

$$P = \frac{1}{2} \times 1.23 \times 11309.7 \times 15^3 = 23.47 \text{ Mw}$$

Illustration 2

A wind turbimes travels with the speed is 20 m/s and has blade length of 30 m. Caculate the wind power.

Solution :

Given Wind speed v = 20 m/s

blade length $l = 30$ m

Air density $\rho = 1.23$ kg/m^3

Area $A = \pi l^2 = \pi \times 30^2 = 2827.43 \text{ m}^2$

The wind power formula is given by ,

$$P = \frac{1}{2}\rho AV^3$$

$$P = \frac{1}{2} \times 1.23 \times 2827.43 \times 20$$

$$P = 13.91 \text{ MW}$$

WIND ENERGY IN INDIA

In India, there are some high wind energy regions. They are

(i) Islands of Bay of Bengal and Arabian Sea.

(ii) Coastal parts of Gujarat, Tamil Nadu and Some parts of Rajasthan, Karnataka and Western parts of Madhya Pradesh. Govt. of India has proposed to install number of projects to tap the wind energy.

(iii) Wind power generation capacity in india has significantly increased in recent years. As of the end of March 2017 the total installed wind power capacity was 32.17 GW, mainly spread across the south, West and North regions. By the end of 2015, India has the fourth largest installed wind power capacity in the world. Tamil Nadu's wind power capacity is around 29% of India's total, which is the highest power generator in any state of India by wind energy.

3.10 ALTERNATIVE OR NON-CONVENTIONAL SOURCES OF ENERGY

With the development of technology and the invention of new devices and machines, the demand for the consumption of energy is increasing day by day. Our life has become more comfortable than our ancestors. This is because we have a good network of transport like scooters, three wheelers, buses, cars, trucks, aeroplanes, ships, etc., many devices like radios, televisions, VCRs, tape recorders, music systems for our entertainment, various machines like tractors for ploughing fields; pumps and motors to draw underground water, computers, fax machines, telephones and mobiles etc. All these devices or machines need energy in one form or the other for their operations.

For our energy requirement, we mainly depend upon the conventional sources of energy (or non-renewable sources) like coal, petroleum, natural gas etc. These sources are limited in quantity and can be finished completely (i.e., exhausted) in bound to come when these sources of energy will be out of stock. This situation would create an energy crisis on the earth. To overcome this energy crisis, the scientists have accelerated the search and use of renewable sources of energy like the solar energy.

3.10.1 ADVANTAGES OF CLASSIFICATION SOURCES OF ENERGY

(i) It helps us to decide which of the non-renewable sources of energy (like coal, petroleum, natural gas and fissionable materials) need to be conserved for future generations.

(ii) It also helps the scientists to accelerate the pace of developing new technologies suitable for harnessing energy from the renewable or non -conventional source of energy.

3.11 SOLAR ENERGY

The energy emitted by the sun in the form of heat and light (i.e. radiation) is known as solar energy.

The Sun contains mainly light elements like hydrogen and helium. When the nuclei of these elements fuse together at extremely high temperature in the core of the Sun, a large amount of energy is radiated in the form of heat and light continuously by the Sun. This process is known as Nuclear fusion. All the planets of the solar system receive the energy emitted by the Sun. The energy is emitted by the Sun in the form of radiation. These radiations are visible rays, infra - red rays (i.e., heat radiation), ultraviolet radiation, gamma rays, X - ray and radio waves. It may be noted that only some fraction of the total energy emitted by the Sun reach the surface of the earth.

Measurements have shown that the outer edge of the earth's atmosphere receives solar energy equal to 1.4 kilojoule per second per square metre (1.4 kJ/s m^2). This amount is known as Solar constant.

Hans Bethe, proposed that the enormous release of energy from the sun is due to nuclear fusion. For this discovery he was awarded the 1967 noble prize in physics.

3.11.1 SOLAR CONSTANT

Solar constant is defined as the energy received from the Sun in one second by the unit square metre area of the atmosphere exposed perpendicularly to the radiation of the sun at an average distance between the sun and the earth.

Or

The amount of heat energy (radiation) absorbed per minute by one square centimeter of a perfectly black body surface, placed at a mean distance of the earth form the sun, in the absence of the atmosphere, the surface being held perpendicular to the sun's rays.

It is generally expressed as calories per minute.

In S.I units its value is 1.388 KW/m^2 $= 1.4\ KW/m^2$

$= 1.4$ kilo joules /sec/sq m

$\therefore$ Solar constant $= 1.4$ kilo joules /sec/sq m Since J/s = Watt (W)

$= 1.4\ KW/m^2$

Traditional Uses of Solar Energy : It is used

(i) for cooking food by using solar cookers.

(ii) for heating water by using solar water heaters.

(iii) for producing steam by heating water to produce electricity.

(iv) by green plants to make their food.

(v) to produce electricity using solar cells.

(vi) to melt metals using solar furnaces.

(vii) for drying clothes and food grains.

Illustration :

If solar constant is 1.4 k W/m², calculate the solar energy received by 1 m² area in one hour.

Solution :

Here, solar constant = 1.4 k W/m^2

Since Watt (W) = joule/sec (J/s)

$\therefore$ Solar constant = 1.4 kJ/s m^2

It means, energy received by 1 m^2 area in 1 s = 1.4 kJ

Given, Time = 1 h = 60 × 60 = 3600 s

$\therefore$ Energy received by 1 m^2 area in 3600 s = 1.4 kJ × 3600 = 5040 kJ

Illustration :

The solar constant at a place is 1.4 kW/m². How much solar energy will be received at this place per second over an area of 5 m².

Solution :

Here, solar constant = 1.4 kW/m^2 = 1.4 kJ/s m^2

This means energy received per second by 1 m^2 area = 1.4 kJ/s

$\therefore$ Energy received per second over an area of 5 m^2 = 1.4 × 5

= 7.0 kJ/s = 7.0 kW

3.11.2 APPLICATION OF SOLAR ENERGY

A large number of devices have been developed to harness the solar energy directly. The commonly used devices are : **solar cookers, solar furnaces, solar water heaters, solar power plants** and **solar cells** etc.

3.11.3 METHODS OF COLLECTING SOLAR ENERGY

Solar energy can be used for heating purpose by collecting and focussing on the object to be heated. It can be done as described below:

(i) Sun rays are reflected by plane mirrors on the black containers. Solar radiation are reflected by plane mirrors to fall on the black containers containing uncooked food. The black containers are used because black body absorbs more heat radiation than the white or polished one.
Solar cookers and heaters are based on this principle. This method is used where moderate temperature is required.

(ii) The sun rays are focussed at a point using concave reflectors. The solar radiation falling on the concave reflectors are focussed at a point. Thus, large amount of heat radiation concentrated at a point. Thus, large amount of heat radiation concentrated at a point increases the temperature of that point to a high value.

Solar furnaces and solar power plants are based on this principle. This method is used where relatively high temperature is required.

3.11.4 INTERIOR OF SOLAR COOKER ARE PAINTED BLACK

Black surfaces are good absorbers of heat as compared to white surfaces or smooth surfaces. That is why the interior of solar cookers or other solar energy devices are painted black.

3.11.5 SOLAR COOKER (BOX TYPE)

Construction : It consists of a wooden box (rectangular in shape) in which a metallic box painted black is fitted. The space between wooden box and metallic box is filled with an insulating material like thermocol. The insulating material minimizes the heat lose by conduction and radiation.

The metallic box is covered by a thick glass sheet. A plane mirror reflector is used to reflect the sun rays and attached to the box (Figure). The un-cooked food placed in the black container is put inside the box.

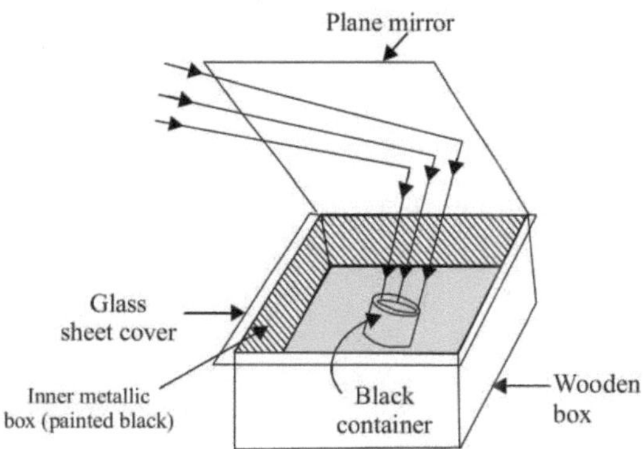

Working :

The plane mirror reflector is adjusted in such a way that maximum sun light falls on it. The light reflected by the plane mirror falls on the thick glass sheet cover.

The heat radiation (i.e. infra -red rays coming from the sun and have short wavelength and are absorbed by the black container or any other object placed in the box and black surface of the box. The heat radiation entered in the box are not able to come out of the box through the glass sheet. Thus, the heat radiation are trapped in the box. The effect is known as green house effect. (For the detail of green house effect, Refer additional topic at the end of this chapter). The temperature inside the box increases from 100° C to 140 °C. Thus, the food in the container is cooked.

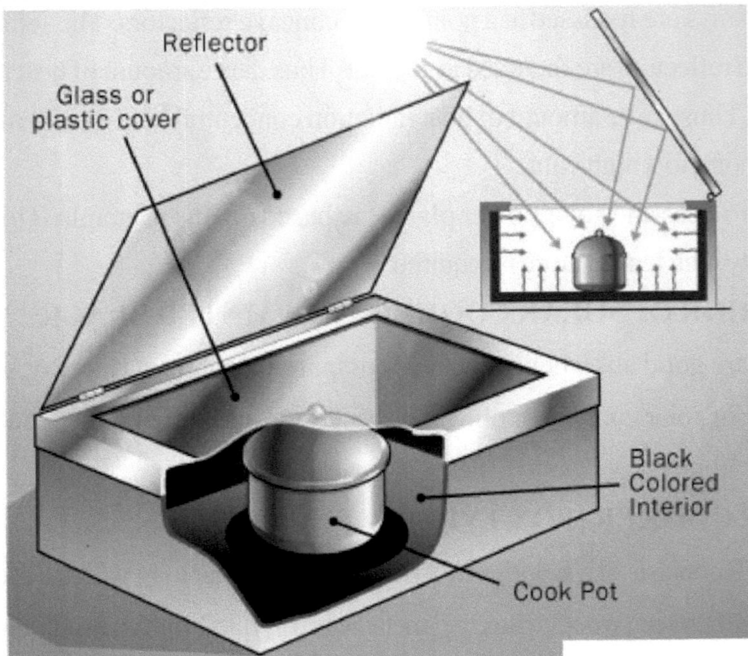

3.11.6 ADVANTAGES OF BOX TYPE SOLAR COOKER

1. **Economical :** The cost of cooking food in the solar cooker is very small as money is only spent to purchase the solar cooker.
2. **Pollution :** No pollution is caused as there is no burning of fuel.
3. **Nutrition value :** of food is preserved as the food is cooked at low temperature and slowly.
4. It can cook two or three dishes at a time.
5. It saves the costly fuel like wood, gas, kerosene oil etc.

3.11.7 DISADVANTAGES OF SOLAR COOKER

(i) Food cannot be cooked at night .

(ii) Food cannot be cooked on a cloudy day.

(iii) Food cannot be cooked quickly as solar cooker takes 4 to 5 hours to cook it.

(iv) Large quantity of food cannot be cooked in the solar cooker.

(v) Food cannot be fried

(vi) The position of the reflecting plane mirror has to be changed time to time so that it always face the sun.

	Spherical reflector type solar cooker		Box type solar cooker
1	It can be used for baking and frying.	1	It cannot be used for baking and frying
2	Spherical reflector is used in the form of concave parabolic	2	Plane mirror is used.
3	High temperature is produced .	3	Low temperature is produced.
4	Its temperature is nearly 180°C-200°C	4	Its temperture is nearly 100°C to 150°C.
5	It is used mostly.	5	It is less used.

3.11.8 SOLAR CONCENTRATORS

Solar concentrators are the devices used to concentrate the solar energy over a small area. When a parallel beam of sunlight falls on a polished concave surface (like concave mirror), then the beam of sunlight concentrates at the focus (F) of the concave surface after reflection (Figure). As a result of this concentrated beam of sunlight, the temperature at point F increases considerably . If we place a piece of paper at F, then it begins to burn after sometime. A concave spherical surface which concentrates the beam of sunlight at a point is called solar concentrator.

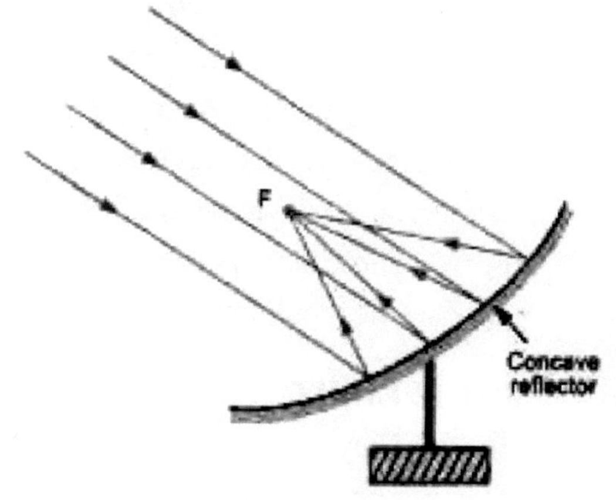

3.11.9 APPLICATION OF SOLAR CONCENTRATORS (SOLAR COOKER)

This type of solar cooker consists of a large concave reflector or solar concentrator (Figure). The sun rays are focussed by this reflector at a point F. The intense beam of sun rays increases the temperature of point F to 200° C. The food to be cooked in a container is placed at point F. The concave reflector must be rotated so that always face the Sun for effective cooking of the food.

Difference between Box Type solar cooker with plane Mirror and Box Type solar cooker with spherical reflector

	Solar cooker with plane Mirror (Box type cooker)		Solar cooker with spherical Reflector
1	Plane mirror is used to reflect the sun light	1	Concave mirror or surface is used to reflect the sun light
2	The temperature inside the box of the solar cooker rises to 100° C to 150°C.	2	The temperature inside the box of the solar cooker rises to 200°C
3	It cannot be used for frying the food and making chapatis.	3	It can be used for frying the food and making chapatis

3.11.10 SOLAR FURNACE

It consists of a large number of movable plane mirrors and a parabolic reflecting surface. Plane mirrors reflect the sun light towards the parabolic reflecting surface. The parallel beam of light falling on the parabolic mirror is focussed at a small area (F) as shown in Figure .

The temperature of the small area where beam of sun light is focussed may be raised to 3000°C.

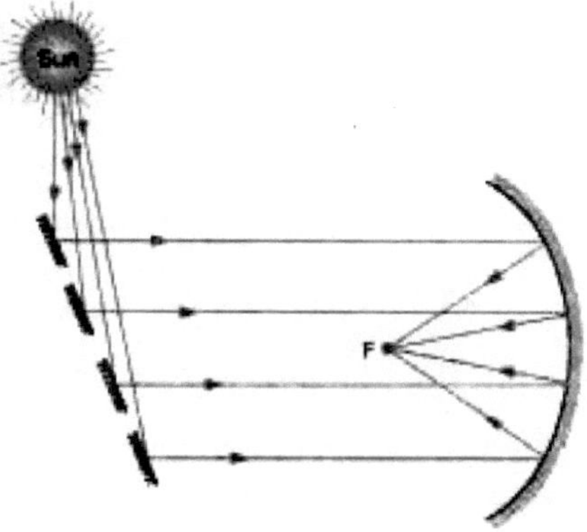

3.11.11 USE OF SOLAR FURNACE

A water reservoir placed at F is heated to produce steam. This steam under high pressure is used to rotate the turbine of a generator to produce electricity. A solar furnace when used to produce electricity is known as solar power tower.

Advantages of Solar Devices

(i) These devices save the costly fuel like wood, gas, kerosene, diesel etc.

(ii) These devices cause no pollution and hence they are environment-friendly.

(iii) The repair and maintenance is very cheap.

3.11.12 LIMITATIONS OF SOLAR DEVICES

(i) They cannot work during night.

(ii) They cannot work on cloudy and rainy days.

(iii) They are less effective during winter season.

(iv) They are not effective in polar regions.

(v) They cannot be used to operate automobiles like buses, cars, ships, and aeroplanes.

(vi) They cannot be used to operate heavy machinery.

(vii) Their initial cost is high.

3.11.13 SOLAR CELL

A device which converts sunlight into electrical energy is known as solar cell.

History of Solar cell

It was discovered more than 100 years ago that sunlight falling on a thin layer of selenium element can be converted into electric energy. But, the efficiency was too low (about 0.7%), so no efforts were made to develop the solar cells.

Semiconductors and Solar cells

A substance whose conductivity lies between those of a conductor and an insulator is known as semiconductor.

Examples: Silicon, Gallium, Sallium and Germanium are Semiconductors.

3.11.14 HOW TO MAKE A SOLAR CELL ?

The layers (i.e. wafers) of semiconductor material like silicon having impurities are placed one over the other. When sunlight falls on these wafers, a potential difference is produced between the two regions of semiconductor's wafers. This potential difference give rise to an electric current. Thus, a device which converts sunlight into electrical energy is called solar cell. A solar cell made of semiconductor (germanium or Silicon having Gallium as impurity) has an efficiency about 10-15%

3.11.15 USES OF SOLAR CELLS

(i) They are used in wrist watches and calculators.

(ii) They are used to generate electricity needed in artificial satellites (i.e. man made satellites).

(iii) They are used to operate electric bulbs and tubes in remote areas where hydroelectricity is not available.

(iv) They are used to operate radio sets in remote areas.

The largest solar furnace in the world is located in France.

3.11.16 ADVANTAGES OF SOLAR CELLS

(i) They directly convert solar energy into electrical energy.

(ii) They are environment - friendly i .e. they do not cause pollution.

3.11.17 SOLAR PANEL

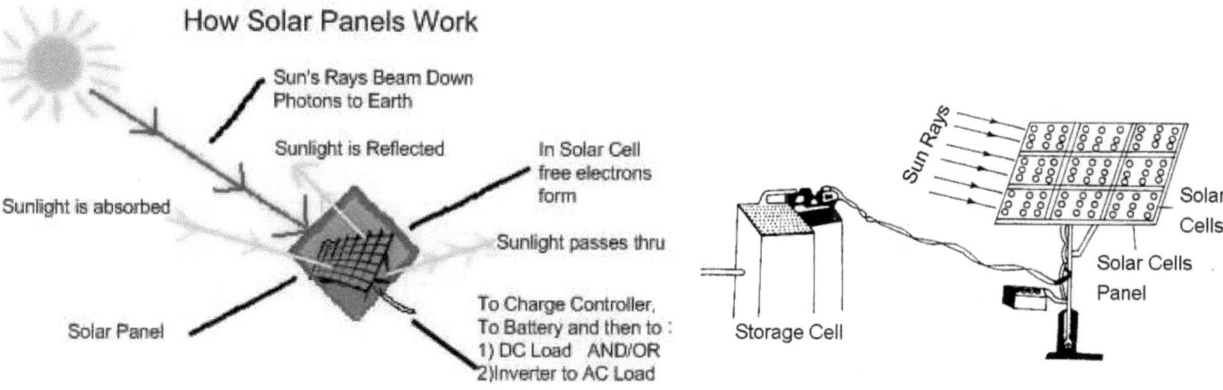

A group of solar cells connected to each other in a certain pattern forms a solar panel (above Figure). A solar panel converts sunlight into electrical energy. The efficiency of solar panel is very large as compared to the efficiency of a solar cell.

During day time, sunlight falling on the solar panel is converted into electrical energy which is stored in a battery connected to it. As soon as sunlight stops falling on it (during night and cloudy day), the battery begins to supply electric current to the appliances connected to it.

3.11.18 LIMITATIONS OF SOLAR PANELS

Solar panels have limited uses. They can not be used to meet our domestic needs of electricity. This is because of the following reasons:

1. The solar cells used in a solar panel are made of pure silicon. The production of pure silicon is very costly affair. These solar cells in a solar panel are joined to each other with a best conductor silver to reduce the resistance of the solar panel to get maximum electricity. But silver metal is also costly. Thus , we find that the cost of fabricating a solar panel is very high.
2. The storage battery connected to a solar panel can supply direct current (D.C.). So only those electric appliances can operate with the solar panel which require direct current. However, the electric appliances which require alternating current (A.C.) cannot be operated with the solar panel.
3. Solar panel can supply the electricity continuously only if the sun shines during day time.

3.11.19 USES OF SOLAR PANELS

(i) They are used to operate electric bulbs and tubes in the remote villages and areas.

(ii) They are used to supply electricity in artificial satellites.

3.11.20 SOLAR WATER HEATER

Solar energy can be used to heat water. In a solar water heater, sunlight is allowed to fall on a box made of a poor conductor of heat. The glass top of the box lets in sunlight and traps heat. Water enters a tube that is painted black to increase the absorption of heat. It is bent several times to increase its length inside the box. This allows the water flowing through it sufficient time to absorb heat. Hot water collects in the tank of the heater for use.

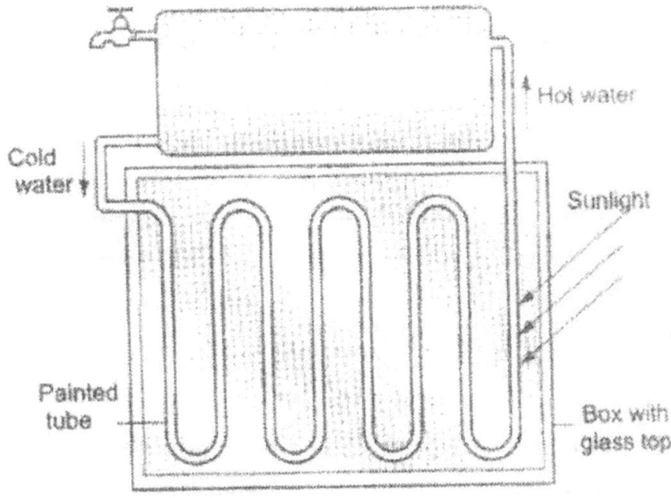

Illustration

A concentrator-type solar water heater has a surface area of 5m2 and it can absorb 80% of the incident solar radiation falling on it, while it reflects the rest. Calculate the energy concentrated by the heater at its focus in a time period of 2hrs, if solar energy incident on it is at the rate of 0.4 KJ/m²s.

Solution

Surface area of the reflector, $A = 5\ m^2$

Energy incident on the solar heater,

$E = 0.4\ KJ/m^2s$

So energy concentrated $= E \times A \times t \times \frac{20}{100}$

$= 0.4 \times 5 \times 7200 \times \frac{20}{100} = 2880\ KJ$

3.12 ENERGY FROM THE SEA OR OCEAN

The sun heats the water in the ocean, rivers, ponds etc. As the specific heat capacity of water ($4200\ J\ kg^{-1}\ °C^{-1}$) is very high, so the water in oceans is a store house of heat energy. The energy from sea or ocean water is available in the following forms :

(i) Energy of sea waves or Sea Waves Energy

(ii) Tidal energy

(iii) Ocean thermal energy

(i) Energy of sea waves or Sea Waves Energy : Due to the blowing of wind on the surface of ocean, very fast sea-waves move on its surface. Due to their high speed, sea waves have a lot of kinetic energy in them. The energy of moving sea-waves can be used to generate electricity. This can be done as follows :

(a) One idea is to set up floating generators in the sea. These would move up and down with the sea-waves. This movement would drive the generators to produce electricity.

(b) Another idea is to let the sea-waves move up and down inside large tubes. As the waves move up, the air in the tubes is compressed. This compressed air can then be used to turn a turbine of a generator to produced electricity.

Limitation of Energy of Sea waves : Energy of sea waves can be extracted only if strong winds blow all the times across the sea. However, as soon as strong winds stop to blow, the generator stops producing electricity. Hence, we cannot depend much on the energy of sea waves.

(ii) Tidal Energy : The alternate rise and fall of waters of the ocean twice in nearly 24 hours is known as tides. The tides are caused due to the gravitational force of attraction exerted by the moon and to some extent by the sun on the water of the ocean. At the time of new and full moon, when the sun and the moon are in a straight line, tides are very high .When the sun and the moon are at right angle from the earth, tides are low. The kinetic energy of water during tides is used to produce electricity.

Tidal power plants are constructed near narrow bays (Figure). During tides, the gates of the dam are opened. The rising water is allowed to fall on the turbine of the generator which produces electricity. Thus, kinetic energy of the water is converted into electrical energy.

During low tides, gates of the dam are closed and hence the water level behind the dam rises. This raised water has potential energy. Again the gates are opened and the water is allowed to fall back into the turbine. This falling water is used to rotate the turbine of the generator. Hence the electricity is produced continuously.

Harnessing tidal energy : Tidal energy can be harnessed by constructing a tidal barrage (or tidal dam) across a narrow opening to the sea and fixing a turbine at the opening of the barrage.

(i) During high tide, when the level of water in the sea rises, sea-water flows into the reservoir of tidal barrage and turns the turbines to generate electricity.

(ii) During low tide, when the level of water in the sea falls, the stored sea-water in the tidal barrage reservoir flows out into the sea and turns the turbines again to generate electricity.

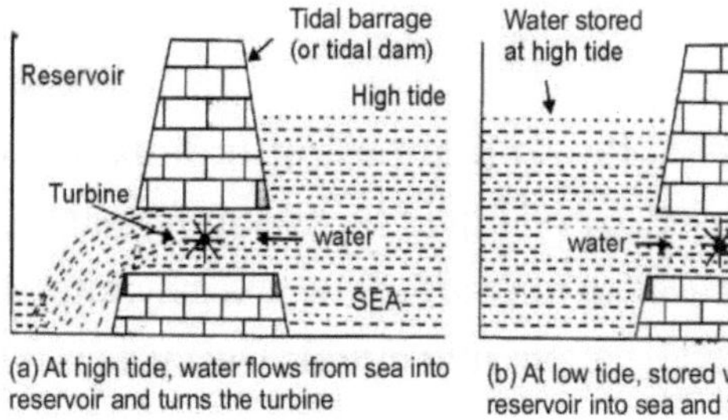

(a) At high tide, water flows from sea into reservoir and turns the turbine

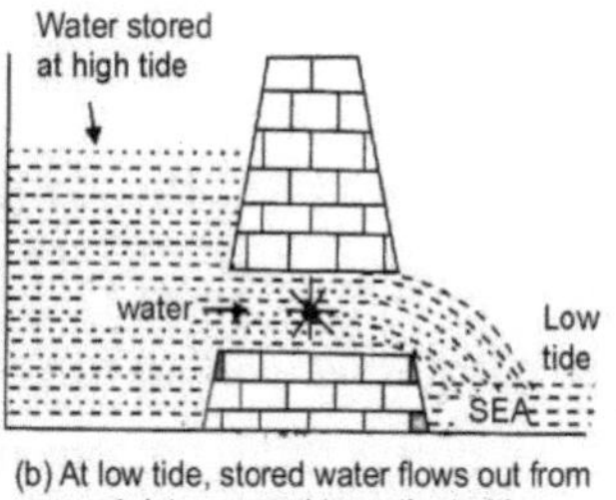

(b) At low tide, stored water flows out from reservoir into sea and turns the turbine.

(a) **Places where Tidal energy is taped :** France and Canada are the leading countries which harness the tidal energy. In India, three sites namely Gulf of kutch (Gujarat), Gulf of Cambay (Gujarat) and Sunderbans (West Bengal) have been identified to construct tidal power plants.

(b) **Limitation of Tidal Energy** : To operate tidal power plant, the difference between the water levels of high tide and low tide should be very large. This much level of tide is not available at all coastal places. Thus, tidal power plants can not be installed everywhere. In other words, tidal energy cannot be major source of energy.

(iii) Ocean Thermal Energy (OTE)

The heat energy due to the temperature difference between the different layers of water in the ocean is known as ocean thermal energy (OTE). The temperature of water at the surface of the ocean is much more than the temperature of water deep into the ocean. Due to this temperature difference, heat energy can be drawn from the sea or ocean water. This heat energy can be used to produce electricity.

(a) **Ocean Thermal energy conversion (OTEC) power plant :**

The devices used to harness the ocean thermal energy are known as Ocean Thermal Energy Conversion (OTEC) power plants.

To operate an OTEC plant efficiently, the temperature of ocean water at the surface should be higher by 20°C or more than the water at certain depth (about 1000 m).

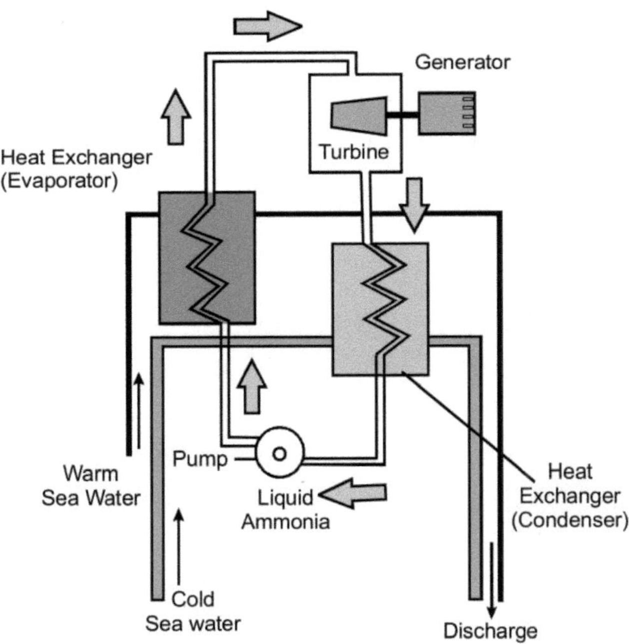

OTEC Power plant using ammonia

Warm surface water is used to boil liquid such as ammonia or a chlorofluorocarbon (CFC). The vapour of such liquid is used to run the turbine and generate electricity. The cold water from the depth is used to convert the vapour into liquid. The cycle is then continued.

LIMITATION OF OCEAN ENERGY :

(i) It is difficult to find suitable sites in and around the ocean for the construction of dams for electricity generation.

(ii) Tides come at a place at intervals of six hours. This also affects the continuous process.

(iii) The strength of the sea waves depends upon the speed of the air flow.

(iv) The temperature of the top surface layer of the ocean is not very high. Therefore, the only low boiling point fluids can be evaporated by using suitable devices to trap ocean thermal energy .

3.13 GEO-THERMAL ENERGY (GEO-THERMAL MEANS EARTH -HEAT)

The earth has three layers i.e. the core, the mantle and the crust. The core is the central part of the earth which is surrounded by the mantle. The mantle is surrounded by the uppermost layer of the earth called magma. This magma consists of molten rocks, gases and steam at very high temperature. Due to some geological changes, the hot magma rises up and is collected in the crust of the earth. The regions in the crust where the hot magma is collected in the crust of the earth. The heat energy stored in the hot spots of the earth's crust is called geo-thermal energy. This energy heats the underground water. The hot underground water comes automatically out of the earth's surface in certain regions where crust is weak in the form of fountains known as hot water springs or geysers.

The steam of underground water is usually taken out by sinking pipes through holes drilled in the earth's crust. This steam under high pressure is used to rotate the turbine of the generator to produce electricity.

Advantages of Geo-thermal energy

1. Geo-thermal energy can be converted continuously into electricity for 24 hours throughout the year.
2. Geo-thermal energy causes no pollution, so it is environment friend
3. The cost of converting geo-thermal energy into electricity is very less
4. It is renewable source of energy.

3.13.1 PLACES WHERE GEO-THERMAL ENERGY BASED POWER PLANTS :

Geo - thermal energy based power plants operate in large number in USA and New Zealand. However, one such plant also operates in Madhya Pradesh (India).

Geo-thermal energy is not derived from the Sun.

3.14 OCEAN WAVE ENERGY

The energy associated with ocean waves is known as ocean wave energy.

In another innovation, the electricity generated is used to electrolyse water to produce hydrogen and oxygen gases. Hydrogen so produced is piped to the shore.

HARNESSING OCEAN WAVE ENERGY

Wind blowing across the surface of the oceans causes ocean waves. The kinetic energy of the huge amount of water that moves along the waves is called ocean wave energy.

The most common devices that can be used for harnessing ocean wave energy are :

(i) Surface–followers using floats or pitching devices

(ii) Oscillating water columns (OWC)

(iii) Focussing devices

The surface–followers consist of a series of floating objects that are pivoted about a rigid shaft along a coastline. The mechanical energy produced in the shaft is then converted into electricity.

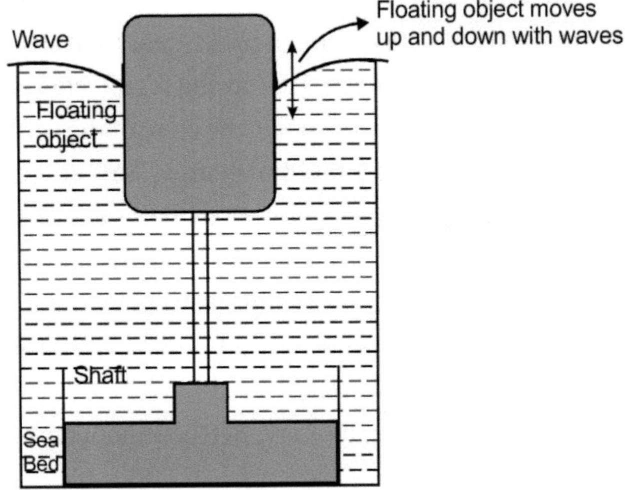

A surface follower used to harness ocean energy

Oscillating water columns (OWC) use the force of the ocean waves entering a fixed device to do mechanical work or generate electricity.

For example, in anchored navigational buoys, the waves compress the air. The compressed air is then used to rotate turbine and generate electricity.

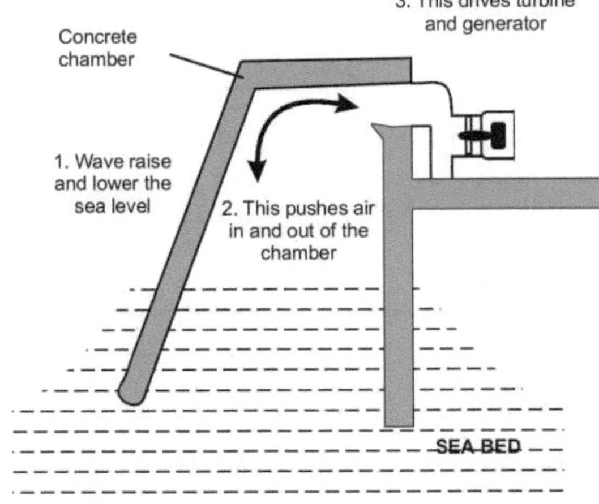

An oscillating water column wave power generator

3.15 ENERGY CRISIS

Fast depletion of the non renewable concentrated sources of energy (fuels) is known as energy crisis.

What are the factors causing energy crisis

The following factors lead to energy crisis;

(i) Increasing population

(ii) Excessive use of non- renewable (conventional) sources of energy.

(iii) Use of less fuel - efficient machines.

(iv) Affluent life - style of the people.

How can the energy cirsis be prevented

To prevent energy crisis we should

(i) slow down the use of conventional fuels

(ii) use renewable sources of energy like wind energy, solar energy, hydroenergy, geothermal energy and biomass energy.

(iii) use more fuel - efficient machines and electrical appliances.

(iv) save energy whenever and wherever possible.

3.16 NUCLEAR ENERGY

Antoine Henri Becquerel, a Franch physicist discovered that uranium emits radiation spontaneously. The spontaneous emission of radiation by uranium or heavy elements is known as radioactivity. A substance or element that shows the property of radioactivity is known as radioactive substance or radioactive element.

In 1897 , Rutherford found that the radiation emitted by radioactive elements are of three types (i) alpha particle (alpha particle is a helium nucleus i.e., a helium atom which has lost its two orbital electrons), (ii) beta particle (beta particles are the streams of fast moving electrons) and (iii) gamma rays (radiation of small wavelengths).

When a radioactive substance emits radiation its mass decreases. Suppose M be the mass of a radioactive substance before emitting the radiation and M' be the mass of the substance after emitting the radiation. Therefore, the decrease in the mass of the substance is given by

$$\Delta m = (M - M')$$

This decrease in mass (Δm) is converted into energy E according to Einstein's mass–energy relation, $E = \Delta mc^2$, where $c = 3 \times 10^8 \text{ m s}^{-1}$ is the speed of light in vacuum. The energy E is known as nuclear energy.

Definition : The energy obtained from the conversion of nuclear mass is known as nuclear energy.

3.16.1 UNITS OF NUCLEAR ENERGY

Nuclear energy is expressed in electron - volt (eV). One electron -volt is the energy acquired by an electron while passing through a potential difference of one volt.

$$1\ eV = 1.6 \times 10^{-19}\ C \times 1\ V$$

$$= 1.6 \times 10^{-19}\ CV$$

$$1\ eV = 1.6 \times 10^{-19}\ J\ (\because 1\ CV = 1J)$$

Bigger unit of nuclear energy is mega electron - volt (MeV)

$$1\ MeV = 10^{6}\ eV \times 1.6 \times 10^{-19} J = 1.6 \times 10^{-13} J$$

Nuclear energy is obtained by the splitting of a heavy nucleus into light nuclei and by combining light nuclei to form a large nucleus. The process of splitting of a heavy nucleus is known as nuclear fission. The process of combining light nuclei to from a large nucleus is nuclear fusion.

3.16.2 BINDING ENERGY

The particles present in the nucleus (protons and neutrons) are called nucleons. The sum of the individual mass of various particles in the nucleus must be equal to the nuclear mass. But this is not so. The nuclear mass is somewhat less than the sum of the individual masses of various nuclear particles. The difference between the actual nuclear mass and the expected nuclear mass (sum of the individual masses of nuclear particles) is referred to as mass defect. The mass defect can be converted into equivalent energy by means of Einstein equation ($E = mc^2$).

The energy equivalent to mass defect is responsible for holding the nucleons together and is called binding energy of the nucleus.

The binding energy per nucleon is a measure of the stability of nucleus. Binding energy may also be considered as the energy required to separate the individual particles of the nucleus.

Mass defect m in amu can be directly obtained by using the following formula.

$$\mathbf{\Delta m = [Zm_p + (A - Z)\, m_n] - m_N}$$

where z is atomic number

A is mass number

m_p is mass of proton

m_n is mass of neutron

m_N is mass of nucleus.

3.16.3 NUCLEAR REACTIONS

In nuclear reactions, the nucleus of an atom undergoes a change forming new atoms and releasing a tremendous amount of energy. New atoms (or new elements) can be produced in a nuclear reaction, which is not possible in the case of a chemical reaction. Thus, a nuclear reaction can convert one element into another element. Some of the nuclear reactions take place in nature on their own in order to attain stability. This process is called as Radioactivity. However nuclear reactions can also be invoked artificially to obtain large amounts of energy.

Such reactions are of two types :

(a) Nuclear fission

(b) Nuclear fusion

3.16.4 NUCLEAR FISSION

The process of splitting a nucleus is known as nuclear fission.

Otto Hahn and Strassman found that uranium –235 bombarded process is known as nuclear fission. The neutrons used in the fission of uranium nucleus have low energy and are known as thermal neutrons. During the fission of uranium two or three neutrons are also emitted along with the release of large amount of energy besides the products of the fission.

3.16.4.1 DEFINITION OF NUCLEAR FISSION

The process of splitting a heavy nucleus into two comparatively lighter nuclei along with the release of large amount of energy when bombarded with a thermal neutron is called nuclear fission.

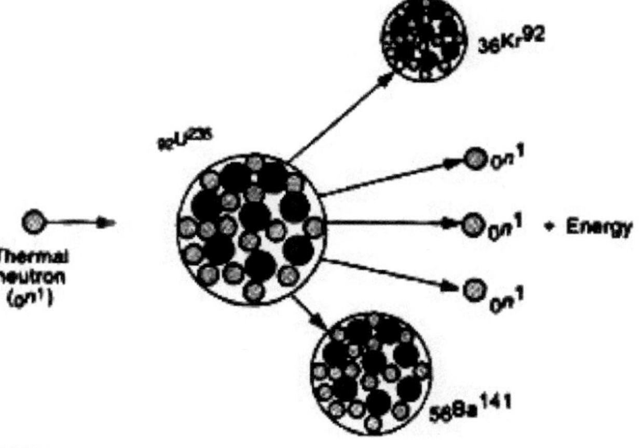

Nuclear fission of $_{92}U^{235}$ when bombarded with a slow neutron (known as thermal neutron) is given below:

$$_{92}U^{235} + {}_0n^1 \rightarrow {}_{56}Ba^{141} + {}_{36}Kr^{92} + {}_0n^1 + \text{energy}$$

This fission is represented as shown in figure.

The energy released per fission of $_{92}U^{235}$ (an isotope of uranium) is about 200 Me V.

Atomic Power Plants and Research Centres in India.

(i) Bhabha Atomic Research Centre at Trombay near Mumbai : This centre has been established to carry out research work to use nuclear energy for peaceful purposes.

(ii) Tarapur Atomic Power Station (in Maharashtra) was the first atomic power station established in India.

(iii) Rajasthan Atomic Power Station at Rana Pratap Sagar near Kota.

(iv) Narora Atomic Power Station at Narora in U.P.

(v) Madras Atomic Power Station (now known as Indira Gandhi Centre for Atomic Research) at Kalpakkam in Tamil Nadu.

India gets most of uranium from the Jaduguda mines in Jharkhand. The uranium obtained from these mines is taken to Nuclear Fuel complex situated at Hyderabad for processing. At this complex , the fuel elements are formed after enriching the uranium. These fuel elements are then sent to different Nuclear power plants.

3.16.4.2 Process of Nulear Fission

The process of nuclear fission is explained by the Liquid drop model of the nucleus. The **liquid drop model** of the nucleus to explain the process of fission was proposed by **Yakov Frenkel, Neils Bohr and John Wheeler**. According to the liquid drop model of the nucleus it is said that in just the same way that a drop of water might become unstable if another small drop hits it, the uranium nucleus becomes unstable and breaks up when hits by a neutron. In this model, the uranium nucleus is treated like a drop of a liquid, which is not compressible and has a uniform positive charge. It is imagined that a stretchable skin–like membrane surrounds the drop like nucleus and holds all the protons and neutrons together inside its body. In the stable stage, the uranium nucleus, like a drop of water is spherical in shape. The nuclear fission of uranium– 235 isotope by means of a slow moving neutron can be explained diagrammatically as follows:

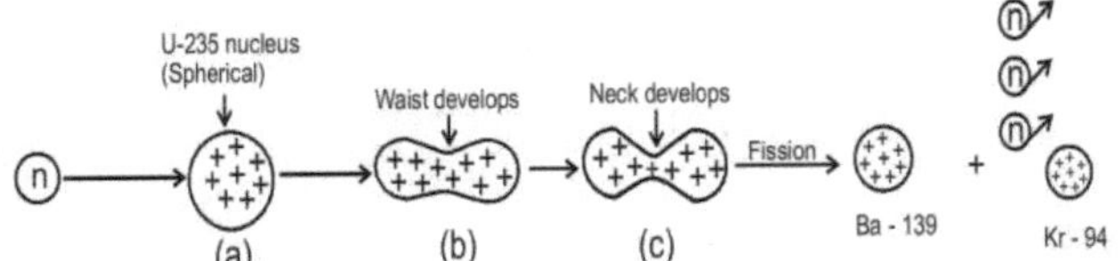

Figure (a) shows that uranium nucleus to be spherical. In this spherical nucleus the nuclear particles like protons and neutrons are very close together because of which the nuclear force of attraction and the electrostatic force of repulsion are very delicately balanced. Now, when a slow moving neutron attacks the uranium–235 nucleus and enters into it, then the delicate balance of force inside the nucleus is disturbed. The energy of neutron is transferred to the nucleons (protons and neutrons) and by gaining this energy, the nucleons start oscillating more and more. Due to increased oscillations of the nuclear particles, the skin-like outer membrane of the nucleus gets stretched, the nucleus gets elongated and a waist develops in it. When the nucleus gets elongated then the distances between nuclear particles (protons and neutrons) increase. This increased inter-particle distance weakens the nuclear force of attraction so that the electrostatic force of repulsion becomes more dominant. Due to the increased repulsion between the protons, a neck develops in the nucleus as shown. The formation of neck decreases the nuclear force further and the increased repulsion between protons ultimately leads to the breaking up of the **uranium–235** nucleus to form two smaller nuclei of **barium–139** and **krypton–94**, along with the emission of three neutrons.

3.16.4.3 CHAIN REACTION

A reaction in which the particle which initiates (starts) the reaction is also produced during the reaction to carry on the reaction further and further is called a chain reaction. Once started a chain reaction will go on propagating by itself, until one of the reactant is all used up. The fission of uranium–235 by means of slow moving neutrons is a chain reaction, because this reaction is started by neutrons and neutrons are also produced during this reaction. The neutrons produced during the fission of a uranium atom initiate the fission of more uranium atoms, and this process goes on, like an unending chain, with the liberation of a large amount of energy at each step. The chain reaction taking place during the fission of uranium–235 can be represented more clearly with the help of a diagram.

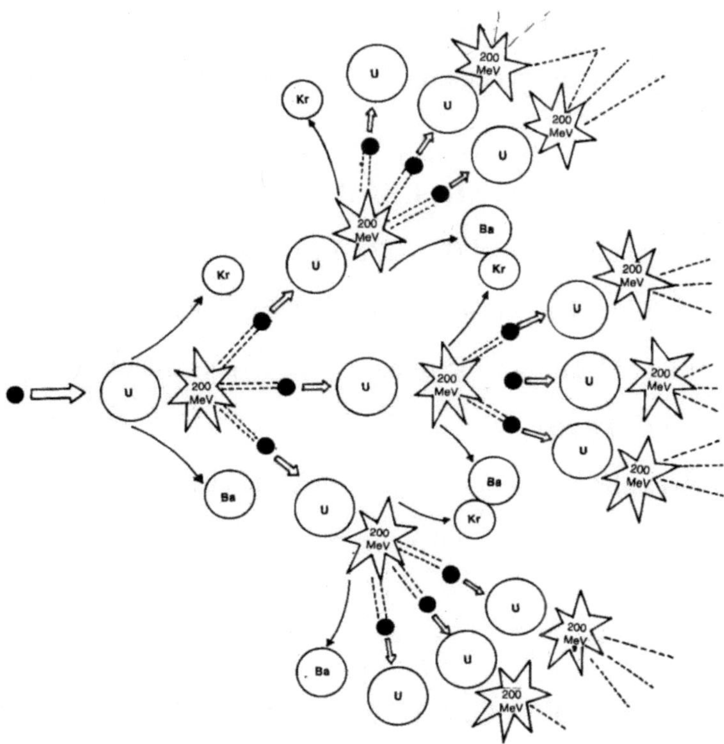

The fact that only 1 neutron is used up in each fission process but 3 neutrons are produced, makes the fission process in uranium–235 a self-sustaining process or self-propagating process called chain reaction. If on the other hand on an average less than 1 neutron had been produced per fission, then the reaction would have died down like a fire in a wet fuel. It should be noted that a chain reaction involves a large number of uranium atoms. So, a chain reaction cannot occur in a very small lump of uranium–235 isotopes, but it can take place in a sufficiently large mass of uranium–235 isotopes. The minimum mass of uranium–235 atoms or any other fissionable material which can support a chain reaction is called critical mass of that material.

3.16.4.4 HAZARDS OF USING NUCLEAR ENERGY (POLLUTION FROM NUCLEAR FISSION)

Nuclear fission causes more serious pollution problem than the fossil fuels. Nuclear fission radiates nuclear radiation namely alpha particles (α – particles), beta particles (β – particles) and gamma rays ($-\gamma$ rays). These radiation are very harmful to the living organisms. The long and constant exposure of living organism to these radiations cause many diseases or disorder in the human body like :

(i) The nuclear radiation can change or damage the structure of cells in the human body.

(ii) They cause diseases like cancer, leukemia and blindness.

(iii) They cause genetic disorder in a human body.

(iv) They cause sterility in young generation.

3.16.4.5 ADVANTAGES OF USING NUCLEAR FISSION ENERGY OVER FOSSIL FUELS

(i) A small quantity of nuclear fuel (U – 235) gives a large amount of energy by the process of nuclear fission. While large quantity of fossil fuel is required to produce large amount of heat. For example, 1 kg of Uranium 235 releases energy equivalent to the energy released by the burning of 2500000 kg coal.

(ii) In a nuclear power plant, the nuclear fuel is inserted once to get energy over a long period of time. On the other hand, in a thermal power plant, fossil fuel is to be supplied constantly to get energy.

3.16.4.6 DISADVANTAGES OF NUCLEAR FISSION ENERGY OVER THE FOSSIL FUEL

1. Nuclear fission causes more serious pollution problem than the burning of fossil fuel. The radiation emitted during nuclear fission are very harmful. They cause dangerous diseases like cancer, leukemia and sterility.

2. The biggest problem of using nuclear fission energy is the safe disposal of nuclear waste. Nuclear waste continues to emit harmful nuclear radiation. No method has been evolved for the complete elimination of the nuclear waste. But no such problem is faced in the disposal of the fossil fuel waste. For example burning if coal give rise to ash which can be thrown in the fields.

3.16 NUCLEAR FUSION

Definition : The process in which two or more light nuclei fuse together (or combine) to form a heavy nucleus alongwith the release of energy is called nuclear fusion.

Ex.: (i) When two nuclei of deuterium (d or $_1H^2$) fuse together, the following products are formed:

$$d + d \rightarrow t(\text{tritium}) + p\ (\text{proton}) + 4.0\ \text{MeV}$$

$$_1H^2 + {}_1H^2 \rightarrow {}_1H^3 + {}_1H^1 + 4.0\ \text{MeV}$$

(ii) When tritium ($_1H^3$) fuse with deuterium ($_1H^2$), the following products are formed :

$$_1H^3 + {}_1H^2 \rightarrow {}_2He^4 + {}_0n^1 + 17.6\ \text{MeV}$$

(iii) When two protonium fuse together, deuterium (d), positron (e^+) and neutrino (v) are formed i .e.,

$$p + p \rightarrow d + e^+\ v + 0.42\ \text{MeV}$$

$$_1H^1 + {}_1H^1 \rightarrow {}_1H^2 + {}_1e^0 + v + 0.42\ \text{MeV}$$

Positron (e^+) is identical to electron .The only difference between positron and electron is that positron has +1 charge and electron has – 1 charge. Neutrino is a neutral particle (i.e., no charge) and its rest mass is zero.

3.16.5.1 PROCESS OF A NUCLEAR FUSION TAKES PLACE

The fusion of nuclei does not take place so easily as it seems to be. In fact, nuclei are positively charged and hence they repel each other when come closer to each other. These nuclei can be fused together if they move with very high speed to overcome the force of repulsion between them. This can happen if the temperature is very high (about 10^7 K). At this temperature, the electron of the hydrogen atom is completely detached and hence we get a bare nucleus (i.e. naked nucleus) and free electron. The collection of bare nuclei moving with very high speed and free electrons is known as Plasma. Since the number of bare nuclei (positively charged) is equal to the number of electrons (negatively charged) hence net charge on Plasma is zero. These bare nuclei of hydrogen move with very high speed (because speed is proportional to the temperature) and hence fuse together to form helium nuclei. During the fusion of hydrogen nuclei, a large amount of energy is released.

3.16.5.2 SOURCE OF ENERGY OF THE SUN -NUCLEAR FUSION

Hans Bethe in 1939 suggested that the source of energy of Sun and other stars is thermo-nuclear or nuclear fusion reactions.

The sun is a huge mass of hydrogen gas and the temperature in it is extremely high.

In the sun the small deuterium atoms (isotope of H atom) collide and fuse together to form bigger atoms of helium. Each time an atom of helium is formed, tremendous energy is released in the form of heat and light. It is this energy which makes the sun shine. The main reaction taking place in sun is :

$_1H^2 + {}_1H^2 \xrightarrow{\text{N fusion}} {}_2He^4 +$ Enormous amount of energy
Deuteron Helium
(heavy hydrogen) (nucleus)

$_1H^1 + {}_1H^2 \longrightarrow {}_2He^3 +$ large amount of energy

Protium Deuteron Helium

$_1H^2 + {}_1H^3 \longrightarrow {}_2He^4 + {}_0n^1 +$ large amount of energy
Deuterium Tritium
(HeavyH) (Veryheavy h)

Nuclear fusion reactions of various isotopes of hydrogen to form helium are going on inside the sun that produces such a great amount of energy which is radiated by the sun. Because of this energy, sun emits radiations (light) of different wavelengths of all the sun's radiation. It is the infra –red radiations which carry heat energy and hence heat up the earth.

3.16.5.3 HYDROGEN BOMB

The nuclear fusion is the basic principle involved in the preparation of hydrogen bomb.
A hydrogen bomb is actually an uncontrolled nuclear fusion process.
A hydrogen bomb consists of an arrangement of nuclear fission in the centre. It is surrounded by a mixture of deuteron 2H1and lithium – 6 isotope (3Li6).
The nuclear fission provides heat and neutrons. The neutrons are used in converting lithium isotope into tritium 3H1 and the heat liberated is required for the fusion between 1H2 and 1H3 to start. The fusion reactions are then accompanied by the liberation of a large amount of energy.

3.16.5.4 ADVANTAGES OF NUCLEAR FUSION OVER NUCLEAR FISSION PROCESS

1. The energy released in nuclear fusion is much more than the energy released in nuclear fission reaction.
2. In a nuclear fusion, hydrogen nuclei fuse together to form a helium nucleus which is stable. Helium nucleus does not emit any type of harmful radiation. So we can dispose off it easily. On the other hand by products of nuclear fission reaction emit harmful radiation. Hence the disposal of these product is a big problem.

3.16.5.5 DISADVANTAGE OF NUCLEAR FUSION

It is still in the experimental stage to have controlled nuclear fusion to produce electricity. The main problem is to contain the ingredients of nuclear fusion at a extremely high temperature.

3.16.6 DIFFERENCE BETWEEN NUCLEAR FISSION AND NUCLEAR FUSION

S.No	Nuclear Fission	Nuclear Fusion
1	In a nuclear fission, heavy nucleus splits up into lighter nuclei.	In a nuclear fusion, light nuclei combine together to form a heavy nucleus.
2	In a nuclear fission, harmful nuclear radiation are emitted.	In a nuclear fusion, no harmful radiation are emitted.
3	A nuclear fission starts when a slow neutron bombards the heavy nucleus (like Uranium-235).	A nuclear fusion starts when light nuclei are heated at a extremely high temperature.
4	Nuclear fission is a chain reaction i.e. it multiplies very fast.	Nuclear fusion is not a chain reaction.
5	Nuclear fission reactions can be controlled to produce electricity.	Nuclear fusion reactions are still uncontrolled and cannot be used to produce electricity.
6	Nuclear fission reactions produce a large amount of energy	Nuclear fusion reactions produce must more energy than the nuclear fission.
7	Temperature plays no role to start nuclear fission reaction.	Temperature of the order of 10^7 K is required to start nuclear fusion reaction.
8	By-products of nuclear fission are radioactive and emit harmful radiation.	By-products of nuclear fusion are not radioactive and hence do not emit harmful radiation.
9	Nuclear fission causes more pollution.	Nuclear fusion causes no pollution.
10	In a nuclear fission, the disposal of nuclear waste is a big problem.	In a nuclear fusion, no such problem is there.

3.17 ENVIRONMENTAL CONSEQUENCES (IMPACT OF INCREASING DEMAND OF ENERGY ON ENVIRONMENT)

Modern life style of people and dependence on machines operated with energy in the form of heat and electricity for our day to day work has increased the demand for more energy. Consequently, the pace or speed of exploiting more and more sources of energy has been increased. More use of fossil fuels for fulfilling the demand for more energy is polluting air around us. Air pollution is a great danger to the living beings. Although some of fuels like LPG and CNG are considered as clean fuels but extraction and transportation of these fuels cause environmental pollution. At present our focus has been diverted to extract energy from non-conventional sources of energy like the wind the sea and the sun to conserve conventional sources of energy like the wind the sea and the sun to conserve conventional sources of energy. The energy obtained from non-conventional sources of energy from non-conventional sources poses a great threat to the environment. Global warming is another problem, we are facing because of the increased use of energy from fossil fuels. Thus we conclude that the increasing demand of energy is disturbing the ecological balance.

3.17.1 HOW LONG WILL AN ENERGY SOURCE LAST ?

We have discussed a large number of sources of energy like fuels, biomass, hydro power ,the sun, the wind, geothermal energy, nuclear energy etc. These sources of energy are divided into two categories.

(i) Renewable sources of energy or in exhaustible sources of energy

(ii) Non-renewable sources of energy or exhaustible sources of energy.

3.17.2 RENEWABLE SOURCES OF ENERGY

The sources of energy which are inexhaustible (i.e. which can never be finished) and are being continuously supplied by nature are known as renewable sources of energy. These sources of energy are also known as non-conventional sources of energy.

For example:

(i) Wind (ii) Hydro Power

(iii) The sun (iv) Ocean Tidals Energy

(v) Interior of the Earth (vi) Biogas

(vii) Plants, vegetable waste etc.

3.17.3 NON-RENEWABLE SOURCES OF ENERGY

The sources of energy which are exhaustible (i.e. which can be finished) and have been formed in nature long ago are known as non-renewable sources of energy. These sources of energy are also known as conventional sources of energy.

For example : (i) Coal (ii) Petroleum (iii) Natural Gas (iv) Fissionable materials like Uranium.

Non - renewable sources of energy like coal, petroleum and natural gas have a huge deposit under the earth. However, the continuous extraction of these sources for the purpose of usable energy is a matter of concern and worry because ultimately the deposit if these sources will be completely finished. It may be noted that the formation of fossil fuels take very long period. Therefore, we should use these fuels judiciously so that their deposit may last long.

On the other hand, renewable sources of energy will last forever. For example, it is estimated that the sun would continue to shine for another 5 billion years. Therefore, the sun as the source of energy will be available for a very long period of time. Similarly, bio-mass as the source of energy will be available for a longer period of time if we grow more and more plants periodically (i.e. at regular intervals of time). The wind energy will be at our disposal as long as the sun exists. Geo-thermal energy is another source which will be available forever.

LET US RECAPITULATE

- Energy is the essential requirement for each and every activity in our life.
- The various sources of energy are the sun, the wind, water, fossil fuels etc.
- The sun is the ultimate source of all forms of energy.
- A good source of energy is one which supplies large amount of useful energy, easily available, economical and cause minimum environmental pollution.
- Thermal power plant generates electricity by burning fossil fuel like coal and oil.
- LPG is a petroleum gas liquefied under pressure. Its full form is liquefied Petroleum Gas.
- CNG is compressed Natural Gas.
- Main constituents of CNG is methane.
- Electricity produced by flowing water is known as hydro - electric power.
- A plant used to produce hydro -electric power is known as hydro -electric power plant.
- Potential energy of water stored in a dam is converted into kinetic energy of the falling water. This kinetic energy of falling water is converted into the kinetic energy of the armature of the generator which in turn is converted into electric energy.
- Biomass is material which contains carbon and other combustible material.
- Plants, wood animals and plants waster are the examples of biomass.
- Gobar gas or bio-gas is the example of a bio - mass energy source.
- Main constituent of a biogas or gobar gas is a methane gas.
- Biogas plant is of two types: (a) Fixed-dome type, (b) Floating gas holder type.
- Kinetic energy of wind is known as wind energy.
- Wind energy is used to produce electricity.
- The region where large number of wind mills are erected to produce electricity is called wind energy farm.
- The minimum speed of wind to operate generator to produce electricity is about 15 km/h.
- Constant and rapid use of conventional sources of energy would ultimately exhaust these sources and hence a need for tapping energy from alternate or non-conventional sources of energy is seriously felt.
- Solar energy is the energy emitted by the sun in the form of heat and light.
- Solar constant is defined as the energy received from the sun in one second by a unit square metre area of the outer edge of earth's atmosphere exposed perpendicular to the radiation of the sun at an average distance between the sun and the earth.

- Value of solar constant = 1.4 k W/m^2.
- Solar devices like solar cooker, solar furnace, solar water heater, solar panels and solar cells are used to harness solar energy.
- Water due to its high specific heat capacity (4200 J kg^{-1}°C^{-1}) is a store house of heat energy.
- Energy from sea or ocean water is available in the form of (i) energy of sea waves (ii) Tidal energy and (iii) Ocean thermal energy (OTE).
- The heat energy obtained from the conversion of nuclear mass is known as nuclear energy.
- Nuclear energy is obtained by two processes known as nuclear fission and nuclear fusion.
- Nuclear energy is expressed in electron - volt(eV)

  $1 \text{ eV} = 1.6 \times 10^{-19}\text{J}$

  $1 \text{ MeV} = 10^6 \text{ eV} = 1.6 \times {}^{-13}\text{J}$
- Nuclear Fission is the process of splitting a heavy nucleus (say Uranium) into two comparatively lower nuclei along with the release of large amount energy when bombarded with thermal neutron.
- Nuclear reactor is a device used to carry out controlled chain reaction.
- Nuclear fusion is the process of fusing or combining together two small nuclei to form a comparatively big nucleus with the release of large energy.
- Nuclear fusion reactions occur at very high temperature (10^7K).
- Nuclear fusion reactions occurring in the interior of the sun are responsible for the energy of the sun. In other words, nuclear fusion reactions are the sources of energy of the sun.
- Sources of energy are classified into two categories (i) conventional or non-renewable sources of energy and (ii) Non-conventional or renewable sources of energy.
- Extraction and transportation of energy from various sources of energy cause environmental pollution.
- The energy from various sources of energy must be used effectively to conserve energy.

CONCEPT APPLICATION LEVEL - I [NCERT Questions]

Q.1 A solar heater cannot be used to get hot water on
(A) a sunny day (B) a cloudy day (C) a hot day (D) a windy day
Ans (B) a cloudy day

Q.2 Which of the following is not a example of a bio-mass energy source?
(A) wood (B) gobar gas (C) fossil fuels (D) bio-mass
Ans. (C) fossil fuels

Q.3 Most of the sources of energy we use represent stored solar energy. Which of the following is not ultimately derived from the Sun's energy?
(A) geothermal energy (B) wind energy
(C) fossil fuels (D) bio-mass
Ans. (A) geothermal energy

Q.4 Compare and contrast fossil fuels and the Sun as a source of energy.
Ans. (i) Energy of fossil fuels comes from the solar energy. However, fossils fuels are the non-renewable sources of energy. On the other hand sun is a renewable source of energy.
(ii) Fossil fuels cause pollution but solar energy does not cause pollution.
(iii) Energy is supplied by fossil fuels at any time of the day but sun supplies energy only when it shines.

Q.5 Compare and contrast bio - mass and hydro - electricity as source of energy.
Ans.

Q.6 What are the limitations of extracting energy from
(a) the wind (b) Waves (c) Tides ?
Ans. (a) (i) We cannot depend upon wind energy as it is available only when strong wind blows. The appliances or machines operating with wind energy stop working as soon as wind stops. The minimum speed of wind to operate generator to produce electricity is 15 km/h.
(ii) The use of wind energy is limited to certain places where strong winds blow most of the time.
(b) Energy of waves can be extracted only if strong winds blow all the time across the sea.
(c) Tidal power plant can extract energy form the waves only when the difference between the water levels of high tide and low tide is very large.

Q.7 On what basis you classify energy source as
(a) Renewable and non-renewable ? (b) Exhaustible and inexhaustible?
Are the options given in (a) and (b) the same?
Ans. (a) Renewable Sources of Energy are those which are continuously supplied by nature. For example the sun the wind.
(b) Non-Renewable Sources of energy are those which have been formed in nature long ago under certain conditions of temperature and pressure. Non-renewable sources of energy take longer period of time for their formation. For example fossil fuels like coal petroleum.
(c) Inexhaustible Sources of Energy are those which supply continuous energy for unlimited time. In fact exhaustible sources of energy are also termed as non -renewable energy sources. But wood is ans exception as it can be made renewable by growing more plants periodically. Inexhaustible sources of energy are termed as renewable sources of energy.

Q.8 What are qualities of an ideal source of energy ?

Ans. (i) It supplies useful energy continuously.

(ii) It does not cause environment pollution.

(iii) It is economical.

Q.9 What are the advantages and disadvantages of using a solar cooker ? Are there places where solar cookers would have limited utility ?

Ans. Advantages :

(i) There is no cost of cooking food in a solar cooker

(ii) No pollution is caused when food is cooked in a solar cooker

(iii) Nutrition value of food is preserved when food is cooked in the solar cooker

(iv) Two or three dishes can be cooked at a time

Disadvantages :

(i) Food cannot be cooked at night and on a cloudy day using a solar cooker

(ii) The cost of making solar cooker is high.

(iii) Food cannot be cooked quickly with the solar cooker

(iv) Large quantity of food cannot be cooked with a solar cooker.

(v) Chapatis cannot be made with solar cooker.

Solar cooker will have limited utility at places where the sun shines for shorter period of time or where the sun rays never reach.

Q.10 What are the environmental consequences of the increasing demand for energy ? What steps would you suggest to reduce energy consumption ?

Ans. (i) More use of fossil fuels for fulfilling the increasing demand for energy is polluting air (i.e. the environment).

(ii) L.P.G and CNG are considered as clean fuels but the extraction and transportation of these fuels cause environmental pollution.

(iii) The use of large number of sources of energy is causing global warming.

Suggestions

(i) Burning fuels must be extinguished as soon as their use is over.

(ii) Bulbs tubes and other electrical appliances must be switched off as soon as you leave your room.

(iii) The engines of the vehicles must be switched off when these vehicles are stopped for more than a minute to save fuel.

CONCEPT APPLICATION LEVEL - II

SECTION-A

Q.1 What is good source of energy?

Ans. (i) It should supply enough amount of useful energy.
(ii) It should be easily stored.
(iii) It should be easily transported.
(iv) It should occupy less space for storage.
(v) It should supply useful energy in a controlled manner.
(vi) It should be easily available or accessible.
(vii) It should be cheap i.e., it should be economical.
(viii) It should cause minimum environmental pollution.

Q.2 What is good fuel?

Ans. A fuel which provides large amount of heat energy without causing pollution.

Q.3 If you could use any source of energy for heating your food, which one would you use and why?

Ans. We would use microwave oven for heating our food. This is because the nutritional value of food is not lost when heated in a microwave oven.

Q.4 What are the disadvantages of fossil fuels?

Ans. (i) They cause environmental pollution.
(ii) They cause global warming.
(iii) They do not supply enough heat energy.
(iv) The by - products of burning fuels cause acid rain which pollute water resources.

Q.5 Why are we looking at alternate sources of energy?

Ans. Because the conventional sources of energy may completely be exhausted one day if their use at the present rate continues.

Q.6 How has the traditional use of wind energy and water been modified for our convenience?

Ans. These energies have been converted into electrical energy using electric generators.

Q.7. What kind of mirror-concave, convex or plane would be best suited for the use in a solar cooker. Why?

Ans. Concave mirror, because it focuses the sun rays at a point to raise the temperature at the point.

Q.8 What are limitations of the energy that can be obtained from oceans?

Or

List any four limitations of the energy obtained from oceans.

Ans. (i) Energy from oceans is available only when high tides are in the ocean
(ii) Power plants used to convert ocean energy into electric energy do not operate continuously.
(iii) Energy of ocean waves can be extracted blow all times across the ocean.
(iv) Tidal power plants can not be installed everywhere.

Q.9 What is geothermal energy?

Ans. The heat energy stored in the hot spots of the earth's crust is called geothermal energy.

Q.10 What are the advantages of nuclear energy?

Ans. (i) A small quantity of nuclear fuel gives a large amount of energy.

(ii) In a nuclear power plant, the nuclear fuel is inserted once to get energy over a longer period of time.

Q.11 Can any source of energy be pollution free ? Why or why not?

Ans. No source of energy is there which is pollution free. However, some sources of energy cause more pollution and some sources of energy cause less pollution.

Q.12 Hydrogen has been used as a rocket fuel. Would you consider it a cleaner fuel than CNG ? Why or why not ?

Ans. Hydrogen causes less air pollution than C.N.G. because burning of hydrogen produces water vapours and burning of CNG produces CO_2. When the concentration of CO_2 increases in the atmosphere, then the temperature of the atmosphere increases. This effect is known as green house effect. The increased temperature of the atmosphere affects life on the earth.

Q.13 Name two energy sources that you would consider to be renewable. Give reasons for your choices.

Ans. (i) Bio-mass is considered as a renewable source of energy because forest can be replenished

(ii) Water is also a renewable source of energy as water is continuously available to use due to water cycle in nature.

Q.14 Give the name of two energy sources that you would consider to be exhaustible. Give reasons for your choices

Ans. (i) Coal (ii) Petroleum.

They will be exhaustible when continuously extracted. Moreover, the formation of these fuels under the earth takes a longer period of time.

Q.15 Name the two forms of energy usually used at our homes .

Ans. Heat and electricity.

Q.16 Name two gases other than carbon -dioxide that are given out during burning of fossil fuel and contribute towards acid rain formation.

Ans. (i) Sulphur dioxide (ii) Nitrogen dioxide

Q.17 Name two renewable or non-conventional sources of energy.

Ans. (i) The sun (ii) The wind

Q.18 Name two non renewable or conventional sources of energy.

Ans. (i) Coal (ii) Petroleum

Q.19 Define solar constant.

Ans. It is defined as the energy received from the sun in one second by unit square meter area of the earth's atmosphere exposed perpendicularly to the radiation of the sun at an average distance between the earth and the sun . The value of solar constant = 1.4 kWm^{-2}.

Q.20 How is charcoal obtained from wood?

Ans. Charcoal is obtained from wood by heating the wood in the absence of air. This process is known as destructive distillation of wood.

Q.21 Name two activities in our daily life in which solar energy is used.

Ans. (i) For cooking food using solar cookers. (ii) For drying clothes and food grains

Q.22 Name the component of sunlight carrying maximum heat.

Ans. Infra - red rays

Q.23 Name the component of sunlight that is absorbed by ozone layer of the atmosphere.

Ans. Ultra - violet rays

Q.24 Which surface absorbs more heat - black or white surface?

Ans. Black surface absorbs more heat than the white surface

Q.25 Name the device which directly converts solar energy into electric energy.

Ans. Solar cell.

Q.26 What is the range of temperature attained inside a box type solar cooker then placed in the sun for two to three hours?

Ans. From 100°C to 140°C

Q.27 A solar cell transform energy of one from into another from. What are these two forms of energy?

Ans. Solar energy (sunlight) to electrical energy.

Q.28 State one limitation of solar energy available from solar cells.

Ans. These cells do not operate during night and on a cloudy day.

Q.29 What is the main basic cause for winds to blow?

Ans. The pressure of a region where maximum sunlight falls decreases as compared to the region where minimum sunlight falls. The air moves from a region of high pressure (i.e., cold region) to the region of low pressure (i.e., hot region). This moving air is the wind.

Q.30 What is the minimum wind velocity required to obtain useful energy with a wind mill?

Ans. 15 km/h

Q.31 What is a wind farm?

Ans. The region where large number of wind mills are erected to produce electricity is called wind farm.

Q.32 Name the kind of energy possessed by wind.

Ans. Kinetic energy

Q.33 Name a part of India where wind energy is commercially harnessed.

Ans. Kanyakumari in Tamil Nadu.

Q.34 Name the leading country for expatiation of wind energy.

Ans. Denmark.

Q.35 Name the factor which enables the ocean to act as a store house of energy.

Ans. The high value of specific heat capacity of water enables the ocean to act as a store house of energy.

Q.36 What is a biogas?

Ans. Biogas is a mixture of four gases namely methane, carbon dioxide, hydrogen and hydrogen sulphide.

Q.37 Name the main constituent of a biogas.

Ans. Methane gas.

Q.38 Name two main combustible components of biogas.

Ans. Methane gas and hydrogen gas.

Q.39 What is a fossil fuel?

Ans. The combustible substance formed from the dead remains of the animals and plants which were buried deep under the surface of the earth over millions of years is called fossil fuel.

Q.40 Give two examples of fossil fuels.

Ans. Coal and petroleum.

Q.41 Justify in one sentence that hydropower (hydel electricity) is a renewable source of energy.

Ans. Since hydropower is derived from the renewable source of energy i.e., sun, so it is also a renewable source of energy.

Q.42 What is nuclear energy?

Ans. The energy which is obtained from the conversion of nuclear mass is called nuclear energy.

Q.43 Is nuclear energy derived from the sun like other forms of energy.

Ans. No. Nuclear energy is derived from the nuclear mass.

Q.44 What is a nuclear fission?

Ans. The process of splitting of a heavy nucleus into lighter nuclei is known as nuclear fission.

Q.45 Which process is carried out at a higher temperature ? Nuclear fission or nuclear fusion?

Ans. Nuclear fusion.

Q.46 Charcoal is a better fuel than wood. Why?

Ans. The following are the cause due to which charcoal is better fuel than wood :

(i) Charcoal does not produce smoke on burning.

(ii) Charcoal causes no pollution.

(iii) The amount of heat produced by the burning charcoal is more than h eat produced by the wood

(iv) Charcoal is easier burn than wood.

Q.47 Deforestation : Explain its effect.

Ans. Deforestation means cutting of trees in large number. Deforestation causes many problems like floods, erosion of fertile land and environmental imbalance.

Q.48 Red shirt looks red. Why?

Ans. When sun light falls on the red shirt, it absorbs all the colour of visible light except red colour. Red shirt reflects red colour and so it looks red.

Q.49 Black shirt looks black. Why?

Ans. When sunlight falls on a black shirt, it absorbs all colour of visible light. No colour of visible light is reflected by it and hence it looks black

Q.50 Why is the emphasis on changing over from patrol/diesel driven automobiles to CNG driven vehicles?

Ans. CNG is a natural gas. It is a clean fuel. And it does not produce pollution.

Q.51 Why do we use peat, the lowest grade of coal, for domestic purposes?

Ans. This is because we do not require very large temperatures.

Q.52 Mention any four areas where solar cells are being used as a source of energy.

Ans. The four areas where solar cells are used is given as below :

(i) Research centers (ii) artificial satellite

(iii) Radio transmission and wireless transmission (vi) Traffic light

Q.53 What is a photo electric cell?

Ans. The device which converts light energy into electrical energy is called photo electric cell.

Q.54 Define photon.

Ans. Light travels in the form of small bundle of energy or small pocket of energy. Energy of each bundle or each pocket is called photon

Q.55 Name the different types of photo electric cells?

Ans. Three different types of photo electric cells are :

(i) Photo emissive cell. (ii) Photo voltaic cell. (iii) Photo conductive cell.

Q.56 Explain why is it difficult to burn a wet piece of wood.

Ans. The main cause is ignition temperature. An ignition temperature is necessary for burning wood. The water in wet wood keeps the temperatures of wood below its ignition temperatures therefore it is difficult to burn wet wood.

Q.57 Can a bottle of kerosene be a source of energy? Explain.

Ans. Bottle of kerosene in constant form is not a source of energy. But when a wick is placed in the kerosene, and then lit, it gives energy. This is called lantern or stove.

Q.58 Which type of coal is normally used for cooking?

Ans. Peat.

Q.59 Which variety of coal has the maximum heating capacity?

Ans. Anthracite

Q.60 Can solar energy be a dependable source of energy in Greenland? Why?

Ans. Because Greenland has only short summers and long dark winters.

Q.61 What is OWC?
Ans. Oscillating Water Columns

Q.62 Give an example of a non-bio mass energy source?
Ans. Atomic energy.

Q.63 Name any two disadvantages of using dry dung cakes as a fuel?
Ans. Two disadvantages of using dry dung cakes as a fuel are :
(i) Burning of dry dung - cakes cause pollution of the air.
(ii) Dry-dung cakes after burning leave a large quantity of ash.

Q.64 What are the factors which cause energy crisis ?
Ans. Causes of energy crisis are:
(i) Increasing population
(ii) Affluent life- style of the people
(iii) Use of less fuel-efficient machine
(iv) Excessive use of non-renewable source of energy.

SECTION-B [PREVIOUS YEARS QUESTIONS, (1 MARK)]

Q.1 Name any two nuclear fuels used for the process of nuclear fission. **[SAI-2015]**
Ans. Uranium, Plutonium, Thorium.

Q.2 Which elements are used to make a solar cell? **[SAI-2013]**
Ans. Silicon and Gallium.

Q.3 Name the reaction responsible for large energy production in the Sun. **[SAI-2013]**
Ans. Nuclear fusion.

Q.4 Mention the source of energy in the working of a hydropower plant. **[SAI-2013]**
Ans. Hydropower plants convert the potential energy of falling water into electricity.

Q.5 Write the percentage of methane in biogas. **[SAI-2014]**
Ans. 75 %

Q.6 Why is a biogas plant a safe and efficient method of waste disposal ? Justify. **[SAI-2013]**
Ans. Biogas plant produces biogas which burns without smoke and leaves no residue. The slurry left behind is an excellent manure.

SECTION-C [PREVIOUS YEARS QUESTIONS, (2 MARKS)]

Q.1 What is a good source of energy ?
Ans. A good source of energy is one which :
(i) does a large amount of work per unit volume or mass,
(ii) is easily accessible,
(iii) is easy to store and transport,
(iv) is economical

Q.2 What is a good fuel ?

Ans. A good fuel is one which :

(i) has high calorific value, i.e., produces large amount of heat on burning completely in air or oxygen,

(ii) produces less smoke on burning,

(iii) has low cost and is easily available,

(iv) has an ignition temperature that is well above the normal temperature

SECTION-D [PREVIOUS YEARS QUESTIONS, (3 MARKS)]

Q.1 What are the problems associated with the construction of big dams ? **[SAI-2010,2013]**

Ans. (i) Big dams can be constructed only in a limited number of places, preferably in hilly terrains.

(ii) Large areas of agricultural land and human habitation are to be sacrificed.

(iii) Large ecosystem is destroyed.

(iv) Submerged vegetations rot under anaerobic conditions and release methane gas.

(v) It creates the problem of rehabilitation of displaced people.

Q.2 (i) Name three forms in which energy from ocean is made available for use.

(ii) What are the limitations of energy that are obtained from oceans ? **[SAI-2013]**

Ans. (i) The three forms of energy that can be obtained from the ocean are tidal energy, wave energy and ocean thermal energy.

(ii) There are several limitations to harness these types of energies :

(a) Tidal energy depends on the relative positioning of the earth, moon and the sun.

(b) High dams are required to be built to convert tidal energy into electricity.

(c) Very strong waves are required to obtain electricity from wave energy.

(d) To harness ocean thermal energy efficiently, the difference in the temperature of surface water (hot) and the water at depth (cold) must be 20°C or more.

Q.3 Give any three reasons that make large scale use of nuclear energy prohibitive. **[SAI-2013]**

Ans. (i) The radioactive materials required for fission emit harmful gamma rays which cause cancer, leukemia and other genetic disorders.

(ii) In case of an accident, it will explode like a very big nuclear bomb destroying lives around the plant.

(iii) Difficulty in handling nuclear waste.

Q.4 Explain the working of a simple turbine. **[SAI-2013]**

Ans. The simplest turbine has one moving part, a rotor-blade assembly. The moving fluid acts on the blades to spin them and impart and energy to the shaft rotor which turns the of the dynamo and converts mechanical energy into electrical energy.

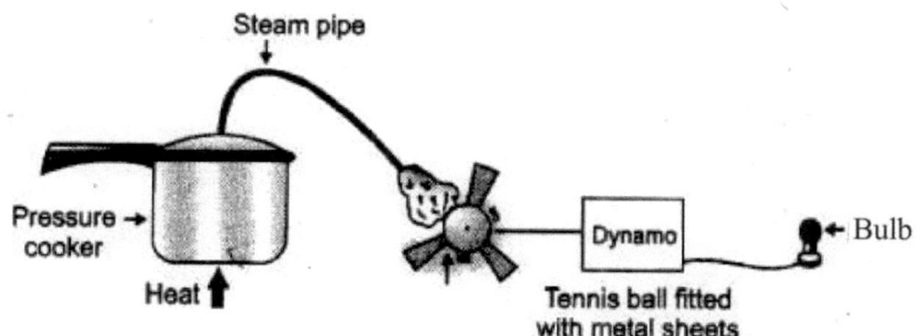

Q.5 Ramesh is a student of standerd X. He organized many activities in his school to convey the students about the various advantages and disadvantages of using renewable and non-renewable sources of energy. Many students of the school took part and concluded about the best choices of energy sources on this basis.

Answer the following questions:

(i) What activities Ramesh might have assigned for the students?

(ii) Name any two renewable sources of energy.

(iii) Which two values are reflected in Ramesh's thought and action? **[SAI-2014]**

Ans. (i) Debate, essay writing, drawing making.

(ii) Wind energy, Solar panel, Biogas.

(iii) Global issues like -Protection of environment/Global warming etc.

Q.6 (a) Describe the structure of a windmill.

(b) Give one example to illustrate that energy from windmill was used to do mechanical work. **[SAI-2015]**

Ans. (a) A windmill consists of a huge structure erected at some height on a rigid support. At the top of windmill there are blades like a fan. The rotatory motion of the windmill is used to turn the turbine of the electric generator that generate the electricity

(b) In water lifting pump, (rotatory motion of windmill, was used to lift water from well).

Q.7 Explain how hydroelectricity is produced. **[SAI-2015]**

Ans. High rise dams are constructed to obstruct the flow of water. Water level rises and in this process potential energy of water increases. Water from high level is carried to the turbine which runs the generator and electricity is produced.

Q.8 Explain how is geothermal energy harnessed to produce electricity ? **[SAI-2015]**

Ans. Molten rocks from deeper part of the earth pushed upwards and trapped in regions (hotsports) containing water. Underground water which comes in contact with hot spots turns into steam. Steam is routed through pipes to run turbines of electric generator to produce electricity.

CONCEPT APPLICATION LEVEL - III

SECTION-A

- **Fill in the blanks**

1. Hydro power plants convert the potential energy of falling water into __________.
2. The phenomena, in which, the nucleus of a heavy atom, when bombarded with low-energy neutrons, can be split apart into lighter nuclei, is called __________.
3. Ultraviolet radiations have a wavelength range of __________ to __________.
4. Infrared radiation constitute __________ of the sunlight.
5. The heat in the sunlight is due to __________ radiation.
6. __________ utilizes the heat of the sun for cooking.
7. Solar cell converts __________ energy into __________ energy.
8. The other name of solar cell is __________.
9. Flowing water contains __________ form of energy.
10. Wind contains __________ energy.
11. The solar energy evaporates the water from __________, __________ and
12. Wind, flowing water and the sun are __________ sources of energy.
13. The examples of non - renewable sources of energy are __________, __________ and __________.
14. Solar constant is __________.
15. __________ layer in the upper atmosphere absorbs most of the ultra - violet rays emitted by the sun.
16. Planck's constant h = __________.
17. __________ mirror is used to reflect the sun light in the solar cooker.
18. __________ mirror is used to reflect sunlight in spherical reflector cooker.
19. The temperature inside the box of the solar cooker rises to __________.
20. A device used to convert wind energy to mechanical energy of the machine is __________.
21. Energy of each photon E = __________.
22. Solar cells are made of __________.

SECTION-B

- **Multiple choice question with one correct answers**

Q.1 The word 'energy crisis' stands for
(A) Energy destruction
(B) Energy creation
(C) Conversion of energy from usable form to less usable form
(D) None of these

Q.2 Device that converts the potential energy of flowing water into electricity is
(A) Solar cooker (B) Thermal power plant
(C) Hydro power plant (D) Bio-gas plant

Q.3 Which is the ultimate source of a all forms of energy?
(A) The sun (B) The moon (C) The wind (D) The air

Q.4 Which of the following is the non - renewable source of energy?
(A) Wind (B) sun (C) petroleum (D) biogas

Q.5 Which of the following is the renewable source of energy?
(A) natural gas (B) petroleum (C) coal (D) wind

Q.6 Deforestation is the cause of
(A) Sunrise (B) energy (C) flood (D) wind

Q.7 Solar constat is equal to
(A) 1.4 KW /m^2 (B) 5.2 KW /m^2 (C) 3.1 KW /m^2 (D) None of these

Q.8 The energy liberated by wood on burning is
(A) 25 kJ (B) 27 kJ (C) 20 kJ (D) 17 kJ

Q.9 The energy liberated by charcoal on burning is
(A) 30 kJ (B) 33 kJ (C) 35 kJ (D) 36 kJ

Q.10 Amount of charcoal produced on the destructive distillation of 1 kg of wood is about
(A) 0.25kg (B) 0.50kg (C) 0.75kg (D) 1.25kg

Q.11 Box - type solar cooker attains temperature in the region of
(A) 150-200°C (B) 50-100°C (C) 170-300°C (D) 100-140°C

Q.12 Reflection type solar cooker attains temperature in the range of
(A) 10-150°C (B) 400-450°C (C) 200-250°C (D) 500-550°C

Q.13 Solar energy is available at
(A) day time (B) night time (C) middle day (D) none of these

Q.14 Solar cooker works during
(A) night (B) day (C) middle of day (D) none of these

Q.15 Energy possesses by the body by virtue of its motion is called
(A) kinetic energy (B) potential energy (C) solar energy (D) air

Q.16 Energy possesses by the body by virtue of its position is called
(A) kinetic energy (B) potential energy (C) solar energy (D) air

Q.17 The calorific value of natural gas is
(A) 17 kJg^{-1} (B) 10 kJg^{-1} (C) 30 kJg^{-1} (D) 55 kJg^{-1}

Q.18 What is the percentage of carbon in bituminous?
(A) 30-90% (B) 65-70% (C) 10-15% (D) 30-40%

Q.19 Solar cells are made of
(A) metals (B) insulator (C) semiconductor (D) none of these

Q.20 The major source of energy in India is –
(A) Nuclear (B) Petroleum (C) Hydro (D) Coal

Q.21 Bio-gas is produced in a bio-gas plant, by decomposition of complex compounds of the cow-dung slurry. This process is done by : Micro-organism in the
(A) Presence of Oxygen (B) Absence of Oxygen
(C) Presence of N_2 (D) None of the these

SECTION-C

- **Multiple choice question with one or more than one correct answers**

Q.1 Limitations in harnessing the kinetic energy of flowing water in hydro power plants is/are

(A) The speed of flowing water should be higher than 15 km/hr

(B) The dam's can be constructed only in a limited number of places

(C) Large ecosystems are destroyed when submerged under the water in dams

(D) The dams need a high level of maintenance

SECTION-D

- **Comprehension**

The solar energy reaching unit area at outer edge of the earth's atmosphere exposed perpendicularly to the rays of the sun at the average distance between the sun and earth is known as the solar constant. It is estimated to be approximately 1.4 Kj per second per square metre or 1.4 Kw/m^2. A rocked is flying at the outer edge of earth's atmosphere. Sun rays are incident perpendicularly on the metal surface of rocket of area 10 m^2.

Q.1 Solar energy incident on metal surface in 10 sec. is

(A) 1.4 KJ (B) 14 KJ (C) 140 KJ (D) None of these

Q.2 In how much time will metal surface receive 42 KJ of solar energy.

(A) 3 sec (B) 30 sec (C) 300 sec (D) None of these

Q.3 Solar energy received by unit area of metal surface in 10 sec. –

(A) 1.4 KJ (B) 14 KJ (C) 140 KJ (D) None of these

SECTION-E

- **Assertion & Reason**

Instructions: In the following questions as Assertion (A) is given followed by a Reason (R). Mark your responses from the following options.

(A) Both Assertion and Reason are true and Reason is the correct explanation of 'Assertion'

(B) Both Assertion and Reason are true and Reason is not the correct explanation of 'Assertion'

(C) Assertion is true but Reason is false

(D) Assertion is false but Reason is true

Q.1 **Assertion:** In nuclear fission, a tremendous amount of energy is released if the mass of the original nucleus is just a little more than the sum of the masses of the individual products.

Reason: The difference in mass, Δm, between the original nucleus an the product nuclei gets converted to energy E according to equation

$$E = \Delta m C^2$$

where C is speed of light in vacuum.

SECTION-F

- **Match the following (one to one)**

  Column-I and **column-II** contains **four** entries each. Entries of column-I are to be matched with some entries of column-II. Only One entries of column-I may have the matching with the same entries of column-II and one entry of column-II Only one matching with entries of column-I

Q.1

Column-I *(Device)*	**Column-II** *(Limitation)*
(A) Hydro power plants	(P) Efficient commercial exploitation is difficult
(B) Wind mill	(Q) Special grade silicon is limited
(C) Solar cell	(R) Wind speed should higher than 15 km/h
(D) Ocean-thermal-energy conversion plants	(S) Large eco-systems are destroyed

SECTION-G

- **Match the following (one to many)**

  Column-I and **column-II** contains **four** entries each. Entries of column-I are to be matched with some entries of column-II. One or more than one entries of column-I may have the matching with the same entries of column-II and one entry of column-II may have one or more than one matching with entries of column-I

Q.1

Column I	**Column II**
(A) Hydro power plants	(P) Produces electricity
(B) Solar Cell	(Q) Converts solar energy into electric energy
(C) Thermal power plant	(R) Converts potential energy of falling water into electricity
(D) Wind mill	(S) Converts kinetic energy of air into electricity

ANSWER KEY

Knowledge Base Questions:

1.	C	2.	B	3.	D	4.	D	5.	A	6.	A	7.	A
8.	C	9.	C	10.	A								

CONCEPT APPLICATION LEVEL - III

SECTION-A

1.	electricity	2.	nuclear-tission	3.	400 nm to 700 nm
4.	one-third	5.	infrared	6.	Solar cooker
7.	solar, electrical	8.	photoelectric cell	9.	mechanical
10.	kinetic	11.	oceans, rivers	12.	renewable
13.	coal, petroleum, natural gas			14.	1.4 KW/sq.m
15.	The ozone layer	16.	6.625×10^{-34} J s	17.	Plane
18.	Concave	19.	200°C	20.	wind mill
21.	hv	22.	semiconductors		

SECTION-B

Q.1	C	Q.2	C	Q.3	A	Q.4	C	Q.5	D	Q.6	C	Q.7	A
Q.8	D	Q.9	B	Q.10	A	Q.11	D	Q.12	D	Q.13	A	Q.14	B
Q.15	A	Q.16	B	Q.17	D	Q.18	B	Q.19.	C	Q.20	D	Q.21	B

SECTION-C

Q.1 B,C

SECTION-D

Q.1 C 2. A 3. B

SECTION-E

Q.1 A

SECTION-F

Q.1 (A)-(S),(B)-(R),(C)-(Q),(D)-(P)

SECTION-G

Q.1 (A)–(P,R), (B)–(P,Q), (C)–(P), (D)–(P,S)

Printed by Libri Plureos GmbH in Hamburg,
Germany